STUDIES IN ANGLICAN HISTORY

Series Editor

Peter W. Williams, Miami University

Sponsored by

the Historical Society of the Episcopal Church

Prayer, Despair, and Drama

Prayer, Despair, and Drama

Elizabethan Introspection

Peter Iver Kaufman

University of Illinois Press
Urbana and Chicago

Publication of this work has been supported by a grant from
the Historical Society of the Episcopal Church.

This book is printed on acid-free paper.

Library of Congress Cataloging-in-Publication Data
Kaufman, Peter Iver.
    Prayer, despair, and drama : Elizabethan introspection / Peter
Iver Kaufman.
        p.   cm.—(Studies in Anglican history)
    Includes bibliographical references and index.
    ISBN 0-252-02222-X (alk. paper)
    1. Spirituality—England—History—16th century.   2. Calvinism—
England—History—16th century.   3. Spirituality—Church of
England—History—16th century.   4. Church of England—
Doctrines—History—16th century.   5. Anglican Communion—
England—Doctrines—History—16th century.   6. England—Church
history—16th century.   7. England—Intellectual life—16th
century.   I. Title.   II. Series
BR757.K38   1996
274.2'06—dc20   95-32477
                                                                      CIP

Series Editor's Preface

Peter W. Williams

Studies in Anglican History is a series of scholarly monographs sponsored by the Historical Society of the Episcopal Church and published by the University of Illinois Press. It is intended to bring the best of contemporary international scholarship on the history of the entire Anglican Communion, including the Church of England and the Episcopal church in the United States, to a broader readership.

Peter Kaufman, a broad-ranging historian of Christianity at the University of North Carolina at Chapel Hill, takes as his theme in *Prayer, Despair, and Drama* the interconnections between religion and literature in Elizabethan works. Kaufman argues that "therapeutic despair" was a staple of the psychology of English Calvinism during this period and that the agony of wrestling with the question of one's salvation was the norm for spiritual progress. This fundamental expectation, expressed copiously in the devotional literature of the late Tudor era, informs not only explicitly religious but also ostensibly "secular" writing. In exploring this connection, Kaufman focuses on works by major writers such as Edmund Spenser, Christopher Marlowe, John Donne, and, most particularly, William Shakespeare and his *Hamlet*. In doing so, Kaufman enriches greatly our understanding of these classics of English literature as documents informed by an essentially *religious* sensibility.

Contents

Acknowledgments

I long thought I started this book several years ago when I put aside early modern politics for a while and became fascinated by the drama, literature, and religion of what colleagues called the late Renaissance or the Elizabethan age. But I've since had to reconsider. It now seems that twenty years earlier, Professor Jerald Brauer's seminars, tutorials, and interests influenced me more than I then imagined. An early draft of " 'Much in Prayer' " was delivered at the University of Chicago during the conference on "Reinterpretation in the History of Christianity" honoring Jerry on the occasion of his retirement in 1991. His characteristically perceptive responses and those of Richard Strier, Martin Marty, John Corrigan, and Clark Gilpin helped me build momentum.

Anne Hall agreed to a duel each week in a seminar on late sixteenth-century literature and religion and gave me quite an education. I will always be grateful for the ways in which Anne, Stephen Greenblatt, Debora Shuger, and John Stachniewski welcomed a poacher and let him make away with some of their ideas. My debt to others is chronicled in the annotations; those to Bill Bouwsma and Peter Lake deserve special recognition. And, for other kinds of help, assistance that ranges from a few nods of encouragement to unfailing goodwill and from stylistic suggestions to splendid counterarguments that compelled me to reconsider, I thank Karen Bruhn, Melissa Bullard, David DeFoor, Terry Evens, Darryl Gless, Ritchie Kendall, John Van Seters, and particularly Carolyn Wood. Three lively colleagues and friends continue to teach me why and how we should teach history. In a sense, they are collaborators in all that I do, though I may make it difficult for them to own up to it on occasion. To John Headley, Albert Rabil Jr., and Grant Wacker, this "occasion" is dedicated.

*   *   *

The first chapter here is a revision of a paper published in the *Journal of Religion*, 1993. Thanks to Salim Kemal and Ivan Gaskell, I have been able to discuss some of the literature that came to my attention after completing this book; "The Constant Inconstancy of Elizabethan Character" will appear in the series they edit for Cambridge University Press, in *Performance and Authenticity in the Arts*. Peter W. Williams, editor of the series Studies in Anglican History, his two tremendously thoughtful readers, and the staff at the University of Illinois Press have made submission and revision pleasurable experiences.

In what follows, I have modernized punctuation but retained the original spelling.

Prayer, Despair, and Drama

Introduction

This is a book about the rituals and ideas that made late Tudor Calvinism "a more spiritual and reflective religion" and about a corresponding reflexivity in sonnet and soliloquy. Among many Elizabethan Calvinists, assurance of election amounted to pious dis-ease, a disorienting, though an ultimately consoling, self-inventory. Emphasis in reformed Christianity, notably in England, it has been said, shifted from devotion to deliberation. No argument here; one can readily agree that reflection replaced devotion, if one narrowly conceives of devotion as reverence for saints, shrines, and shrivers. But I want to examine deliberation *as* devotion and then to place my findings on what has been called "the full internalization" of Protestantism, that is, the English Calvinist construction of a prodigal identity or self, alongside Spenser's Redcrosse, Marlowe's Faustus, Hamlet's resolve, and John Donne's "inward researches" to see whether correspondences encourage us to think of an aesthetics of experience that conditioned or structured Elizabethan self-consciousness.[1]

Prayer, Despair, and Drama is a small book, busy with religious sentiment, prayers, poems, and plays, and it tries to accommodate or argue with many colleagues who have been to them before me. Chapter summaries are compulsory, but readers may be best served if I preface them with something of the historical context, with a sketch of the fate of religious reform in sixteenth-century England.

*   *   *

One could say Elizabeth and English Protestantism were born to gether. To marry Elizabeth's mother, Anne Boleyn, the eighth Henry had to divorce the English church from Roman Catholicism, for Pope Clement VII refused to annul the king's first marriage. Had Clement obliged Henry, the king's "great matter" would have ended there, for he was taken with Anne, not with the reformed doctrine. In fact, he had written against Luther with help from his trusted adviser, Thomas More (1521). And More was unalterably convinced that the "feeling faith" of continental Protestants and their impressionable English disciples distorted religious truth, which only church authority, attentive to the Roman Catholic tradition, could protect.

Yet from 1534, England had no use for Rome's protection. During Elizabeth's first fifteen years and Henry's last, the king's government ruthlessly repatriated the English church, dissolved its monasteries, confiscated and redistributed their properties, and spent their revenues. If nothing else, the considerable material advantages of such reform kept Henry VIII from contemplating any reconciliation that might have required restitution. Besides, the king was counseled by the shrewd opportunist, Thomas Cromwell, and, for the remainder of his reign, by Thomas Cranmer, Archbishop of Canterbury, who was increasingly influenced by continental reformers and interested in prospects for greater English participation in international Calvinism. But Cranmer had to tread carefully; his sovereign proved, in time, as indecisive in church reform as he was inconstant in affairs of the heart.

Only when Elizabeth's half-brother Edward succeeded their father did Cranmer have the chance to "Calvinize" the English church. By 1548 the Chantries Act took full effect, eliminating the masses that once sped the souls of deceased patrons through purgatory (which was itself shortly legislated out of existence). Priests were allowed to marry; obligatory confession, denounced. In 1549, a set of English rituals replaced the Latin liturgies, and revisions three years later made the English Prayer Book more consistently Calvinist. Lecturers imported from the continent had a similar effect on the minds of those preparing for the ministry at Cambridge and Oxford. The 1553 articles of faith declared against the adoration of images and saints and for the doctrine of divine predestination. Then Edward died.

The accession of Elizabeth's older half-sister Mary made it hard for English Calvinists, at home and in diaspora, to identify God's will with their fate, for Mary and her husband, Philip II of Spain, were intent on reestablishing English Catholicism. The government executed Cranmer and his closest colleagues. Would God have predestined or permitted such a disappointing turnabout and left the elect at the mercy of monarchs only too eager to reimpose their faith on the realm?

But after five years, God's plan, if no more intelligible, should have seemed at least less menacing. Reginald Pole, the papal legate, insisted that restitution precede absolution and reunion with Rome, and such insistence slowed Catholicism's and Mary's progress. Philip eventually broke Pole's resolve, but it hardly helped matters when he fell afoul of Rome for other reasons and was excommunicated by Pope Paul IV. Recatholicization survived neither Mary nor Pole, who died within hours of each other.

Elizabeth was crowned queen in 1559. Her religious settlement restored the 1552 Prayer Book and replaced Mary's bishops with reformers. To many, if not most, English Calvinists, this "triumph of Protestantism" left but one challenge: to round up and reeducate reluctant Catholics. But a restless minority saw the settlement as an invitation to further reform, to root out remnants of "popery" in the reformed church, remnants that more complacent Protestants thought unobjectionable and, some said, necessary for "good order." Edward Dering, Walter Travers, and William Fulke made it abundantly clear that they thought Elizabeth and England had gotten off to an excellent start in 1559 but that they still awaited a more perfect reformation, and ever more impatiently so.

During the 1560s, the agitation for further reform was essentially a Cambridge phenomenon and largely confined to controversies over worship. At the start of the next decade, however, Thomas Cartwright, Lady Margaret Professor of Divinity, was deprived of his position for having advocated, *inter alia*, consistorial or presbyterial church government. John Whitgift, his chief critic and Master of Trinity College at the time, was subsequently rewarded with an appointment to the episcopal bench (1577), which he had defended and kept defending. Cartwright and his allies, notably John Field and Thomas Wilcox, continued to press for more sweeping reform of liturgy and polity, petitioning parliament with verve but to no avail. The queen resented their impertinence. The likes of Matthew Sutcliffe, Dean of Exeter, scolded them for failing to think through their alternatives to prevailing church administration. But it was Whitgift, Archbishop of Canterbury from 1583, who was seen by the persistent and more radical reformers to stand squarely and all-too-dependably in the way of further reform.[2]

Whitgift was not oblivious to the church's enduring abuses and in-
equities. He was disturbed, for instance, that only small portions of ap-
propriated tithes were reaching incumbents while unconscionably large
amounts remained in patrons' coffers. But making headway against such
scandals required the government's cooperation and the archbishop had
to purchase it with his own. He may secretly have agreed with Edmund
Grindal, his predecessor at Canterbury, who angered the queen by refus-
ing to proscribe pastors' unsupervised public conferences (prophesying),
but he consented to their suppression and planned to devise exercises
"not lyke unto that which they called prophecies . . . but some other more
private, such as shall seeme best to our selves both for the peace of the
churche and their better instruction."[3]

Whitgift also understood that he would more easily get and retain
government cooperation if he could count on overwhelming clerical cooperation, so he legislated liturgical uniformity and frowned on dissent,
denying the pulpit to the discontented. Even friends compared his dedication to combat nonconformity with that of the Spanish inquisitors.
Enemies thought him and the English episcopacy still closer to Catholicism. They easily conceded the bishops' Calvinism but charged that if
they were forced to chose between their reformed opinions and the dig-
nities and perquisites of their office, English officials would drop the
doctrine. John Udall's fictional bishop, Diotrophes, confided that he had
come to terms with papists in his diocese. They helped him defend episcopacy ("beare up oure authoritie") against learned critics' pamphlets,
and he forbade those same critics of Catholicism from preaching ("wholsome barking"). Presumably Udall and his friends knew Whitgift had
ordered recusants to surrender their rights of patronage to local bishops,
but, to such implacable critics, the surrender seemed no solution, only
badly camouflaged collusion.[4]

Dissidents believed their "wholsome barking" depleted the ranks of
sinners in England and hastened church reform. Whitgift and his associ-
ates found it "disdainful," "spightful," full of "curious and willful contradictions," and intolerably disruptive during the late 1580s. They stepped
up efforts to silence their critics and were awarded an unwanted notoriety
in the anonymous Marprelate satires that branded them as "petty popes."
Against Marprelate, it was said that the church's chief executives were
major factors in England's unparalleled piety and that there was "never a
more learned clergy in anie church since the apostles' time." No thanks

to "disordered and seditious schismatics," who, left to themselves, "infect[ed] the commonwealth with factions." So they simply could not be left to themselves. John Udall was imprisoned, as was Cartwright. John Penry, suspected of having fathered Marprelate, was executed in 1593.[5]

Looking back on such terribly unsettling consequences of the Elizabethan settlement, apologists for the dissidents put their distinctive spin on the story. They associated the excitement and freedom identified with Elizabeth's accession with the increased incidence of scriptural study and "godlie talk." But, as Josias Nichols pointed out, all that study and conversation eventually raised questions about the church's customs that, upon informed inspection, seemed unscriptural as well as "unprofitable." Yet "the greater sort . . . being old barrels which could holde no newe wine [had been] addicted partly to poperie and partly to licentiousnesse." Nichols praised Edmund Grindal for bridling reactionaries; nonetheless "a newe and freshe assault" followed the "goodlie space of quietnesse" when Whitgift succeeded Grindal at Canterbury. The new archbishop weighed in with the "old barrels," insisting that dissidents subscribe to the queen's supremacy, the Prayer Book, and the articles formulated by the episcopal bench. Nichols explained that Whitgift's quarry had no quarrel with the queen's prerogative but that they considered the other provisions absolutely unacceptable. The result of continued pressure and resistance was "a great division."[6]

Partisans from both sides fired insults across the divide. Conformists dubbed their critics "precisionists," "anabaptists," "peevish puritanes." Dissidents hurled "petty popes" and "old barrels" to the right, "donatists" and "anabaptists" to the left, when some among them grew more irascible and separatist. It is seductively simple to draw polemically charged names into a historical narrative but dangerous to use them descriptively. "People falslie termed puritanes," for example, get stuck with the epithet, excusable perhaps because dissidents later came to embrace the name. Still, anachronism is just about unavoidable. Despite a growing body of literature that thoughtfully qualifies and reclassifies, naming never ceases to be controversial. Even "Calvinist" seems something of a violation, for Walter Travers objected in 1583 that only misguided Catholics immortalized founders (Dominican, Franciscan, Scotist, Thomist).[7]

But naming is necessary. Travers's objection may be set aside, because on both sides of the "great division" English Protestants battled for bragging rights to John Calvin's legacy. *Prayer, Despair, and Drama* is concerned with those Calvinists, dissidents and conformists alike. Their hold on and in this book depends on their tenacious interest in the revealing as well as the consoling character of religious experience. Until we more completely parse it in the following chapters, the experience they countenanced and expected of reformed Christians will seem like an odd, if not impossible, mix of despondence, vertigo, and ecstasy. They were sure that it compassed intense sorrow for sin, "holy desperation" for mercy, and eventual, wondrous assurance of election and salvation. They called it piety; I will call them pietists.

William Perkins, prominent among them, taught at Cambridge from the 1580s to his death in 1602. He was friendly with leading conformists, known lately as "Calvinist Episcopalians," one of whom, James Montagu, preached his funeral sermon. Yet enemies of episcopacy in England and puritans in New England celebrated and circulated his work. Perkins, then, seems to have straddled the "great division"; his career confounds those working with the familiar names and classifications, "Puritan," "Anglican," and the like. His practical divinity, however, virtually begs on his behalf for the name "pietist" because it typically concentrates on defining works of faith, which "concurre to justification" as "signs" and "effects" of election (never its causes), in terms of an internal struggle with remnants of sin and doubt in regenerate and reformed Christians.[8]

The absence of struggle, for Perkins, was the sum and substance of impiety. He detested religious indifference. He scowled at Christians feverishly preoccupied with the "assurance of lands and goods to themselves and to their posterity" while they were "drowsie," spiritually numb, and "slacke in making sure to [them]selves the election of God." That was a sad yet also a predictable situation—predictable, from Perkins's perspective, because it seemed to him that only part of the reformed program reached reformed Christians. They learned well enough that no church had custody of "the over-plus of the merits of Christ." But they had never been compellingly told, or perhaps they had forgotten, that Christianity was a summons to self-criticism and repentance. They took for granted the "endlesse efficacie" of Jesus's atonement and just assumed that God would directly apportion grace to the generally faithful, more or less morally scrupulous, and routinely modest. Perkins countered that God predestined only those few whom he elected. They could obtain assurance of election and strength to persevere in righteousness if they intensely and often experienced uncertainty and dis-ease and took "nothing to [them]selves but shame and confusion." Their humility and "holy desperation" generated a feeling of repentance that grew "little by little," conspicuously in their prayers but in "godlie talk" and scriptural study as well. Much of Perkins's work, exhortation and explanation, pairs piety with prayerful self-concern and with "serious invocation of pardon," both of which fashion the pietists' prayerful prodigal self. Pietists, then, did not pray for what God had not given them; they prayed to inspire a prodigal's remorse and to refortify the confidence that God's most fundamental gift, election, had been theirs all along. The reasons for election were mysterious; the results were demonstrable and reassuring to those who "descend[ed]" into their hearts, rebelled against the rule of sin within, and warded off diabolical doubts about God's vast mercy and about their own recuperation.[9]

*   *   *

The first chapter of *Prayer, Despair, and Drama* comes upon pietists "much in prayer" and discovers just how important their prayers were. To critics who charged that they evinced a morbid self-interest, pietists replied that appeals to God both "pressed down" and "stirred up." The "down" and "up," they claimed, were sensible together, sinister apart. They had in mind a dialectic between faith and doubt, an "interchangeable course," to quote one, that swerved between good cheer and grief. To present that course, I have drawn on some of the pietists' many efforts to distinguish "godly sorrow" from "feigned repentance" and "sudden qualms," and I have recounted their quarrels over the relative values of scripted and impromptu prayers. The purpose is simply to illustrate pietist devotion, yet the first chapter concludes with a glance ahead at performance art to put the pietists' self-absorption in another context, ideally a suggestive and useful context, but also to prefigure the connections made in the third chapter between prayer and drama, specifically between pietists' prayers and Hamlet's self-absorbed asides.

The second chapter returns to the sixteenth century, to the Elizabethan Calvinists who reserved a special place in reformed orthodoxy for self-absorption. At the time, as I just noted, advocates of "all this looking to our selves" were blamed for spreading gloom. Those charges resurface in the late twentieth century as scholarly observations, the gist of which is that such concentrated "looking" and self-lacerating marked either the late Renaissance disintegration of the self or the dislocations that attended and thwarted early modern attempts at integration. All three chapters of *Prayer, Despair, and Drama*, but none more than this second, which looks closely at the practical divinity or theology behind the prayers, subject observations and charges of that character to significant qualification and argue that, for the late Tudor pietists, coming unglued was a precondition for coming together, *religans*, for reforming the self and conforming to God's will.

Pietists instructed preachers that their "wholesome barking" must disconcert auditors and get them to "plow up their hearts." The task was to teach Christians how to feel about themselves and what to think about their feelings, most urgently when they were coaxed into, and lost in, despair. Pietists' sermons and their literature of consolation invested considerable capital in the discussions of "contrary grace," discernible, they thought, in the first and feeblest tremors of regret as well as in the most wretched sense of desolation. The aim was to redeem the dis-ease induced by pietists' "barking," a dis-ease that "adequated" subjects to their election and to the object of their desire.

Aphorisms abounded: "a grieved spirit is no argument for a faithless heart"; "desire for mercy in the want of mercy is the obtaining of mercy"; unfeigned repentance is "no ordinary three hours matter" but is "to be crushed in peeces in feeling"; "care not for hell, for the nearer we feel it, the farther we are from it." To understand "contrary grace" and the therapeutic role of religious despair, we must restore the pietist practical divinity that generated something of a culture of confirmation in which aphorisms such as these made sense and, moreover, made sense of the wretchedness and irresolution experienced by dutiful pietist pilgrims. Theirs was that "interchangeable course of sorrow and comfort, of faith and fear." Nonetheless, each pilgrim was likely to match John Jewel's disdainful description of the "wavering minded man . . . unstable in all his waies." That course and wavering should be familiar to readers of Spenser's Redcrosse and Marlowe's Faustus. The second chapter closes by considering what pietists might have made of such protagonists.[10]

There is certainly no more conspicuous and curious specimen of Elizabethan wavering than Hamlet. Is he stalling for time, deliberately puzzling his prey and screwing up his courage to kill Claudius? Is he groping for an independent fate, attempting to wriggle free from the role of revenger in which his father's ghost and his script have trapped him? Or is he the consummate expression of late Tudor melancholia?

The third chapter sifts answers to these and cognate questions, because Hamlet's run of self-recrimination so strikingly resembles the prayerful improvisation of the pietists' prodigal self.

The soliloquacious Hamlet is fond of what some now see as "lengthy speeches of self-erasure." The same "some" might say much the same thing about English Calvinists who spent countless hours "erect[ing] an inquisition over [their] hearts," as William Perkins directed. But inasmuch as bruising self-interrogation was therapeutic, practiced to complete a soterially advantageous submission to God's will—in the latter instance—and insofar as Hamlet's brooding self-interrogation led finally to humility and readiness ("readiness is all"), emphasis might better be placed on recomposition and composure than on decomposition and "erasure."

The ritual recomposition or refashioning of the self was the desideratum of pietist prayer and devotional literature. To keep theatrical rituals in an altogether different orbit or to satisfy ourselves with having spotted but superficial similarities hardly seems to make sense. It is not only that we are now learning that religious opposition to the theater was less uncompromising and less effective than scholars once thought. Segregation ill serves our study of the social construction of the self in Elizabethan England, where religious and dramatic cultures interpenetrated. Of course, the distinctiveness of pietist self-formation ought not to be understated. As dissidents increasingly realized how pointless it was to petition past Whitgift, Bancroft, and other apostles of order, they amplified the summons to self-inventory, sorrow for sin, and helplessness before God, which had sounded less stridently before. Shakespeare had entirely other reasons for creating Hamlet, and other results. As library acquisitions attest, the interpretive possibilities associated with those contested reasons and incontestably impressive results are just about inexhaustible. Hamlet cannot exclusively or very easily be enrolled among the pietists' "emblem[s] of alienated agony," but his alienation, agony, and soliloquacious introspection suggest that consequences drawn from a doctrine of divine predestination into pietist devotional literature were part of a larger cultural practice, an Elizabethan therapy of sorts and an aesthetics of experience.[11]

Opinions differ about Christianity's responsibility for anxiety and agony. Jean Deprun thought they were integrally related to piety. God was the supreme object of Christians' desires. He was, in part, hidden, and he was said to be angry. Deprun maintained that, from the time of Augustine through that of Pascal, divine anger was wed to each Christian's purported defection, as effect to cause, and that coupling perpetuated profound dis-ease among the faithful. From a different angle, however, Christianity's successes imposing meaning on experience seem to have allayed anxiety. William Bouwsma suggested that the imposition frequently gave life "a measure of reliability and thus reduce[d], even if it [did not] altogether abolish, life's ultimate and terrifying uncertainties." Inevitably, though, rival consolations competed for the imagination. If not for Marlowe's Faustus, at least for many medieval and early modern Christians, the church effectively countered the regressive pull of magic, to some extent by incorporating its seductively comforting elements. But the church was most successful setting boundaries that made uncertainties and ambiguities more manageable, mostly by mapping relatively clear routes through the uneven terrain of this world and into the next. Protestants were persuaded that Catholicism provoked and manipulated rather than diminished dis-ease. Calvin charged that priests "torture souls with many misgivings and immerse them in a sea of trouble and anxiety." Yet, as Bouwsma found, Calvin also understood that anxiety was an antidote for "worldly security," which was the chief obstacle to faith. Only the unregenerate were carefree. Among the faithful, anxiety was the necessary foil to hope. It was there to be overcome, but stubbornly there, all the same.[12]

So there is something to recommend Jean Delumeau's striking contention that Catholicism and Calvinism alike prospered through *culpabilisation*. Delumeau collected many more bits and pieces of evidence than did Deprun to document a confessionally bipartisan campaign to terrify Christians. Catholics and Protestants harped on the narrowness of the "narrow gate" (Matthew 7:13) and "door" ("strive to enter by the narrow door; for many I tell you, will seek to enter and will not be able to": Luke 13:24). Pessimistic preaching stressed the dire consequences of even the smallest transgressions. Frescoes and woodcuts kept tormented spirits, cadavers, and gaping caskets before Christians' eyes. Fear near totally eclipsed forgiveness. The result, according to Delumeau, no mean practitioner of *culpabilisation* himself, was an alleged "de-Christianization" of early modern Europe.[13]

To say I take a different approach is an understatement, although to say more now will keep me introducing indefinitely. Yet I was interested to see that Delumeau cast John Donne as the epitome of Elizabethan pessimism and that John Stachniewski, who appraised Donne independently and far more thoroughly, caught and emphasized his "dominant mood of despair." But when the speaker in Donne's *Holy Sonnets* begs for "repair" and thus performs his repentance by dramatizing the tension between faith and doubt, the poet seems to me to give voice to the pietists' program for rehabilitation. *Prayer, Despair, and Drama* concludes with a look at the *Holy Sonnets,* a final look at the Elizabethan aesthetics of experience that stretched some years into the seventeenth century. For Delumeau, guilt and fear constitute a constant refrain. For Stachniewski, the last word is "despair." My last word is "Donne." [14]

Notes

1. Patrick Collinson, *The Birthpangs of Protestant England: Religious and Cultural Change in the Sixteenth and Seventeenth Centuries* (London: St. Martin's Press, 1988), 95, for "full internalization"; and C. John Sommerville, *The Secularization of Early Modern England: From Religious Culture to Religious Faith* (Oxford: Oxford University Press, 1992), 179, for "reflective religion." Four alternative approaches invite preliminary comment: (1) John N. King, *Spenser's Poetry and the Reformation Tradition* (Princeton: Princeton University Press, 1990), to my mind, is among the most nuanced and engaging efforts to find doctrine or theological themes "at work" in Elizabethan literary culture. That challenge has kept literary historians and several historical theologians preoccupied for generations. (2) Joel Fineman, *Shakespeare's Perjured Eye: The Invention of Poetic Subjectivity in the Sonnets* (Berkeley: University of California Press, 1986) brilliantly elaborates the structuring of early modern self-consciousness without even a nod to religious deliberation. All converges on "the rhetoric or rhetoricity of praise." (3) Hamlet was sure that a play was just the thing to "catch the conscience" of his unrepentant king; Martha Tuck Rozett, *The Doctrine of Election and the Elizabethan Tragedy* (Princeton: Princeton University Press, 1984) suggestively speculates on the Calvinist conscience and the didactic function of drama. (4) Anne Ferry, *The "Inward" Language: Sonnets of Wyatt, Sidney, Shakespeare, Donne* (Chicago: University of Chicago Press, 1983) labors to document the lack of correspondence. *Prayer, Despair, and Drama,* on the whole, is compatible or collateral with the first and, as a whole, addresses an oversight in otherwise generative attempts to parse "poetic presence" and subjectivity. I shall have little more to say, then, about advocates of the first two alternatives. Specific reservations about the third and fourth, as well as arguments and counterproposals are included in what follows, as are my arguments with colleagues similarly interested in Elizabethan sentiment but apt to construe religious and dramatic despair as symptoms of late Tudor "destabilization" and "dislocation." For "patterns of

prodigality" in other Elizabethan fiction, see Richard Helgerson, *The Elizabethan Prodigals* (Berkeley: University of California Press, 1976), 1–15.

2. See, for example, Sutcliffe's *A Treatise of Ecclesiastical Discipline* (London, 1590), 146–50.

3. Quoted in Hirofumi Horie, "The Origin and the Historical Context of Archbishop Whitgift's *Orders* of 1586," *Archiv für Reformationsgeschichte* 83 (1992): 249.

4. John Udall, *The State of the Church of Englande laide open in a conference betweene Diotrophes, a byshop, Tertullus, a papist, Demetrius, an usurer, Pandocheus, an inne-keeper, and Paule, a preacher of the word of God* (London, 1588) C4r, E2v, H2r. Udall snatched Diotrophes, "who likes to put himself first," from 3 John 9. For Whitgift's order, see the documents appended to John Strype, *The Life and Acts of the Most Reverend Father in God, John Whitgift, D.D.* (London, 1718), 117; and, for recent corroboration of his critics' suspicions, Wallace T. MacCaffrey, *Queen Elizabeth and the Making of Policy, 1572–1588* (Princeton: Princeton University Press, 1981), especially 101–14.

5. Leonard Wright, *A Summons for Sleepers* (London, 1591), 17–21. For Penry and the authorship of the Marprelate satires, see Leland H. Carlson, *Martin Marprelate, Gentleman: Master Job Throkmorton Laid Open in his Colors* (San Marino, Calif.: Huntington Library, 1981), 271–313.

6. Josias Nichols, *The Plea of the Innocent wherein is averred that the ministers and people falslie termed puritanes are injuriouslie slaundered for enemies or troublers of the state* (London, 1602), 6–11.

7. Walter Travers, *An Answere to a supplicatorie epistle of G. T. for the pretended Catholiques* (London, 1583), 352. For the name game, notably, Paul Christianson, "Reformers and the Church of England under Elizabeth I and the Early Stuarts," *Journal of Ecclesiastical History* 31 (1980): 463–82; Patrick Collinson, "A Comment Concerning the Name Puritan," *Journal of Ecclesiastical History* 31 (1980): 483–88; and Peter Lake, "Puritan Identities," *Journal of Ecclesiastical History* 35 (1984): 112–23.

8. William Perkins, *A Reformed Catholike*, in *Works*, vol. 1 (London, 1612), 574. See *inter alia*, Harry C. Porter, *Reformation and Reaction in Tudor Cambridge* (Cambridge: Cambridge University Press, 1958); R. T. Kendall, *Calvin and English Calvinism to 1649* (Oxford: Clarendon Press, 1982); and Patrick Collinson, *The Religion of Protestants: The Church in English Society, 1559–1625* (Oxford: Oxford University Press, 1982), particularly 82–85. For "Calvinist Episcopalians," Nicholas Tyacke, *Anti-Calvinists: The Rise of English Arminianism, 1589–1640* (Oxford: Oxford University Press, 1987).

9. William Perkins, *The True Gaine*, in *Works*, vol. 1 (London, 1612), 650, 664; *Exposition of the Symbole or Creede of the Apostles*, in *Works*, vol. 1, 292; and *A Treatise of Man's Imagination*, in *Works*, vol. 2 (London, 1617), 478.

10. Richard Greenham, *A Letter Consolatorie*, in *The Works of the Reverend and Faithfull Servant of Jesus Christ, M. Richard Greenham*, ed. Henry Holland (Lon-

don, 1605), 265; and John Jewel, *An Exposition upon the two epistles of the Apostle St. Paul to the Thessalonians* (London, 1594), 196.

11. For "emblems," see Michael MacDonald, "*The Fearefull Estate of Francis Spira:* Narrative, Identity, and Emotion in Early Modern England," *Journal of British Studies* 31 (1992): 32-61; for religious opposition to the theater, Paul Whitfield White, "Calvinist and Puritan Attitudes Toward the Stage in Renaissance England," *Explorations in Renaissance Culture* 14 (1988): 41-55.

12. Jean Deprun, *La philosophie de l'inquietude en France au XVIIIe siècle* (Paris: J. Vrin, 1979), 123-28; William Bouwsma, *A Usable Past: Essays in European Cultural History* (Berkeley: University of California Press, 1990), 170-73; and Bouwsma, *John Calvin: A Sixteenth-Century Portrait* (Oxford: Oxford University Press, 1988), 32-48. Also consult Keith Thomas, *Religion and the Decline of Magic* (New York: Scribner's, 1971), particularly 636-40.

13. Jean Delumeau, *Le péché et la peur: La culpabilisation en Occident XIIIe-XVIIIe siècles* (Paris: Fayard, 1983), 244-45, 315-16, 568.

14. John Stachniewski, *The Persecutory Imagination: English Puritanism and the Literature of Religious Despair* (Oxford: Clarendon Press, 1991), 254, 291.

1

———⟨⟨⟩⟩⟨⟩———

"Much in Prayer"

The sixteenth-century reformers were anything but shy. They dreaded what they saw as the slush of unscriptural ceremonies in their churches, and they did not hesitate to say as much to their more politically influential and more circumspect coreligionists, the princes of Germany, the magistrates in the Swiss cantons, and the monarchs of England. They selectively and aggressively quoted the Bible to cautious friends and critics, notably to apologists for tradition. The reformers favored, among other passages, the one which informed that a person's faith, not a church's solemn liturgical occasions or the priests presiding over them, could exorcize demons, even move mountains (Matthew 17:20). In fact, those reformers were known for an outspoken, exclusive, consuming faith in faith. Yet despite their solafideism, none forgot that the statement suggesting the omnicompetence of faith was followed by one enjoining prayers (17:21).

Theodore Beza, John Calvin's successor in Geneva, conceded that faith could do little without "conscientious prayer," so it comes as no surprise that his many avid readers and admirers in England insisted on the importance of praying. A number of them publicly regretted the survival of prescribed and "popish" prayers in their reformed churches, but even those plaintiffs—according to John Geree, in 1646, particularly those plaintiffs—were "much in prayer." Geree said so after looking back on nearly seventy years of religious controversy. He referred particularly to the implacable critics of Roman Catholic ritual and of its apparent comeback during William Laud's tenure at Canterbury and Arminian ascendancy, critics who hated what was left of Catholic worship in their Prayer Books but loved to pray "in closet, family, and publicke assembly."

"Much in prayer," they "esteemed that manner of prayers best wherby the gift of God's expressions were varied according to present wants and occasions, yet [they] did not account set forms unlawfull."[1]

Geree's report is tremendously compressed. It simply does not explain why Protestants who were persuaded that divine will was immutable and that they had been chosen or elected would so anxiously trouble their God with the contents of their troubled consciences. (If God had already forgiven their trespasses, why did they hurl their petitions heavenward? If God arranged all things in advance, even their wickedness and remorse, why did they painstakingly detail the former and prayerfully labor the latter?) Moreover, Geree's account virtually elided the perceived incompatibility between set and varied forms of prayer. Did Geree forget the prayer wars that kept Elizabethan Calvinists feuding for decades? In 1572, the standardbearer during the Cambridge campaigns to reform polity, Thomas Cartwright, declared that reading set prayers or reciting them from memory could not be called praying. Others defended the practices and objected to impromptu and allegedly aimless and unruly prayers. The dispute raged; Cartwright's friends clamored, more persistently than he, that "set forms" were "unlawfull," and just before the century's end, Richard Hooker protested that many reformed Christians still belligerently maintained that "prayers were no otherwise accepted of God than beinge conceaved allwayes newe, accordinge to the exigence of present occasions."[2]

I want to recover Elizabethans' reasons for praying and to look closely at the controversy over prescribed forms of prayer. All Calvinists agreed that scripture commended prayer and that the commendation was sufficient reason for copying the practices current and uncontested among Jesus Christ's first followers. Calvinists disagreed, however, about what those practices were. Some said there had been no set liturgies and read prayers among the disciples and apostles. Such formalities, they argued, were afterthoughts, contrivances that unduly restricted free, pious, and prayerful expression. They said as well that set forms of prayer promoted complacency and precluded candor.

Claims about candor betray the widely held assumption that authenticity amounted to correspondence between personality and performance, between the grief, guilt, and longing lodged in the deeper strata of consciousness (personality) and the confessions, petitions, and expressions of gratitude that break the surface and constitute pietists' prayerful performances. Yet prayerful performances were encouraged to create, rather than simply to correspond to, prodigal personalities. Prayers tapped into the residue that experience left in memory. They also retrieved what instruction and indoctrination deposited in conscience. But the pietists expected prayers to fashion each petitioner's intense inwardness, to conjure up and compose identity, as well as to articulate it. This fashioning or conjuring is terribly important for my purposes because it reduces the textbook distance between Reformation piety and late Renaissance drama.[3]

Praying Up the Prodigal

Comatose Christians mumbled their prescribed prayers in church. They understood nothing. They displayed little or no devotion. They were the casualties of an incomplete reformation, according to those who pressed for completion. But a case could be made that the critics of alleged incompletion had imagined those hapless casualties and their mumbling or at least that proponents of prescribed prayers were doing what they could to obviate listless worship. For Calvinists generally concurred that the Catholics were wrong to pray by the clock, to prescribe times for prayer and thus to restrict the liberties of the faithful. Any Christian who did not "often repaire to the fire of praier," they said, would certainly be daunted by the challenges of this chilly world.[4]

Such sentiment, which admiring Calvinists had lifted from Catholic devotional literature, specifically the "often," could have suggested to some the advantage of impromptu prayer and the disadvantage of scripts. But sentiment and phrasing, the well-advised frequency, summoned others to double their efforts to make their scripts for prayers integral parts of the Christian's life. Pastors resourcefully churned out their formulae to prepare petitioners "in their families" for public worship. Thomas Becon, Edward Dering, and John Daye, to name only the most conspicuous, published sets of home remedies for lethargy, meditations that they brewed as medicine for indifference and irreligion, prayers to assist "every Christen man to lamente his owne cause before the merciful eies of divyne majeste."[5]

Many Calvinists were convinced that it was not just possible but also advisable "to lamente [one's] owne cause" with another's words, but several thought otherwise, presuming it was not simply inadvisable but absolutely impossible. The difference of opinion started the prayer wars, about which we will hear more shortly. At present, though, I am interested in the point put quite well by Thomas Knell, a noncombatant. In 1581, Knell's *Godlie and Necessarie Treatise* released readers from any obligation they might feel to repeat verbatim the volume's prayers, nonetheless it supplied a checklist of required preparatory exercises and preferred attitudes, all to generate intense feeling, Knell confided. The pietists' program was to bring Christians "to greater feeling," as Dudley Fenner stipulated, "not only by doctrine but by experience." Proponents of unscripted prayer proclaimed the importance of greater feeling and demanded that liturgical experience be deregulated. Defenders of set liturgies and scripted prayers also insisted on the importance of greater feeling, which, they said, was why the experience of prayer ought to be controlled.[6]

In prayer, an appreciable portion of that greater feeling was forwarded to God in sighs and statements expressing need and gratitude. Petitioners lavished the other considerable portion on their searches for signs of election to intensify their laments, as they were counseled. Searches began in an odd place, in the shadows cast by their memories of wickedness. Their preachers' responsibility was to dwell on those shadows and to be certain that they occasioned something of a crisis of confidence. From their pulpits they were also to remind sinners of the plight of the impenitent, the stated purpose of which, as one might expect, was to inspire remorse, rededication, and godliness.[7]

William Perkins influentially sketched the lines connecting pulpit, personal feeling, and prayer. He taught at Cambridge from the 1580s until his death in 1602, then and thereafter the most widely read and revered of the pietists. Perkins suspected that even the most passionate sermons might stimulate only a modicum of remorse. Preachers, he said, must go after their parishioners, who could only ascertain signs of their election and thus learn of their salvation when the enormity of their sins "pierceth to the heart and taketh hold of the affections." The elect, quite simply, are those who "feele continually the smart and bitternes of their owne sinnes."[8]

Catholicism struck the Calvinists as having forgotten that, soterially, pain preceded gain and conditioned each petitioner's requests for divine grace and mercy. Perkins flatly asserted that Catholics could not pray effectively. They were too arrogant, he said; they appealed to God as if their causes were just rather than justifiably lost. They looked to earn or merit the kingdom of heaven; Perkins believed they were groping for some entrance other than "God's mercie gate." Neither their arrogance nor their purported virtue served them well, no matter how many penances or prayers they performed: "hee which prayeth truely must be touched inwardly with a lively feeling of his owne misery." [9]

Laurence Chaderton, Master of Emmanuel College for nearly forty years and close friend of Perkins, redrew the boundaries and floated a different explanation for the Catholics' failures. They prayed ineffectively, he alleged, but not because of their arrogance. In fact, they were usually humble, but their humility was a symptom of "wavering faith." They were driven to extremes of self-abasement by substantial skepticism about their election. Chaderton held that doubts and uncertainty, not pride, moved the Catholics to earn their redemption. Yet uncertainty kept them from serious self-inquiry. By contrast, Calvinists were confident in their recuperation and could determinedly and comprehensively "examine the very bottome of [their] heartes and rippe up all the inwarde and secrete corners of [their] consciences." [10]

Not every Calvinist at Cambridge, though, was preoccupied with the Catholics. For most, their side of the tracks concerned them more than the other. Henry Smith was often seen and heard around the colleges in the 1580s before becoming one of London's more celebrated preachers. He was not known to have commented at any length on the Catholics' temerity or timidity. Instead, he concentrated on getting the Calvinists to feel their misery more intensively. He was displeased that so many of them had become experts at exculpation. "Sins and excuses [were] twins," Smith said, describing his parishioners' prayers. They "mince sins as though they needed no forgiveness," he continued and echoed his colleagues' calls for that "lively feeling of misery," the sure symptom of election. So "backe-reckoning," among the elect, was bloodletting. Prayers were probing, bruising confessions.[11]

Maybe one expects only Malvolio, William Shakespeare's paper puritan, to place a premium on misery. But we will progressively understand why the pietists ascribed estimable qualities to that "lively feeling of misery" if we remember that the doctrines of divine election and predestination were primarily parts of what Thomas More contemptuously called "feeling faith." After he had surveyed the full range of his opponents' opinions and arguments, More teased them about their faith in feeling. He concluded that emotional attachment was their court of last resort. So if Martin Luther or William Tyndale or any of their apprentices "felt" the truth of his or her faith, notwithstanding a formidable consensus to the contrary, that faith would need no further confirmation. Subsequent predestinarian pietism was something of an outgrowth of what More perceived and parodied. Predestination, for many Calvinists, was only secondarily, if at all, a vexing doctrinal corollary to the Calvinist assertion of divine sovereignty. It was primarily an apprehension mediated by experience and by that "greater feeling" commended in devotional literature. Faith in God's sovereignty and clemency (and assurance of election) came with one's heartfelt anguish and remorse. In his letter "full of Christian consolation," Edward Dering mentioned a combination of dis-ease and comfort, a rather curious and striking one that we will have several occasions to recall: "care not for hell," he advised, "for the nearer we feele it, the further we are from it." [12]

William Perkins knew how confused pietists were likely to get, searching for signs or assurances of their election in the swirl of feelings, longings, and regrets. It would be easy, for example, to mistake repentance for a first sign, because it was "first in appearance" (by which Perkins meant first to appear as a rounded or fully articulated resolve). Moreover, ordinarily a preacher urged repentance on those hearing the gospel for the first time, a strategy that seemed to suggest that repentance, "an utter disliking" of sin combined with the resolve to reform, was an initial rather than a final phase in sanctification. But actually, anguish and remorse, ingredients for what Elizabethan pietists termed "godly sorrow," were the first signs of election and sanctification. Perkins dug up an analogy to press the point.

> If any marvell how repentance follows sanctification . . . I answer that all other graces are more hidden in the heart, whereas repentance is open and sooner appeareth to a man's owne self and to the eyes of the world. It is like the bud on the tree, which appeareth before the leafe, the blossome, the fruit; and yet in nature, it is the last; for a man must be renewed and come to an utter disliking of his owne sinnes before he will turne from them and leave them. [13]

Perkins's enviable reputation, I suspect, was due in no part to his gardening, but his point is not lost here, and he went on to add that the "more hidden" graces assured that the elect never completely consented to sin.

Still, it was a struggle for them to withhold consent. The elect "partly will and partly abhorre that which is evil." Perkins noticed, as had the apostle Paul before him, that "a striving within," a tension between "would do" and "should do," deterred the elect from settling in their wicked ways, and prayer gave that "striving" texture. It exacerbated anguish, remorse, and tension, but, Perkins ruled, prayer also "tame[d] the flesh." In meditation, another of Perkins's tactics for "taming," one mulled over the problem of consent, but prayer, described as a "groveling" confession, was an apt vehicle for humbling self-incrimination, anguish, and remorse, although it was more than that. Prayerful performances did not simply record the tremors of "godly sorrow"; they were its very source and mainspring.[14]

With only subtle signals at the start, godly sorrow was not all that readily distinguishable from vague regret or mannered self-reproach. That was why Perkins, Chaderton, Smith, and others encouraged Christians to intensify their experiences of misery, to search ever more diligently for specks of sin, to "rippe up the inward and secrete corners," if they wanted to improve their chances for finding the surest tokens of their election. Every Calvinist would have heard that "slight and superficiall" sorrow was inadmissible evidence. Roger Fenton, preaching at Gray's Inn, confirmed that prayer was no time for "sudden qualmes," which produced only what John Preston later and euphemistically called "vanishing purposes," because they were feigned and fugitive rather than sincere and steadfast. They were a far cry from the determination to improve that pietists identified with unfeigned repentance.[15]

Beza of Geneva was clear about the distinction when he wrote about the apostle Paul's commendation of "godly grief." He could not imagine that the apostle intended to compass as "godly" the vulgar and less intense sorrows prompted by fears of punishment (*dolor formidine poena territus*). That *dolor*, or possibly one of Fenton's "sudden qualmes," brought Hamlet's uncle Claudius to his knees: "pray can I not. . . . My words fly up, my thoughts remain below" (3.3.38, 97). Certainly it was not the sorrow that Lawrence Tomson, with Beza's gloss before him, identified as sorrow and repentance "unto salvation."[16]

Pietists emphasized the difference between godly sorrow and feigned or faint regret until it came to resemble the disparity between a doze and death. Generally, they figured that fears of punishment were something of a dead end, yet Niels Hemmingsen had declared them a "first steppe unto life," and his exposition of the Twenty-fifth Psalm circulated in a

London translation during the 1580s. Still, there is little other evidence that continuity caught on. Popular compendia assembled for pastoral use stressed the discontinuity between worldly sorrow, disquiet stemming from a natural aversion to punishment, and godly sorrow, the "greefe and displeasure of mind which we feele for offending God." According to Thomas Wilson's *Christian Dictionary*, worldly sorrow was fear of divine justice and retribution; godly sorrow presupposed God's mercy. The distinction was so fundamental it will be reasserted in the next chapter's study of wretchedness and redemption. For now, it stands to suggest that petitioners during prayer did not offer the contents of their troubled consciences to alter God's will and win reprieve but to change themselves from frightened sinners into sorrowful but confident penitents, in conformity, of course, with God's plan for the elect.[17]

The plan awaited implementation, but Calvinist preachers did not wait patiently, for they imagined that the doctrine of divine predestination did not preclude their best efforts to inspire the desired changes. They gathered that their task, as noted, was to impress on the impenitent the risks they ran. Predestinarians on the continent were excellent models. At Heidelberg, Hieronymus Zanchius lectured on the foolish expectations that kept Catholics from anguish and soterially advantageous remorse. The Catholics, he said, assumed that friends' prayers would help them and that they could purchase with bequests what only godly sorrow would gain. Zanchius commenced to disabuse them, stressing Christians' responsibilities for significant choices, without sacrificing the idea that God had already determined the fate of the elect: "here life is either lost or gotten." Elizabethan pietists detailed the getting. "Touched with the finger of God's grace," John Phillip wrote in 1584, Christians withdraw their consent from sin and turn to God, returning "like prodigall sons." As often as they prayed their sorrow to their supremely clement father, offenders turned into penitent prodigals.[18]

Transformations of that sort intrigue present-day observers, some of whom suspect that Calvinists "much in prayer" were really redirecting hostility: the pietists covertly hated God but found it was safer and theologically more sensible to hate themselves. Conjectures about such displacement appear to feed the frenzy among literary historians who write almost rhapsodically about "experiences of dislocation" in Elizabethan England, discovering dislocation and self-cancellation nearly everywhere—in sermon, sonnet, and soliloquy. We will want to deal at greater length with their discovery in the third chapter, but even here we cannot afford neutrality.[19]

Inasmuch as they promised that prayers would "rippe up all the inwarde and secrete corners of consciences," pietists seem to welcome the immigrant ideas about self-destruction smuggled from the late twentieth century. Their insistence on the frequency and intensity of prayerful performances also appears to warrant, if not welcome, twentieth-century speculations about compulsive devotional behavior, "obsessive introspection," and deliberate decentering. But the presumption of all latter-day guesswork is that somewhere, prior to prayer, the self more or less peaceably awaited decomposition. Some presume it was the victim or object of pietist inquiry and indictment, decimated during a thrashing and agonized search for signs of election. Some presume it was an integrated, tyrannical, executive self, the impresario or subject of the literary or religious rituals of interrogation, inventory, contrition, and submission that ended by destroying its integrity and tyranny. Too rarely, however, have selves been understood as dramatic effects, instead of causes, of their performances. But that approach invites us to reconsider apparent dislocation and disintegration and to make prayerful "rip[ping]" part of pietist renovation and regeneration. Whereas, to the pietists at prayer, authenticity often meant correspondence between personality and performance, a broader perspective on the cultural dynamics of religious experience and expression shows that prayers were not just formulations of agents' intentions or narrative traces of some psychodynamic process operating behind or beneath intention. Prayers shaped worshipers as well as worship. "Much in prayer," the petitioner, "touched with grace," created and became a prodigal self.

Pressed Down and Stirred Up

Thomas Playfere is not quite in the same league as the twentieth-century critics of agonized introspection, but in 1596, while prosecuting his unsuccessful candidacy for the mastership of St. John's College, Cambridge, he expressed serious and, for his time, psychologically sensitive reservations about fellow Calvinists' devotions. His sermon on the power of prayer turned into a register of complaints against "pety novelties" of the more extreme pietists. He doubted their claims about the stirring character of private prayers. Unless Christians' petitions were recited publicly and in unison, Playfere said, "that small spark of zeale which is in us may quickly bee put out and that little droppe of devotion . . . may quickly bee dried up."

What gives this sermon its special relevance to our study of prayerful performances, however, is Playfere's burly opposition to the pietists' self-inventory and self-accusation. "We may look back a little," he allowed, but too much memory hobbled prayer. Shame and sorrow "presseth down." They slowed progress and prohibited perseverance in righteousness. That was why the apostle Paul instructed Christians to "lay aside every weight and sin" (Hebrews 12:1). Playfere made that remark a milestone in the history of the human imagination, adding that, if Paul returned to attend late Tudor worship, he would have been distressed by reformed Christians doting on their vices. "All this looking to our selves is more than needs"; it was self-indulgent, Playfere fussed, and, worse still, it played into Satan's hands. Shuffling through a heap of shortcomings, too scrupulous Calvinists would be distracted from more vital concerns and dragged, he feared, "into the new-found way of Puritanisme."[20]

John Freeman and Richard Rogers saw Satan's work very differently. Freeman charged that the devil danced Christians away from confrontations with their failures. Satan made them rather sleepy—"drowsie," Perkins would have said—and inclined them to pray too infrequently and bundle their sins too neatly, using generalizations rather than their chafing recollections of specific misdeeds. Rogers warned that unvoiced and unprayed guilt and insecurity were the devil's playground. But the *Comfortable Treatise* composed by Robert Linaker shortly before Playfere preached on prayer, in effect, answered that sermon's stiff objections to pious self-absorption most forcefully.[21]

Linaker acknowledged that tormenting "backe-reckoning" might turn back many petitioners, if only because lengthy rehearsals of reprehensible conduct, their own stories of their own misconduct, could convince them they were lamenting their causes in vain, that forgiveness was unlikely. "Pressed down" by the burden of sin and guilt, they would give up praying and thus take a fateful step away from God's mercy.

If prayerful introspection stopped with that step, Satan scored another set of souls. Playfere would hardly have had to labor his point. Yet Linaker garrisoned his counterproposal with scriptural assurances, chief among them, Christ's summons to those "laden with sins." If those sins "lie upon your conscience like some little light feather," Linaker said, there

was cause for despair, for it would signal that confessors and petitioners had no inkling of the magnitude of their offenses. It would show, in
other words, that they were unaware that they had offended a father who
had already forgiven them and would go on forgiving them. So, if they
were not "pressed down," they might just as well give up. But Linaker
celebrated the alternative: if sins "presse and hold you down as a wonderfull weightie burthen," there was cause for confidence, rumpled but
robust. For godly sorrow, with all its torments, and assurance of election were partners. The only catch was that the partnership regularly
had to be renewed. Hence, the pious life regularly was punctuated by
despair. There is no need to unscramble Linaker's lucid comments on
"backe-reckoning" to see a preview of the pietist apology for the feeling of misery or wretchedness and for the therapeutic value of anguished
introspection.[22]

Linaker admitted that he sometimes settled in a soterial trough. "Baren
in prayer," he improvised "babling praiers" at those times and could pack
his laments with only "poore, drie, naked, and sillie stuffe, both for words
and matter." Yet he looked back on his sorry states almost immodestly because his halting performances and his despondence actually brought him
closer to Christ, who had also experienced "exceedingly great anguish"
only to receive, and be revived by, God's assurances. Despondence was
not dangerous, then, and it would become less debilitating as it recurred.
The danger, if one can call it that, was in the eye of the critic or skeptic
who thought that pietists grew progressively grim and gloomy, brooding over the sufficiency of their sorrow or about some surplus of sins left
unpardoned. The elect learned they had recourse to divine grace. They
learned—as we will come to see more clearly in the third chapter—that
the frontier between melancholy and the reformed Christians' godly sorrow was well marked. Sorrow "pressed down" prayerful petitioners, stirring and lifting them up, for sorrow and grief announced God's mercy
to those who prayed earnestly and often.[23]

Prayers "stirre up our selves." We have already heard the "stirring"
described as a stinging, a tousling of sorts, more violently as a ripping
and ransacking. I think Nicholas Bownde expressed this most memorably, with the exception of John Donne. The passage in question was
planted in Bownde's meditation on prayer and in the context of his accusation that some reformed Christians prayed too lethargically. "Prayers
flowe from us like a still streame" and show to the world that petition-

ers' hearts have been hardened and are "senseless and dead . . . like a lake which is without motion." So much for the problem; the solution: "our hearts must be working like a great ocean sea that sometimes cometh with great billowes so that it bringeth up things that are at the bottom of it." The prayerful performances of pietists must elicit inordinate affections, Bownde implied, basically because "great billowes" were necessary if sedimented faults and failures were to be dragged to the surface of consciousness and into petitioners' confessions.[24]

"Great billowes" were necessary as well to overcome reason, which Bownde arraigned as the chief cause of "unbelief." Reason, after all, held that a just judge would never let the guilty go unpunished, whereas surges of sentiment encouraged the elect to see their "wants and weaknes" but also to believe that God would supply strength and grant amnesty. Billowing prayers, therefore, "stirre up our selves in true faith to depend upon God's promises and to acknowledge his benifites towardes us."[25]

I suspect that we have enough to go on: many Elizabethan pietists apparently wanted prayer to do precisely what Plato feared poetry might, that is, to stir passions and sympathies that would suppress rational judgment. For rational judgment would not rebel against common sense. It was likely to find something absurd and hopelessly contradictory in sorrows that simultaneously pressed petitioners down, stirred them up, and afforded them calming or comforting assurances. Sixteen years ago, writing about the theater, Joel Altman glimpsed what just may be the "play of mind" that favored dramatically staged contraries not only in theatrical "interludes of extended quest" but also, I think, in prayerful equivalents of what Donne called "inward researches." On stage, the goal of the Tudor game or play (with "hopeless contradictions") was not to explain propositions but to "mirror minds coming to grips with a complex problem." In prayer, "vexed contraries," Donne would have said, fashioned and became the penitent prodigal self.[26]

Prayer Wars

Richard Rogers was not one to scrub unpleasant experiences and self-criticism from his journal. One entry for 1587 tells of a meeting convened for "the stirring upp of our selves to greater godliness." All went well until adjournment neared and one of the assembled volunteered an extended benediction. The "stirring upp" then ceased, at least for Rogers, whose mind wandered. His diary deplored the inattention and confessed his chronic inability to concentrate: "I am caryed . . . with drouzines and wearisomnes commonly at the praiers of others." And Rogers realized that there was something doubly dishonorable about his unfortunate habit, for he was intolerant of those similarly afflicted, his parishioners who dozed during their pastor's prayers.[27]

Boredom, bad enough, was but a side effect of "bondage," according to the most outspoken Calvinist critics of "stinted, read prayers." They blamed pastors who insisted that parishioners pray in their wakes, who barred impassioned and impromptu prayers from the pews, and who thereby chained petitioners to sentiments other than their own; hence, "bondage." Predictably, charges of this character prompted the advocates of prescribed prayers and "devised leitourgies" to reply, yet it is hard to keep track of the controversy. A number of Calvinists found they could defend both fixed and impromptu prayers. Extremists closed ranks against set forms, yet some disagreements among them left their premises untidy. (We know enough from one source to suggest that critics in exile more hospitably entertained arguments for the utility of fixed and formal prayer.) The general dispute resembled more a tavern brawl than a tug-of-war.[28]

To follow the controversy into the next century is to come across fresh difficulties. Sometime after 1634, John Seldon, with some finality, reported that "the church is settled; no man may make a prayer in publicke of his owne head." Seldon immediately and enigmatically confided, however, that he "hoped wee may be cur'd of our extempore prayers in the same way the grocer's boy is cur'd of his eating plums, [that is,] when wee have had our belly full of them." Could the church's "settlement" have been that inconsequential, so much so that remedy was expected to come with and from excess?[29]

Seldon's preferences for decorum during worship reflected concerns articulated often during the prayer wars of the 1590s. Thanks largely to two Essex ministers, John Greenwood and George Gifford, we possess plenty of evidence for that chapter of our story. Greenwood put the case for impromptu prayer so plainly that neither Gifford nor we could mistake it. He conceded that pastors should pray with and for their parishioners about the "publick affaires of the church," should pray, for example, for peace in the realm, relief from drought in the fields, and repair of dry rot in the fabric. Yet Greenwood then declared that it was impossible for anyone to undergo and express for someone else the intense experiences of dislocation and renovation, which we must now associate with the ritual creation of the penitent prodigal. Parishioners must lament their own causes. "To lay forth our wantes and estate of our owne soule," Greenwood said "cannot be done by reading an other man's writings, alwayes singing one song, customably repeating in superstition certaine words, our hearts never ripped up, examined." He was sure that one borrowed another's sorrow when one repeated another's prayers and that borrowed sorrow was not godly sorrow. Those certainties, coupled with his prejudices against episcopacy, earned Greenwood several short terms in prison from 1586 until his execution for sedition seven years later. But the argument that scripted prayers were illicit and that parasite piety was profitless survived him, as did George Gifford's often repeated opinion that the case against set prayers was uninformed and insensitive.[30]

Uninformed, Gifford said, because the critics of set prayers had not appreciated the similarities between prayers and sermons. Prescribed prayers, like sermons, were the words of others that nonetheless prompted "deeper sighing and sorrowing" than ordinary language used by even the most pious laypersons.

> The cause of all sighing and sorrowing . . . is the sinne and miserie which is within us, which we may the better behold and *expresse* by instruction. I have greevous sinne . . . which I doo partlye knowe, and can make some moane therein and praye. I come into the publike assembly where I hear the minister preach the word, which doth more fully laye open and display my sinne and misery. I am thereby driven into deeper sighing and sorrowing, with vehement praier in my heart unto God. Shall it be saide that I doo now fetch the cause of my sorrowing from an other man's speech in the time of my begging at God's hands? If not, then why should I be said to fetch the cause from the boke, which also doth instruct me? The like may be said when the congregation dooth pray with their pastor: they fetch not the cause of their sighing from him but are stirred up by him.[31]

And the case was insensitive, because critics of prescribed prayers apparently never stopped to think what their freedom from fixed forms might mean to worshipful yet unlearned persons who could lament nothing without help. Gifford contended that leadership was more valuable than liberty to the unlearned, to those "not otherwise able" to "poure

forth their hearts." Without the prayers of a carefully trained and or-
dained ministry, maybe John Greenwood could send syllables soaring,
give voice to godly sorrow, and gain assurance of election. The liturgies,
in that case, were not scripted for him but for less literate Christians
whose consolation, Gifford said, should be the concern of all.

Gifford admitted that weaker Christians, along with "great heapes . . .
of false Christians" mixed with their more genuinely and articulately
contrite neighbors. But it was unworthy of the better part, he scolded,
to throw out the incompletely reformed. He recalled that Augustine had
made precisely that point against the Donatist separatists in the fifth century and saw himself as a second Augustine befriending the weak and
berating the arrogant and inconsiderate who thought themselves strong
and who cast off from the church to experiment with impromptu prayer
and other practices. They were the Donatists *redivivi*, "ignorant blinde
scismatikes, which imagine they knowe more than all the churches of
God in the earth."[32]

Gifford himself was an outcast, deprived of his pulpit in 1584 and later
forbidden to preach anywhere in Essex. But while Greenwood obsti-
nately registered his opposition to authorities and insisted on the wheel,
Gifford eventually reconciled himself to those authorities and was re-
instated. He met occasionally with the leading moderates at Cambridge,
Chaderton and Perkins, who likely shared his interest in the unlearned,
"the most [who] are ignorant, weake, short of memory, dull and slow, and
need all helpes to stirre themselves up." And they probably shared as well
Gifford's nightmare: "every frantike spirit" sounding its private confessions publicly could make a bedlam of every Essex and East Anglian
church. Gifford, for his part, agreed with Chaderton and Perkins that
self-inventory and self-accusation were critically important, but his position on the front line against advocates of impassioned impromptu prayer
kept him from using the imagery of ripping, ransacking, battering, and
billowing. Instead, he adroitly juggled the language of feeling with that
of learning: "looke how much more a man feeleth in hymselfe the increase of knowledge," he wrote of the elect. As for the reprobate, they
"feeleth . . . darkened in [their] understanding." Gone from Gifford's
work are hints that Calvinism could have sanctioned billowing sentiment
and delirious self-deprecation. "Every one," he said, "must come home
to him selfe," but the homecoming was relatively subdued.[33]

Gifford, then, could be enrolled among late Tudor apostles of re-

straint, who increasingly prefixed the adverb "duely" to acknowledg-
ments that prayer and meditation should "stirre the affections." Their
complaints and cautions about "overcharged imaginations," however,
might never have acquired campaign or crusade momentum, had it not
been for two tenacious archbishops of Canterbury, John Whitgift and
Richard Bancroft, and Matthew Sutcliffe, the prolific dean of Exeter from
1588, who was particularly severe on "giddy spirits." "Ever seeking and
searching," those "spirits," Sutcliffe said, turned solemn worship into a
carnival with their "disorderly prayers."

> The spirit of God doeth in divers places of scripture exhort and
> stirre us up to praier, yet better it were not to pray then as some do
> withoute signe of humilitie, devotion, or religious reverence, yea
> without premeditation, order, or gravitie, to powre foorth sound-
> ing words. For God doth rather punish such men for their pro-
> phane contempt and senselesse presumption, then graunt their
> petitions. . . . [A]mong us then is a sort of seditious and schismati-
> call fellowes that are very presumptuous in this behalfe. Sometimes
> lay men and women upon very small occasion, yea upon no occa-
> sion, will take upon them suddenly to powrre forth their disorderly
> prayers, and divers fantastike preachers they are, that as they allow
> them, so cannot wel like of any prescripte form of prayer. Therefore
> doe they take upon them to make extemporall prayers, most piti-
> full and unlike to Christian prayers; for order, confused; for sense,
> absurd; for their needlesse repetitions, vaine; for their great out-
> cryes, ridiculous; for the multitude of words, very tedious. Prayers
> certes without devotion, good reason, or gravitie.[34]

Nearly fifty years earlier, Thomas Becon commented on "the rory-
ing of the throte, the shakynge of the head, the knockynge on the brest"
that frequently accompanied spontaneous prayer. Becon dismissed the
dramatic effects as "unfrytful," as "nothing." To Sutcliffe, however, such
special, convulsive effects—"humming, sighing, and groaning"—were
ominous signs of a "raging desire for innovation" that could very well destroy church order and discipline. Enthusiasts, he believed, "scarce know
the difference betwixt Christian praying and bitter cursing," and he heard
anger rumbling through their "extemporall" prayers. Sutcliffe generally was contemptuous of fervency without understanding, "zeal without
reason," but he was quite apprehensive, it seems, about fervency itself.

Zealots attracted crowds. Their confusion was contagious and usually seditious. A multitude, Sutcliffe gathered, "is more likely to doe anything then to reforme the church." Anything and everything from those "over-charged imaginations" stoked his own imagination, but had he wanted to cook up a seditious stew of anger, "roryng," and cursing, he could have done no better in fiction than what Edmund Copinger, William Hacket, and Henry Arthington did in fact.[35]

Edmund Copinger thought he was receiving special revelations from God, but he could get no one to take him seriously until he met Hacket, an itinerant preacher whose "dexteritie in conceiving extempo-rall prayers" subsequently captivated Arthington as well. The trio de-cided to warn England against Archbishop Whitgift, to warn the queen that her reign and realm were doomed unless she removed the prelate from her council and his see. Whitgift, by the late 1580s, seems to have been fairly effectively suppressing dissent against the prevailing church government and prescribed forms of worship.[36]

One day, while Copinger was soliciting support on the London streets, he chanced upon Job Throckmorton, a passerby who would have made a tremendously valuable ally. Throckmorton funded and probably col-laborated in John Penry's popular literary assaults on episcopacy, and he let himself be lured to Hacket's lodgings on this occasion to hear the realm's self-styled savior at prayer. Sutcliffe assumed that presence at this prayer meeting denoted partisanship. He thought he finally caught a prey that had been successfully eluding him. But Throckmorton as-sured him that he found the performance ludicrous and disapproved of the display. Hacket's prayer, he said, was "like the wild goose chase [with] neither head nor foot, rime nor reason." He insisted that the sounds of Copinger's and Arthington's rapturous assent, groans and hums, made him want to leave, and he did leave, he claimed, never to return.[37]

Still, to Sutcliffe, the coming betrayed far more than the going. That Throckmorton could have been drawn to see Hacket "and judge his gift in prayer" suggested complicity and political, as well as religious, sub-version. It suggests also that reputations in the early 1590s were made by virtuosity in prayer. And it seems safe to say that Henry Arthington hoped for as much when he challenged Whitgift to something of a duel.

Arthington composed the rules. He and Whitgift were to appear be-fore the queen. He was to pray first, confessing his sins, but also incrimi-nating his opponent. He would ask "that God's vengeance may presently consume me, both body and soule into hell for ever," if the archbishop "be not as deepely guiltie as I have charged." If Arthington survived his imprecations, then Whitgift was "to fal down in like sort and make the same praier," to pray "that the like vengeance may fall upon himself, if he be so gilty as I have charged." Arthington said he would willingly and directly submit to the hangman, if his opponent arose, though it was Hacket who went to the scaffold. A disturbance in the city streets during the summer of 1591 spurred authorities to take the trio into custody. Copinger refused food and starved to death in prison. And Arthington, who never got the opportunity to outpray the archbishop, escaped by betraying the others and abjuring his "conspiracy" and heresy.[38]

Richard Cosin was one of Whitgift's students at Cambridge. In the 1590s he came to his former teacher's defense, taking great pains to prove that Hacket, Copinger, and Arthington were not madmen. They were sinister not sick, he said, real dangers not deranged renegades. Many pietists, however, asserted quite the contrary. They were embarrassed by the rage and rancor that accompanied the impromptu prayers of the alleged rebels. Josias Nichols in Kent thought Hacket and his small, impressionable company had been "bewitched . . . by a mad and frantick spirit." He regretted the episode and looked ahead joylessly to the hard "choice" forced on him and on all other pietists by the apostles of restraint who were exploiting the Hacket affair to press the case for conformity: henceforth Nichols and the others would have to "administer praiers and sacraments by one form."[39]

Impromptu, impassioned prayers were once taken as remedies for demonic possession, but by 1600 they were routinely thought to be signs of demonic possession. Cosin, Sutcliffe, and Richard Hooker simply refused to consider "endles and senseles effusions of indigested prayers" as "things of the spirit." Edward Topsell said of them that "without the spirit of God they speake evill of the things of the spirit, deeming our earnestnes in praier to be raving." But in prayer, as in late Elizabethan theater, what T. S. Eliot called "the bombastic," the billowing and oratorical, lost ground to conversational and controlled *modi discendi*.[40]

Prayerful Performance

After putting the prayerful improvisations of the penitent, prodigal self in the context of the pietists' practical divinity, we can then return, in the second and third chapters, to the Elizabethan stage. It may be help-ful here, though, to anticipate and reflect for a moment on the pietists' prayers in light of what nowadays is said about performance and, first, about the performances of those soliloquacious characters in late Tudor England who probed the problems of guilt and irresolution as assidu-ously, it would seem, as did the Calvinists "much in prayer."

Dramatists directed those playing Hamlet and Faustus, to name the obvious pair, to look within, with various measures of self-mockery, self-reproach, perplexity, and panic. Lately, as noted, literary historians take such scripts as symptoms of a crisis, loss, or absence of identity. Franco Moretti comes upon soliloquacious characters "painfully absorbed" in themselves, not just searching inward, but caving inward and signaling, he says, the near collapse of Tudor civilization. Catherine Belsey thinks the subject in soliloquy so dissolved in signifying practice that playgoers dis-cover subjectivity only as they project it on Elizabethan protagonists. If correspondences between prayerful performances and soliloquies hold, however, as I intend to demonstrate, observations of that kind will seem much less tenable.[41]

But evidence for prayer is less revealing than historians would like to have it. Pietists who preferred unscripted prayer and were among the most introspective Calvinists left few traces of their devotional lives. We have their apologists' explanations and their critics' objections, but it would be infinitely more helpful to have the "voices" of petitioners *in medias res*. Yet when we contemplate what we do have, we learn that rum-maging through woes and showing, if only to oneself, what ordinarily surpassed all show, were ritual preconditions for regeneration. Hence, in prayer, if not also in soliloquy, "disjunction" and suspenseful hyper-reflexivity were hardly parts of what Moretti and others depict as an Elizabethan "dynamic of destruction"; they were stages in the reformed Christian's renewal, repeatable as often as prayerful performers were af-flicted by doubts and despair.

Shakespeare's soliloquies and self-questioning sonnets are art. That much seems incontestable, but what of the prayers of Elizabethan pietists? To say they were theology-becoming-art is prattle, one may ar-gue, as long as relatively narrow ideas about the beautiful are central to the exercise of aesthetic judgment. For then only delicately com-posed scenes of consciousness—John Donne's *Holy Sonnets*, for example —would pass as both prayers and objets d'art. Much the same applies

when concepts of the sublime replace classical concepts of the beautiful, although, in that event, connoisseurs could more plausibly consider
the billowing sentiments and unyielding imprecation of much late Tudor
prayer as artful. But prospects for aesthetic reflection on prayer are most
promising when questions of significance jostle ideas about the beautiful
and the sublime, that is, when those questions of significance complicate
the tradition of interpretation that assumes art's meaning or meanings
lay hidden, awaiting players and spectators guided by informed critics.
Any determination of significance requires attention to the plurality of
perceptual responses, comparably less deference to informed critics, and
less devotion to preconceived standards.

To concentrate on the issue of significance in aesthetic judgment is to
accommodate the avant-garde performances, which Allan Kaprow calls
"happenings," wherein unscripted responses of performers and spectators are incorporated into performances that occasionally parody or
offend against prevailing standards. The introduction of significance invites further reflection on the artfulness of "indigested prayers" because
significance is and was then identified with change. Sixteenth-century
pietists expected prayers to change petitioners. Now, those formulating
the aesthetics of the avant-garde expect profound change from significant performances or happenings. They welcome plurality but not arbitrariness and anarchy. Michael Kirby, for one, will not leave questions
of significance to perceivers' or performers' whims. He sets a standard,
measuring significance as a profound change in consciousness, not just
some perceptual change but a cumulative, cultural change. Significance
therefore resembles a promissory note. In fact, identifying change with
significance seems to me to be part of the avant-garde's efforts to create
contexts of expectation and appreciation for varied irreverent expressions, a way, that is, to disseminate the confidence that emancipations in
art will disperse in, and change, culture. And that, too, has special relevance to the evaluation of prayerful performances.[42]

For historians have distinct advantages. They cannot peer ahead to
forecast significance and change, but they can look back intelligently.
That does not mean that historians of performance can infallibly track
the dispersions of art into culture. Their evidence, for instance, will not
permit them to assert any causal connection between the prayerful improvisations of the penitent prodigal and staged self-analyses in Elizabethan soliloquies. Yet striking correspondences may disclose precisely

what changes were considered significant for the rehabilitation or regeneration of character.

The apologists for impassioned prayer emphasized changes that were ordinarily occasioned by pietists' desires to lament "their causes" before God. Fundamentally, petitioners ceased thinking that their sins would sink them and came to anticipate that God's mercy would save them. The change signified divine election. It was performed in prayers that thereby became rites of passage as well as rituals of purgation and rededication. In that they were "intended for the introspective attention of the performer," they resembled that species of avant-garde expression that is said to "interiorize" art. But more self-evidently, they anticipated later pietists' spiritual autobiographies, which are aptly called "hazardous expeditions" of self-discovery by those who admire them. But "hazards" in the sixteenth and seventeenth centuries were not those associated with the utter indeterminacy of avant-garde "happenings." Pietists' changes were patterned, and, as we will see, patterns so dictated the trajectories of change that the prayerful rituals of purgation and rededication were also rituals of containment.[43]

For now, though, we may conclude—and without bidding prayer farewell—that the pietists' performances exhibit the virtuosity of sixteenth-century self-fashioning. And we might suggest, if only tentatively at this time, that character and identity were not erased by introspection, as Moretti, Belsey, and like-minded critics claim. Neither were they liberated to the extent promised by the proponents of "extemporall" prayer. Character seems to have been contained by what Leo Bersani, referring to later fiction, terms "the exertion toward significant form" that "serves the cause of significant, coherently structured character." The confessions, petitions, and thanksgiving (prayer's customary format) serve as beginnings and endings do in Bersani's stories. They "provide a temporal frame in which individuals don't merely exist but move purposefully from one stage of being to another." In prayer, the petitioners move from self-accusation to contrition and from godly sorrow to assurance.[44]

Concentrated attention to prayer and to the prayer wars of the late sixteenth century will make it difficult for historians of piety to postpone to the seventeenth century the "devotional recovery" in English Calvinism. Such attention should also scale down debts to Jesuit poetry and meditation thought to be quite high by the literary historians who have traditionally kept the books on the "inward researches" of Protestant poets. But my principal point here has been that pietists "much in prayer" were not so much researching their innermost feelings as creating them. I think reference to sorrow and assurance was predominantly productive rather than denotative, and I will continue to argue that the purpose of Elizabethan pietists who wrote about prayer was to give what Lionel Trilling, in a related context, called "rough concreteness" to the practical divinity of late Tudor Calvinism. The pietists wanted to structure character and desire and took a special interest in the therapeutic value of despair. I will let them explain as they escort us through the next stretch.[45]

Notes

1. John Geree, *The Character of an Old English Puritane or Non-conformist* (London, 1646) A2r. For Beza's exposition, see *Jesu Christi Novum Testamentum, Thedoro Beza interprete* (London, 1574) 27r. Also see Peter Lake, *Anglicans and Puritans? Presbyterianism and English Conformist Thought from Whitgift to Hooker* (London: Unwin Hyman, 1988), 239-41.

2. Richard Hooker, *Of the Laws of Ecclesiastical Polity* 5.26.2 (Cambridge: Harvard University Press, 1977-82); and *Puritan Manifestoes*, ed. W. H. Frere and C. E. Douglas (New York: Franklin, 1972), 114-15, for Cartwright's *Second Admonition.*

3. For identity as "a cultural artifact," see Stephen Greenblatt's seminal *Renaissance Self-fashioning: From More to Shakespeare* (Chicago: University of Chicago Press, 1980), particularly 255-57.

4. For the influence of Catholic devotional literature, see Francis Mere, *Palladis Tamia* (London, 1598), citing here and amply elsewhere Louis of Granada's *Of Prayer and Meditation.* Consult also the critics of incompletion, William Whitaker, *An Answere to the Ten Reasons of Edmund Campion, the Jesuit* (London, 1606), 257; and John Stockwood, *A Sermon Preached at Paules Crosse* (London, 1578), 117-19.

5. Thomas Becon, *A Newe Patheway unto Prayer* (London, 1542) K3r-K5r; Edward Dering, *Godlye Private Praiers for Householders in their Families* (London, 1574), especially A3r and B3v-B4r; and John Daye, *A Booke of Christian Prayers* (London, 1578) A2v.

6. Thomas Knell, *A Godlie and Necessarie Treatise touching the Use and Abuse of Praier* (London, 1581) B7r and D6v; and Dudley Fenner, *Certaine Godly and Learned Treatises* (Edinburgh, 1592), 114-15. Also see Arthur Dent, *The Plaine Man's Pathway to Heaven* (London, 1601), 280-81; and Lewis Bayly, *The Practise of Piety* (London, 1620), 469-70.

7. Stephen Egerton, *A Lecture Preached by Maister Egerton at the Blacke-friers* (London, 1589) C4v; Nicholas Bownde, *The Unbeleefe of S. Thomas the Apostle laid open for the comfort of all that desire to beleeve* (Cambridge, 1608), 46-50; Edward

Topsell, *Time's Lamentation* (London, 1599), 179, 213-14; and Eusebius Paget, *A Verie Fruitful Sermon necessary to be read of all Christians concerning God's Everlasting Predestination, Election, and Reprobation* (London, 1583) B1v.

8. William Perkins, *A Treatise tending unto a Declaration whether a man be in the Estate of Damnation or in the Estate of Grace*, in *Works*, vol. 1 (London, 1616), 357–65. Also see the sermon preached by Arthur Dent in 1581, at the start of his quarrels with his diocesan, *A Sermon of Repentance* (London, 1630), 8, 27; and Thomas Wilcox, *A Discourse touching the Doctrine of Doubting* (Cambridge, 1598), 113-16.

9. Perkins, *Treatise tending unto a Declaration*, 403.

10. Laurence Chaderton, *An Excellent and Godly Sermon most needeful for the time wherein we live in all Securitie and Sinne* (London, 1610), 32-33.

11. Henry Smith, *The Betraying of Christ*, in *The Works of Henry Smith*, 2 vols. (Edinburgh: J. Nichol, 1866-67) 1:414-18. Also consult Daye, *Prayers* A3v-A4v ("It is requisite there be no brag of righteousness"); Becon, *Newe Patheway* H6r-v; Richard Rogers, *Seven Treatises* (London, 1610), 32-33; and, on the difficulty of cataloging all sins occasioned by one's "owne heart's roaving motions," see Laurence Barker, *Christ's Checke to St. Peter for his Curious Question* (London, 1599) Q3v.

12. Edward Dering, *Certaine Godly and verie Comfortable Letters full of Christian Consolation* (London, 1590) B3r; Lawrence Tomson, *The New Testament of our Lord Jesus Christ* (London, 1576) 229v; and Perkins, *Treatise tending unto a Declaration*, 409-13. For More's criticisms, see, for example, his *Confutation of Tyndale's Answere*, vol. 2 (New Haven: Yale University Press, 1973), 742.

13. Perkins, *Treatise tending unto a Declaration*, 372-73.

14. Ibid., 388-89. For subsequent "devotionalists," see Cynthia Garrett, "The Rhetoric of Supplication: Prayer Theory in Seventeenth-Century England," *Renaissance Quarterly* 46 (1993): 328-56.

15. Roger Fenton, *A Perfume against Noysome Pestilence* (London, 1603) B7r-v; and John Preston, *The Saint's Daily Exercise: A Treatise unfolding the Whole Duty of Prayer* (London, 1629), 133-34.

16. Tomson, *New Testament* 308v; Beza, *Novum Testamentum* 238r, citing 2 Corinthians 7:9-10.

17. Thomas Wilson, *A Christian Dictionary*, 2d ed. (London, 1616), 557-58; William Knight, *A Concordance Axiomaticall containing a Survey of Theologicall Propositions* (London, 1610), 510; William Perkins, *A Treatise of Man's Imaginations*, in *Works*, vol. 2 (London, 1617), 481-82. For continuity, see Niels Hemmingsen, *A Godly and Learned Exposition upon the XXV. Psalme* (London, 1580), 142-43.

18. John Phillip, *A Sommon to Repentance given unto Christians for a Loking Glasse* (London, 1586) D1v and D4r; and Hieronymus Zanchius, *Confession of Christian Religion* (Cambridge, 1599), 255-56. Also consult Rogers, *Seven Treatises*, 68-69; and John Bradford, *Godly Meditations on the Lord's Prayer*, in *The Writings of John Bradford*, ed. Aubrey Townsend (Cambridge: University Press, 1848), 173-80.

19. For "dislocation," see Jonathan Dollimore, *Radical Tragedy: Religion, Ideology,*

and Power in the Drama of Shakespeare and His Contemporaries (Chicago: University of Chicago Press, 1984), 166–69, and the work of other critics cited in the third chapter here. To sample psychoanalytic approaches, see Cynthia Griffin Wolff, "Literary Reflections on the Puritan Character," Journal of the History of Ideas 29 (1968): 13–32; Murray G. Murphey, "The Psychodynamics of Puritan Conversion," American Quarterly 31 (1979): 135–47; and David Leverenz, The Language of Puritan Feeling: An Exploration in Literature, Psychology, and Social History (New Brunswick, N.J.: Rutgers University Press, 1980), particularly 23–40.

20. Thomas Playfere, The Power of Prayer (London, 1633), 2–3, 133–36, 176–77.

21. Rogers, Seven Treatises, 448–53; and John Freeman, The Comforter (London, 1622), 229–30, 251–52.

22. Robert Linaker, A Comfortable Treatise for the Relief of such as are Afflicted in Conscience (London, 1595), 6, 13–14, 34–35, 43–47.

23. See William Perkins, An Exposition of the Symbole or Creed of the Apostles, in Works, vol. 1 (London, 1616), 284; and Perkins, Treatise tending unto a Declaration, 389–90.

24. Nicholas Bownde, Medicines for the Plague (London, 1604), 130–43.

25. William Fulke, The Text of the New Testament (London, 1589) 297r; Richard Greenham, A Treatise of the Sabboth, in The Works of the Reverend and Faithfull Servant of Jesus Christ, M. Richard Greenham, ed. Henry Holland (London, 1599), 360–61; and Bownde, Unbeleefe, 60–62.

26. Joel Altman, The Tudor Play of Mind: Rhetorical Inquiry and the Development of Elizabethan Drama (Berkeley: University of California Press, 1978), 30–31, 240. For Donne's "contraryes," see, inter alia, Roger B. Rollin, "Fantastique Ague: The Holy Sonnets and Religious Melancholy," in Claude J. Summers and Ted-Larry Pebworth, eds., The Eagle and the Dove: Reassessing John Donne (Columbia: University of Missouri Press, 1986), 145–46; Richard Strier, "John Donne Awry and Squint: The Holy Sonnets," Modern Philology 86 (1989): 357–84; Stanley Fish, "Masculine Persuasive Force: Donne and Verbal Power," in Elizabeth A. Harvey and Katharine Eisaman Maus, eds., Soliciting Interpretation: Literary Theory and Seventeenth-Century English Poetry (Chicago: University of Chicago Press, 1990), 223–52; and this study's conclusion.

27. M. M. Knappen, Two Elizabethan Puritan Diaries (Chicago: American Society of Church History, 1933), 69; and Rogers, Seven Treatises, 352–53.

28. For squabbles among separatists, see Joseph Hall, A Common Apologie of the Church of England, in A Recollection of such Treatises as have been heretofore severally published (London, 1615), 739. For separatists' criticisms of scripted prayers, see Horton Davies, Worship and Theology in England from Cranmer to Hooker, 1534–1603 (Princeton: Princeton University Press, 1970), 255, 268–73; Patrick Collinson, "Towards a Broader Understanding of the Early Dissenting Tradition," in C. Robert Cole and Michael E. Moody, eds., The Dissenting Tradition (Athens: Ohio University Press,

1975), 13–19; and Stephen Brachlow, *The Communion of Saints: Radical Puritan and Separatist Ecclesiology, 1570–1625* (Oxford: Oxford University Press, 1988), 160–64, 175. For "bondage," see John Penry, *A Briefe Discovery of the Untruthes and Slanders against the True Government of the Church of Christ* (London, 1588) A3r.

29. Frederick Pollock, ed., *The Table Talk of John Seldon* (London, 1927), 103–4.

30. John Greenwood, *A Fewe Observations of Mr. Giffard's Last Cavills about Stinted Read Prayers and Devised Leitourgies*, in *The Writings of John Greenwood and Henry Barrow, 1591–1593*, ed. Leland H. Carlson (London: Allen and Unwin, 1970), 56–57.

31. George Gifford, *A Short Treatise against the Donatists of England* (London, 1590), 22–25, my emphasis.

32. George Gifford, *Short Treatise*, 42–43; Gifford, *A Plaine Declaration that our Brownists be full Donatists* (London, 1590), 105; Gifford, *Sermons upon the Whole Booke of Revelation* (London, 1599), 189–90; and Hooker, *Laws* 5.35.2.

33. George Gifford, *Foure Sermons uppon the Seven Chiefe Vertues or Principall Effectes of Faith* (London, 1584) E8v–F3r; and Gifford, *Short Reply unto the last printed books of Henry Barrow and John Greenwood* (London, 1591), 18, 70.

34. Matthew Sutcliffe, *An Answere unto a certaine Calumnious Letter published by M. Job Throckmorton* (London, 1595) 60v–61r. Also see S. I., *Bromleion: A Discourse of the most Substantial Points of Divinite* (London, 1595), 382, 394–95; and Joseph Hall, *Art of Divine Meditation*, in *Recollection*, 161–63.

35. Becon, *Newe Pathewaye* C7v–C8r and M4v–M5r; Sutcliffe, *Answere* 80r; and Sutcliffe, *A Treatise of Ecclesiastical Discipline* (London, 1590), 199–202. Doctrine as well as display and discipline divided the overzealous from their critics. For example, William Negus, active in opposing Whitgift and conformity during the 1580s, shows how close to Pelagianism pietists might come during their searches for assurance of election (for "warrantable perswasion"). In remarks published after Sutcliffe's, but probably uttered before, Negus suggests that Christians who do all they can to inflame faith in prayer will receive God's assistance in getting their confessions airborn and their petitions answered. William Negus, *Man's Active Obedience or the Power of Godliness* (London, 1619), 40–42, 137–42. For details of the so-called Hacket conspiracy, see Richard Bauckham, *Tudor Apocalypse* (Abingdon: Sutton Courtenay Press, 1978), 191–204; and Patrick Collinson, *The Elizabethan Puritan Movement* (London: Cape, 1967), 424–25. Peter Lake usefully assesses the immoderate tone of conformist pamphlets (*Anglicans and Puritans*, 111–13).

36. Antagonism against Whitgift can best be appreciated in the light shed by Leonard Wright's generous tribute: "and if that grave reverend and learned father, D. Whitgift, now archbishop of Canterbury, had not stept in in time to withstand subtill and peevish devices, we had ere this daie felt as great hurly burly in the Church of England as was of late yeres . . . in the citie of Munster." Leonard Wright, *A Summons for Sleepers* (London, 1589), 22–23.

37. Job Throckmorton, *A Defence of Job Throckmorton against the Slaunders of Master Sutcliffe* (London, 1594), 23–27; and Sutcliffe, *Answere* 59v and 64r.

38. For Arthington's rules, see Richard Cosin, *Conspiracie for Pretended Reformation* (London, 1592), 33–35.

39. Josias Nichols, *The Plea of the Innocent* (London, 1602), 31–35, 83–85. Nichols promises to use the Book of Common Prayer but refuses to say on oath that it conforms absolutely to the will of God (121, 127). For Cosin's analysis and evidence adduced from Hacket's early career in Northampton, see Cosin, *Conspiracie*, 73–81, his "answere to the calumniations of such as affirme that they were mad men."

40. T. S. Eliot, "Rhetoric and Poetic Drama," in *Selected Essays*, 3d ed. (London: Harcourt, Brace & Co., 1932), 37–42; Hooker, *Laws* 5.25.5; and Topsell, *Time's Lamentation*, 202. For impromptu prayers and exorcisms, see John Darrell, *A Detection of that Sinful, Shamful Lying and Ridiculous Discours of Samuel Harshnet* (London, 1600), 50–51; and Henry Arthington, *The Seduction of Arthington by Hacket* (London, 1592), 14–15.

41. Catherine Belsey, *The Subject of Tragedy: Identity and Difference in Renaissance Drama* (London: Methuen, 1985), 33–48; and Franco Moretti, *Signs Taken as Wonders: Essays in the Sociology of Literary Forms* (London: Verso, 1983), 49, 70–72.

42. Michael Kirby, *The Art of Time: Essays on the Avant-Garde* (New York: E. P. Dutton, 1969), 53, 77–81, 155–57, 169.

43. For "hazards" in the seventeenth century, see Owen Watkins, *The Puritan Experience: Studies in Spiritual Autobiography* (New York: Routledge and Kegan Paul, 1972), 14–15.

44. See Leo Bersani, *A Future for Astyanax: Character and Desire in Literature* (Boston: Little, Brown, 1976), 55.

45. See Lionel Trilling, *Sincerity and Authenticity* (Cambridge: Harvard University Press, 1972), 93–100; and Peter J. McCormick, *Fictions, Philosophies, and the Problems of Poetics* (Ithaca: Cornell University Press, 1988), 131–45, for helpful comments on productive or generative reference. Also see Louis Martz, *The Poetry of Meditation: A Study in English Religious Literature of the Seventeenth Century* (New Haven: Yale University Press, 1954), particularly 3–4, 22, 168–69, 182–83, for influential calculations of Jesuit influence; and U. Milo Kaufman, *The Pilgrim's Progress and Traditions in Puritan Meditation* (New Haven: Yale University Press, 1966), 196–231, for a typically delayed "devotional recovery."

2

Wretched

Peter Pleaseman is the pastor in Robert Wilson's *Three Ladies of London*. His name gives him away: he never burrows beneath the "shew of godliness" he puts on to please parishioners. He never explores his calling, never gives spiritual substance to his ministry. Pleaseman never struggles to please God. Chaderton of Cambridge raised the customary pietist objections to this kind of prelate. His sermon urging students of divinity to "rippe up all the inwarde and secrete corners" of their consciences also swatted at the "swarmes of idle, ignorant, and ungodly curates" who were more interested in what was socially acceptable than devoted to what was spiritually rehabilitating or therapeutic, namely, the self-analysis and self-accusation that led through wretchedness to an assurance of election and redemption. Abraham Fleming guessed that hardly a hundred ministers in all of England worthily professed and practiced reformed Christianity. The rest just "carr[ied] the light of the gospell in their mouthes [while] carrying also in their hands the filthie water of ambition . . . wherewith to quench it." [1]

Pastoring was criticized as posturing long before the late sixteenth century. Religious reformers of nearly every generation echoed the dissatisfaction with hypocrisy expressed early and often in the history of the Christian traditions, as early as charges in the New Testament against scribes, pharisees, and false prophets. Origins, however, do not concern us here. We attend to industrious, prolific, influential critics among the Elizabethan Calvinists to learn what, from their perspectives, Pleaseman's peers should have been doing. Readers of the preceding chapter have already glimpsed the answer: pastors were supposed to spread displeasure. The present chapter is about displeasure and despair, specifically, about the unusual relationship between wretchedness and righteousness in pietist practical divinity and in the literature and drama of the late English Renaissance. We start with the pastors obliged to "rippe," "ransacke," and "plow up [their own and their parishioners'] harts," because the seeds of regeneration were thought to prosper only in broken soil.[2]

John Geree remembered that pietists were "much in prayer" but also that scourging self-examination was their "first care." Nonetheless, one could argue that I am off target, that I have zoned off the wrong period. Pastors in the sixteenth century asked parishioners to "plow up" yet seldom divulged the lay of their own land. But, as Norman Fiering confirms, introspection during the seventeenth century became "a cultural tendency of first-rate importance." Fiering refers here principally to the unprecedented proliferation of personal journals, diaries, and spiritual biographies in New England, all expressing enthusiasm for self-study. And I think it reasonable to infer that many of the later pietists' attempts to compress the dialectic of faith and despair into their narratives of personal regeneration were responses to antinomians who suspected that self-examination was an unwelcome form of self-assertion, a mark against, rather than a mark of, the fideism of reformed religion. In other words, the New England pietists probably determined that the best response to antinomians who pronounced against the possibility of finding evidence of election in the ambiguity of one's innermost guilt, longing, and wretchedness was finding the evidence and explaining the ambiguity. Fiering was absolutely right: there was a lot of soul-searching, finding, and explaining in New England. My sense is that much of the credit or blame, notwithstanding antinomians' provocations, belongs to the older England.[3]

Glances ahead and west will not be irrelevant as we proceed. After all, New England received its first rush of Calvinists from the old and welcomed an impressive crowd—impressive in numbers and erudition—from the colleges and the churches in and around Cambridge. Some of the most influential emigrés had learned from Elizabethan pietists why to look within and what to look for. So I am tempted to submit and, were there time, to argue that late Tudor practical divinity—efforts in East Anglia, Essex, Kent, and elsewhere to lower lofty propositions of reformed doctrines into reformed Christians' stressful lives—explains, in part, so much subsequent explaining. But rather than look ahead or west at the moment, it will be useful for us, in the company of the older England's pietists and dramatists, to look within.[4]

Sin Within

Geree said that self-examination was each pietist's "first care," to which, though, he conspicuously fastened a second: "as an office of charity," the exemplary pietist, he recalled, "had an eye on others." And many of those others did not care for it. They described Geree's "old English puritanes" as snoops. Critics called them "precisionists," referring to their overscrupulous surveillance of neighbors' private lives. John Downhame, however, justified the pietists' "eye on others," adroitly returning to their "first [and preeminent] care" in his *Guide to Godlynesse*. Downhame conjured up the prospect of an overbearing houseguest, an apparent nuisance who "curiously looke[s] into every corner" of every room for evidence of careless cleaning. "He is not a curious carper," according to the *Guide;* the meddler's interest in "our infirmities" makes him "a cheerful helper to reform and amend." His inspection only goads pietists to attend to their "first care" more thoroughly. "We must daily indevour to purge our memories and to cast out of these store-houses the rubbish and trash of sinfull vanities which doe but cumber the roome and take up the place of spiritual riches and heavenly provision."[5]

When William Perkins spoke similarly of self-examination, he yielded greater place in his tale of house-cleaning to Christian revelation. One cannot discern undusted corners in darkness, he said; infirmities too easily go unnoticed. "But let [the reformed Christian] come in the day time when the sunne shineth, and he shall then espie many faults in the house" and see many "motes that flie up and downe." If they search their hearts in darkness and ignorance, Christians "will straightway thinke all is well." But if they see by the sun-bright light of God's law they will discover "many foule corners" and "heapes of sins." For purposes of self-discovery, radiance and filth are compatible in Perkins's parable, which commends sinners' disconcerting confrontations with their sins. "After due examination hath been made, a man comes to knowledge of his sinnes in particular and of his wretched and miserable estate."[6]

The problem, then, was not just dust, the clutter of "sinnes in particular." English Calvinists knew that human nature itself was deeply flawed. Repressive measures would always be necessary to reduce as much as pos-

sible those "sinnes in particular." "We feel them in us," Thomas Becon
said at mid-century, announcing an obligation rather than an established
fact and intimating that no transition from the sordid to the sublime
was likely without that feeling. But Becon also stipulated that Christians acknowledge and "feel" "the leaven of wickedness" responsible for
particular sins, the "little leaven [that] soureth the whole lump." Becon called it "leaven"; John Downhame, "poison"; William Fulke and
others rehearsed Augustine's accounts of concupiscence. And no amount
of steady, scrupulous housekeeping could purge this source of particular
sins that packed the memory with all the debris of regrettable behavior
in the past and thus made recollection a sad and painful exercise for the
pious. Concupiscence all but assured that reformed Christians continued
to fare unwell. It screened or camouflaged itself so cleverly; that is, concupiscence generated a range of desires that kept sinners from discovering the leaven, poison, or lust behind their sinning. Stephen Egerton, a
popular preacher at Blackfriars in late Elizabethan London, stated that,
for all or the better part of their lives, most people made "no reckoning
at all" of their irrepressible "purpose and resolve" to sin. Concupiscence
stayed below but ran the ship. All too often, Egerton admitted, "nothing
standeth betweene us and the actuall committing of sinne, but only the
want of occasion." But pietists were sure that if they candidly confronted
their wretched estates and realized the full extent of the sin within, the
leaven would spoil less of the lump.[7]

George Gifford, when we last left him, was bristling at the thought
of perfectionism, but he also argued that Christians, if not thoroughly,
could progressively emancipate themselves from the sources of sin
within. The Christian will sin, he conceded, but less as a slave to sin. To
get to that point, the strategy was two-fold. The faithful must "mortify"
the affections that offended God. Thereby, they become less and less
"debtors to the flesh." Yet because it was impossible programmatically to
purge altogether the leaven or poison—a perfectly pure Christian was
an oxymoron to Gifford and his colleagues whom textbooks call "puritans"—Christians must throw themselves on God's mercy and learn to
trust their truest sovereign "on whom all abilitie and desire to doe good
dependeth." Pietists implemented both parts of the strategy with their
prayerful performances, which would all have been filled with billowing
sentiment if Nicholas Bownde had his way. But Bownde also specified
that the sabbath had been set aside for additional extended encounters

with the sin within, for ardent meditations that dramatized pietists' dependence on divine clemency. Greatest gain was not anticipated from God's finding Christians both sorry and supplicant—the fate of the elect had already been decided—but from Christians finding the infidelity "lurking in" themselves. Every seventh day, Bownde said, should be dedicated to self-discovery. Sermons should be recounted and scripture studied, not for book-learning but for self-knowledge. Only then could reformed Christians discover or know "howe the case standes betweene the Lord and our selves."[8]

Self-knowledge of this kind was a buoyant, "saving and experimentall knowledge" of God's will as well as a devastating arraignment of self-will. John Downhame refused to be content with "a speculative, idle, and fruitlesse knowledge swimming in the brain." The most penetrating intelligence, he said, usually produced little besides arrogance. Intellectual agility made no one "more godly and religious." The mind possessed a place among other serviceable gifts from God, yet once it tried theoretically to compass a Christian soul's standing before God's justice or the magnitude of God's mercy or, for that matter, any of God's attributes, the mind showed itself to be the devil's instrument. Its monstrous effect was to alienate the theorist from God. At the very start of his *Pathway to Heaven*, Arthur Dent chided those who thought learning and wit "prove a regeneration" and therefore were "things of the essence of religion." Papists, heathen poets, and pretentious philosophers were amply endowed with intellectual gifts, yet their headwork only demonstrated to Dent that the wicked can be counted among "the wise of this world."[9]

But, repaired or "made new," as John Calvin put it, reason was typically supposed to regulate unruly emotions. The pietists' emphasis on regulation acquired such a reputation in England that Leonard Wright, one of the more outspoken critics of Marprelate's satires, insisted that the most fervent pietists were enemies of affect. After listening to their sustained volleys of complaints about immoderation, Wright facetiously thanked them for having plastered "a stoical disposition" on all Christianity. Possibly the Stoic commendation of restraint appealed to some Calvinists, for they knew that the soul was "wrapped with infinite hurtfull passions and perturbations" and they admitted that those passions "work in it a continual disquietnes." But Stoic self-reliance had no appeal, because it was, after all, self-reliance and because pietists did not think every "disquietnes" was "hurtfull."[10]

The Stoic aversion to feeling misery and wretchedness was irreconcilable with the pietists' stress on the importance of experimental knowledge of sin and concupiscence. ("For I know that in me, that is, in my flesh, dwelleth no good thing," the apostle conceded in Romans 7:18.) This Pauline or "Augustinian pietistic emotionality," according to Norman Fiering, was the principal "barrier against the full absorption of the Stoic spirit." John Calvin had declared that "disquietnes" similar to St. Paul's was a symptom of regeneration, so certain was he that the apostle was explicating the emotional conflict generated and perpetuated when the spirit of sanctification confronted vestiges of sin in the faithful. The tension recounted by the apostle did not plague persons unvisited by grace. They remained comfortable in their ignorance, unagitated, complacent, lost.[11]

Drawing lessons from the apostle's inner conflict, Calvin sometimes seems overwhelmed by his foreboding that unremitting personal struggle against sin within would deal debilitating blows to each Christian's faith. But Calvin will not have his readers discouraged. They had to endure disorienting convulsions of regret and desperation, for they were regular patrons of what Andrew Delbanco calls "the internal spectacle of festering sin." They must experience what the apostle Paul experienced, because to feel depravity profoundly was to know God's generosity more perfectly. Paul discussed the paradigmatic "Christian struggle which believers constantly feel in themselves in the conflict between flesh and spirit." The elect simply could not escape it, for that spirit "comes from regeneration," Calvin said, and the ensuing struggle afforded assurance of election. "Who would have such strife in himself but a man, who, regenerated by the Spirit of God, bears the remains of his flesh about with him?"[12]

A number of Catholic exegetes looked on St. Paul's ordeal as Calvin had. They, too, characterized life under grace as a life of conflict, although the nature of the conflict changes as one crosses confessional lines. Catholics believed that resistance to concupiscence must be constant, resistance, that is, in terms of moral choice. Alternatives presented themselves to what Catholic moralists hoped would be a progressively better informed and more pious deliberation. But Calvin thought that contrary affections in the will of every regenerate Christian persistently baffled the most practiced judgment. From his perspective, the Catholic arbiters of moral life were nearly as untroubled as unrepentant sinners, because the arbiters misunderstood the agony of the apostle and minimized the difficulty of fashioning the penitent prodigal self. So, notwithstanding an occasional tremor of doubt or spasm of conscience, the Catholics were relatively integrated personalities, much as inveterate sinners. English Calvinists would not have disappointed Calvin on this count. Torn by the tensions generated by contrary affections, they were told that inner conflict led to confidence and that confidence, if genuine and "effectuall," invariably led to further conflict.[13]

The lesson of pietist devotional literature, when set down this simply, looks inconclusive, circular, and self-defeating. Nonetheless, the summary reflects the instruction John Winthrop received at Cambridge between 1602 and 1605 and then put to use as he pondered his sin within and struggled, he said, for "faith and holiness." He arrived at the university shortly after William Perkins's death. Deprived of the presence of Cambridge's leading theorist of practical divinity, Winthrop poured over his literary remains and later attested their influence on his life, although his crises and conflicts seem to have started after he left the university to administer his family's estates and his new wife's dowry lands. Winthrop managed lands and revenues well enough; he managed as well to acquire an enviable reputation for piety ("I grew to bee of some note for religion"). But he also found that worldly success and, surprisingly, the "generall approbation of good ministers" in his region left "much hollownes and vane glory in [his] heart."[14]

Having sounded the "hollownes," Winthrop, who appeared to others to be conspicuously self-assured, was frequently shaken, haunted by a sense of failure, "put . . . to some plunges." His inadequacies often slammed into his self-esteem like fists. And self-esteem itself seemed irredeemably sinful. He countered by "urg[ing] upon my owne soul" "the doctrine of free justification by Christ." He attacked his self-esteem with inventories of his incompletely repented sins and with reminders of the "leaven" or "poison" that remained within him. But that only "plunged" him deeper into despair: "I could not close with Christ." Here was the rub: "suche discomforts of anguish, feare, and unquietnesse" tempted Winthrop to think that he had deceived himself when he believed that Christ had "closed with" him, tempted him, that is, to doubt that doctrine of free justification. And could "plunges" and doubts be anything but signs of God's displeasure? But from England's ablest preachers Winthrop heard that he should desire, strive for, and welcome the staggering

discovery of his "secrete corruptions." Such knowledge utterly dismayed
the reprobate, but it renewed the regenerate's resolve to be more vigilant
and to pray more earnestly for God's mercy.[15]

In his *Journals*, Winthrop reported a number of personal crises. The
entry for the summer of 1616 is representative: "the couldnesse" of his
prayers in the July heat distressed him, he later said, confiding that he
had been so lethargic he could hardly bring himself to contemplate the
problem. Then, at last, it pleased God "to bringe me to the sight of
my selfe," and what Winthrop saw disturbed him far more than his inability to warm to prayer, which, he learned, was but one symptom of
his "lukewarme religion" and estrangement from God. He saw that he
had grown lazy, cheerless, and tolerant of his imperfections. Had God
granted him the peace he longed for and permitted him to derive some
small comfort from the cold, he probably would have gone uncorrected
and unredeemed. Instead, God would not or could not evict one of the
elect from the company of others. God made Winthrop feel wretchedly,
and Winthrop, for his part, reappraised his doubts and distress, praying
that no peace or comfort henceforth prohibit him from "closing with
Christ." He appreciated the shrewdness of his divine caretaker, who used
the "discomforts of anguish and unquietnesse" to dislodge obstacles between himself and God—indolence, complacence, and arrogance.[16]

Thomas Wilcox knew why reformed Christians were unlikely at first
to find comfort in their discomfort. Wretchedness was not self-evidently
consoling. But initial and recurring distress was part of God's plan: "the
reliques of sinne in the righteous and the sight they have of it and the feare
and griefe of heart that they conceive for it should, for the time, though
not alwaies, bleare and deface . . . hope and joy." Distress documents each
pietist's conquest of "blindnesse and benummednesse of heart." Only the
reprobate "cannot truely conceive, much lesse feele their condemnation,"
because God withheld from them an accusing conscience and deafened
them to their preachers' accusations and appeals.[17]

Sermons were effective antidotes for numbness and hardness of heart.
Late Tudor Calvinists hoisted the pulpit over the altar and insisted that
each parish be supplied with a preacher. During the 1580s the insistence
of some aroused suspicion among others, that is, some pietists so insistently campaigned for "powerful preaching" that they worried episcopal
authorities intent on restricting the pulpit to persons acquiescent to offi-

cial rules for worship. Yet ways were found to finance dissident preachers. Revenues from certain parish properties were set aside sometimes to hire lecturers to supplement the preaching of less "powerful" parish incumbents. Perhaps, as was later said, "a deep instinct in men who were conscious that they were not as good as they ought to be" impelled churchwardens to reach deeper into their pockets to salary some voice to proclaim the sin within, harp on parishioners' wickedness, and drive them to despair.[18]

John Penry goaded and defied authorities who were slow to see that "powerful preaching" and the full disclosure of every Christian's "wretched and miserable estate" served to reform character, save souls, and renew the realm's religion. Penry earned the enmity of Sutcliffe and Bancroft by denouncing "dumb ministers," who rarely, if ever, preached. He was persuaded that "the utter undoing of many a thousand soule" could be blamed on official indifference to the propitious effects of the accusing sermon.

Penry defended his "intermedling" in ecclesiastical affairs in 1590, three years before his execution, by recounting the many blessings God showered on England during Elizabeth's reign, not the least of which was the defeat of the Spanish Armada and the successful persecution of Catholic subversives smuggled into the country from continental seminaries. And what, Penry asked, had been England's response? Canterbury continued to vilify friends of the gospel, who happened also to be advocates of the further reformation of the church, depicting them falsely as enemies of the government. Moreover, church officals circulated relatively toothless homilies and required England's "reading ministry" to repeat the approved yet deplorably uninspiring words.

Inasmuch as you lende your whole force to maintaine and keepe in the church the reading idol ministrie, which you may know wel inough can neither beget faith nor any true aedification in your people and by whom the Lorde accounteth himselfe and his ordinances to be profaned: the very trueth in this, that you stand at this day guiltie in his sight of the defects, ruines, and profanations of his worship and also the utter undoing of many a thousand soule within England. And I do not see what you can alledge for your defence, except you will joyne with that notable seducer of your

people, the Arch[bishop] of Cant[erbury] and affirme eyther that
salvation may be wrooght in your people by hearing the word read
or that reading is preaching.[19]

To God, who delivered the realm from Mary, Rome, and Spain, the authorities' answer amounted to the self-serving supplication Penry paraphrased as "[give me] a gospel and a ministry that wil never trouble my
conscience with the sight of my sinns."[20]

While Penry was dodging authorities and lodging complaints ("pre-
cisian snevill," said the opposition), Edward Topsell came to Cambridge,
where he detected developments the fugitive critic might have thought
promising: would-be preachers were trained at many of the colleges to
compose and deliver sermons that inspired self-indictment, godly sorrow,
and "a lively feeling of misery." Topsell called them "painefull preachers." He was chiefly and conventionally underscoring their diligence, but
the phrase also calls to mind Topsell's concern that they dwell on the
pains and anxieties that resulted from reflection on sin within and on
the prospects for punishment. The aim was to send wretched, repentant
Christians "weeping to heaven."[21]

Obviously, that required parishioners' cooperation; tears could not be
painted on them. Pietists never tired of demanding that sorrow and repentance be "unfeigned." Henry Smith, whose "powerful," "painefull"
preaching was legend in Cambridge when Topsell matriculated and later
in London, instructed Christians on "the way to hear" and, as we have
already heard, to "digest" the words of a sermon so they reverberate and
circulate through the week. During one sermon, Smith stopped to ask
auditors to consider the changes in attitude and behavior they experienced since they heard his sermon the previous sabbath. He implored
them that if they registered absolutely no change, they should remember that even God's patience had limits. "Will not a man be angry to
set his child to school and find him always at his A, B, and C? So God
will be displeased if we be negligent and slack and never take out his lessons, but stand at a stay." Smith knew how distracted from the sin within
his auditors were. He knew they had become inhospitable to preachers
suffering them to hear reams of indictments. Quite possibly, they had
forgotten that God directed ministers to "declare to my people their
transgressions" (Isaiah 58:1). Indeed, they were like the Hebrews who
persecuted Stephen for his accusations and then who held "it as a prin-

ciple that he forgetteth his text who remembreth their sins." Smith understood that auditors were resolved to put off distressing thoughts. How resourceful they were at finding excuses to defer disconcerting meditations! He sometimes stacked the "painefull preaching" of pastors against "the people's little profiting" and thought that, despite deliverance from Mary, Rome, and Spain, England was under some kind of curse.[22]

Although prey to pessimism, Smith persisted. A deluge of excuses greeted indictments from the pulpit, but the pietists told their preachers to start up again at the next opportunity, like the sedulous spider at the waterspout. Smith admitted that the immediate effects of his sermons— "preparatives," he called them—might seem negligible, but it was unwise, even perfidious, to discontinue treatment. Cumulatively, the "preparatives" made the sick "more fit and pliable to receive wholesome medicines." And the persistent preacher's reward was to see furrows line the faces of his parishioners as they acknowledge their mendacity and pack away their reasons to procrastinate, to hear them "groaning and sighing" for mercy as they "plow up their hearts." To judge from Henry Smith's remarks about the people's "little profiting," one could infer that the rewards were few and far between. Yet, at Cambridge, where the cause of further church reform attracted so many "painefull preachers," advocates stated that the sermons preached in the vicinity made them more fervent Calvinists, more godly men, and more effective preachers. The forty preachers who begged Laurence Chaderton not to retire and forsake the pulpit attributed their faith and their own good fortune in spreading the gospel to his words. John Cotton arrived at the university suspecting that pious injunctions and pulpit accusations there would interfere with his studies. Yet because he heard the word of God so "plainly and effectually" preached, he said, he left the colleges ready to launch his ministry and dedicated to perfect his piety.[23]

The Word around Cambridge: Greenham and Perkins

From 1570 and nearly nonstop for twenty years thereafter, Richard Greenham attended to the salvation of souls in and around Cambridge. He preached several times each week in the village of Dry Drayton, not many miles from the colleges. Occasionally he was in the pulpit at St. Mary's, within earshot of the students and fellows. He knew Chaderton well and frequently consulted with Henry Smith. Contemporary admirers predicted a lasting renown for a collection of Greenham's sermons and treatises ("it shall never finde one resting day"), but the pastor of Dry Drayton confided to Thomas Fuller (who relayed it to his son, who relays it to us in his *Church History of Britain*) that failures to influence the villagers depressed him.[24]

Actually, Greenham often remarked on the unfavorable climate for preaching. (He probably heard his friend Henry Smith berating "stiffnecked" parishioners.) But he concluded that unpopularity came with the territory, as did the peril that preachers might be persuaded to please those who displeased God. Pietist pastors, he said, were like Joseph at the pharaoh's court. Joseph had been exceptionally scrupulous, yet he "began to be coloured with the Egyptians' corruptions." His Elizabethan counterparts undertook salvage work of the utmost significance, but it was a thankless job and they were under tremendous pressure. Greenham knew how the wicked "inveagle" and "allure" and "take us slily away from a good conscience." The elect, however, worshiped with the wicked, and they had to be approached, accosted, reproved, and corrected. This combination of temptation and duty was bound to make a good pastor at "pharaoh's court" a bit twitchy, so "we must feare our selves and in everything suspect them." There was no escaping the risk, no escaping the responsibility.[25]

Greenham would have the minister be companionable. Be "zealous against the sinne," he counseled his colleagues, nonetheless, "have a comiseration of the person." The difficulty was that pastors could not be delicate indefinitely because they were obliged by God to pronounce "terrible judgments." Severity was God's extraordinary gift to the ministry and to the rebuked. To spare the rod was to betray the giver and to be uncharitable to intended beneficiaries. So, in the last analysis, comradeship and "comiseration" were less important to Greenham than powerful and "painefull" preaching that was meant to discomfort those who heard it. To censure parishioners was to save them. The "victims" of preachers' assaults would ultimately derive consolation from their effects. Then, they would not just forgive assailants but countenance the prodigious insults and indictments that brought them grief, guilt, alarm, and misery.[26]

Greenham was fond of what a colleague once said about his method of attack: "I was never acquainted well with any but first I displeased him by admonishing him of some sinne." What a superb foil to Peter Pleaseman! And Greenham himself, commenting on his colleague's remark, specified a place for "Christian admonition" in "directing al men to the attaining and retaining of faith and a good conscience."

Worldly wise men call admonition medling and that they that look not to other men's matters are . . . peaceable and learned sober wise men; and they that practise admonition are thought to be unsociable. Caine himselfe was one of this judgement; he was one that looked not after his brother's life. . . . We having learned not the practise of the world, but the practise of the word, looke for another judgement, and breaking through all such shadowes, wee dare and must be busie with our brother. And if neede be, we will sharply deale with him, as plucking him out of the fire. We may not under the colour of peaceablenes, muzzle our mouthes; if I have an eye on the church, I must poynte at sinne; if I be an hand in the church, I must plucke it out: for every sinne not admonished is inrolled among our sinnes.[27]

The purpose of pointing and plucking, for Greenham and other pietist pastors, was to keep each parishioner's conscience "in a bleeding plight." A calloused conscience could hardly provoke the self-accusation and wretchedness into and through which the elect must pass. "Beware of drawing a thicke skinne on our conscience," Greenham cautioned; sermon and prayerful self-inventory kept the conscience exposed and tender, and "the conscience which at every check is melting and resolved into godly grief at feeling the least smart of the least impression of God, his correction, is farthest from hardening and neerest . . . healing." After all this, it would only be surprising had Greenham's *Grave Counsels* been reserved and had he qualified his grand assertion that the preacher's foremost responsibility was "to beat upon the conscience."[28]

Greenham often repeated the apostle Paul's advice to Titus, "rebuke them sharply" (1:13), as if that hard line might not get through to pastors and would-be pastors at Cambridge. Maybe the pastor at Dry Drayton feared that others would prevail upon them to be discreet, courteous, amiable—to "muzzle [their] mouthes." And, of course, it was often awkward to accuse, to cause any Christian pain. But Greenham urged colleagues, if they were ever inclined to equivocate, to imagine how divine vengeance would deal with unrebuked and unrepented sins.[29]

To "beat upon the conscience" and "keepe it in a bleeding plight," pietist preachers learned at Cambridge to compose and deliver sermons that their parishioners would preach again and again in their prayers and family conferences, long after the original "amen." Greenham said lay re-preaching stoked up the accusing conscience. He pressed preachers to plan for enduring effect and insisted that they "sift themselves narrow-lie," lest auditors have any misgivings about their pastor's character and authority, that is, lest parishioners be given cause to suspect that their pastor's sermons had an impeachable source. Critics, though, had gotten confused. According to Greenham, they thought pietists were preaching perfectionism. But he never suggested that either preachers or their parishioners would "live like petie angels . . . dropped out of the cloudes" after self-sifting and "painefull" preaching. The critics' biggest mistake, however, was maintaining that the best sermons left some "elbow roome for policie" or compromise and that the very best conveniently faded from memory whenever the choices confronting reformed Christians rewarded compromise and conformity with this world's irreligious ways. Parishioners, alas, were resourceful enough; they needed no help forgetting. "Good motions die in us so soon"; "motions" that Greenham defined as "a secret and sweet disliking of sinne and an irking of ourselves for the same" quickly dissipated unless sharp reprimands sustained the uneasiness or dis-ease occasioned by the preacher's initial admonitions and accusations.[30]

William Harrison alleged that forgetfulness was no accident. "Good motions" ceased because they were stopped. Good seeds were stolen by "a cunning thief," always ready to snatch sermons from memory before they caused any grief and thus before they did any good. Smart farmers protect their seeds; "as by harrowing of your sowne fieldes, you cover the seed with earth . . . so cover the seede of the worde in the furrowes of thy affections and let it enter deepe into thy heart." Other agrarian imagery illustrates the idea of re-preaching in Harrison's expositions, which direct Christians to chew their wholesome cud, to fetch up what they had heard from the pulpit and to chew it over so it could "work more effectually upon [their] emotions" and "nourish" their souls.[31]

Many purportedly reformed Christians were untroubled by the pietists' sermons and saw no reason to repeat or re-preach them. But could there be any truth to their contention "that above all others, they have the best consciences, because they seldom or never accuse them"? John Downhame speared such conceit. He was sure that reluctance to fret about one's "estate" and fate in light of what was said from the pulpit signaled reprobation. Greenham, Harrison, and Downhame never meant to dignify a sour disposition. Greenham allowed that cheerful souls could have a lively faith, yet he also said that faith regularly reacquainted them with the sin within and induced the most carefree Christians to "common with [their] owne hearts" and to "complaine of [their] lumpish, earthly, and dead spirits."[32]

It is impossible to read very far in Greenham's work without coming across the language of complaint and accusation. Yet that hardly lessens the shock of finding how prominently such language figures in *Sweet Comfort for an Afflicted Conscience*, a treatise that turned self-accusation and affliction into "sweet comforts." Greenham was certain that to convict was to console, yet to get parishioners to convict themselves effectively, he said, pastors must know the tricks and evasions the faithful commonly used to avoid "plowing their hearts" and to forget their "wretched estates." Many reformed Christians accused themselves of "generall sinnes," for example, conferring on their conduct a respectable disgrace, a generic wickedness. They hid from themselves the truth about their specific failures and never discovered how heinous their crimes were and how gracious God had been and would continue to be. Ironically, they were also hiding from genuine comfort and consolation. The scriptural proverb held that "he who conceals his transgressions will not prosper" (28:31), and Greenham's sermon on the text added his curse, as did his *Sweet Comfort*, which emphasized that "the most righteous are their owne greatest accusers."[33]

Greenham counted "three things whereby we may know whether we be in the right way or no." Two of the three refer to those "affections" fairly close to the surface of Christians' lives: the faithful may take their bearings by checking whether they care for nothing more fervently than for God's favor and whether they love God while they undergo hardships. But the third way "we may know whether we be in the right way" is to descend, Perkins would have said, for it refers to "inward corruption and privie temptations." "It is a good token," Greenham allowed, if reformed Christians "travell to see" their sinfulness. At Cambridge stern preachers pushed them off, urged them on, and made sure along the way that they were "burdened," "sickened," and tormented by what they found. The elect had to discover how contemptible they were and experience "grief and anguish" of mind. All this was "a good token" because the pitched battle between spirit and flesh—and between faith and doubt—that followed signaled regeneration. The same stern preachers, then, were shrewd therapists, cunning consolers. They started by inspiring self-contempt but concluded by imparting confidence in election.[34]

Allowing for variation, one might say that Christians had been invited in every age into battles between spirit and flesh, faith and doubt, from the time of the apostle Paul. But Greenham saw history differently. He thought Catholics had fallen under the devil's spell. Knowing full well that Christians' disquiet could defeat him, the devil coaxed Catholics to decorate their churches with magnificent crosses and poignant but distracting images such as depictions of martyrdom. Greenham suggested that Catholics were therefore unable to attend to the exhortations of their worthiest priests, who encouraged them to "profess" the cross rather than admire it.[35]

Reformed Christians worshiped with fewer distractions, although, according to Greenham, many of them were kept from "travelling" to see the sin within by their mistaken expectation that the reformation of character was instantaneous. They equated reform with righteousness, righteousness with repentance, and repentance with a modicum of anxiety followed by a measure of faith. They might think that they had repented during a moment's dis-ease, Nicholas Bownde said as he warned against banking on the sorrow and repentance fashioned in what his father-in-law, Greenham, called "preposterous haste." But their repentance was "so small." And Bownde's warning seems quite close to the point of Greenham's story of a heretic executed at Norwich who asked tearfully at the stake whether he was damned by God as well as condemned by those circling him. He was told that he would be absolved and saved if he repented there and then. "Is your Christ so easily to be intreated," the heretic erupted; "then I defie him!" Greenham did not dispute that some assurance can be derived from sincere repentance. Any slender triumph over sin betokened God's assistance and mercy. But the heretic's would-be consolers had erred, he said; they should have "dealt more bitterly" with him.[36]

Nothing about devotion and consolation was easy. Typically, one started with the sermon, the kind of sermon Winthrop walked miles to hear. From there, one proceeded through self-accusation to crave God's mercy. When the craving was satisfied for a short term, that is, when one felt blessed rather than cursed, it was more than likely that the Christian would experience reversals, because self-satisfaction set in. Managing only mock groans and sighs, the Christian had then to undertake another review of the sin within. "You have felt it your selfe," Greenham wrote to an acquaintance, "that there hath been an interchangeable course of sorrow and comfort, of faith and feare." The course changes from faith to fear seemed to risk divine reprisal, but Greenham made it clear that each turn in the "interchangeable course" was God's doing. In fact, assurance of election derived from the faith in divine oversight and sovereignty and from the consoling cadence and repetition of the experiences of affliction and recovery, from God's "helping hand," both its slap and its stay.[37]

Peter Lake writes about the Elizabethan pietists' efforts to pave over an "anxiety-filled rift" between "the objective reality of the decree of election" (assurance that God has chosen some) and "subjective experience" (doubts that God has chosen them). The first was a matter of doctrine, assent to which afforded a certainty of divine sovereignty. But "subjective experience," the second, was more complicated. "The merest impulse toward God," Bownde's "small" repentance, might allay preliminary doubts, yet the pietists were inclined to pick over "initial stirrings," and to question their sufficiency and authenticity. Lake exploits his excellent sources, commonplace books compiled at Cambridge during the 1580s and 1590s. They enable him to plot portions of Greenham's "interchangeable course." Yet his "rift" separating "objective and subjective levels in Protestant religion" looks more like Lessing's famous "ditch" than the terrain traversed by Perkins, Greenham, Chaderton, and others when they wrote about pietists' pervasive anxieties. At Cambridge, in other words, anxiety was not something to be crossed or gotten over once and for all. It was regularly to be renewed, interrogated or wrestled, and tamed each time pietists descended to their underworlds, encountered the sin within, and entertained grave doubts about their election.

When Lake writes about "nagging doubt," he acknowledges that it "always" plagued his sources at Cambridge. Yet very possibly because he presumes that subjective assurance roughly corresponds to objective certainty, he tends to toss doubt along with anxiety into his "rift." Doubts, he maintains, "incessantly threatened to stand between the subjective experience of the believer and the objective reality of election." But this "between," I think, is misleading. The doubts and anxieties were supposed to be critical parts of the reformed Christian's subjectivity. One could insist that they were subjectivity's defining characteristics. Only provisionally did they prevent the faithful from internalizing the full content of their faith. Hence, while we are still at Cambridge, we might amend Lake's presentation to accommodate more comprehensively the "interchangeable course" commended by Richard Greenham, for whom anxiety filled not just a rift, but filled much, if not all of the righteous life.[38]

William Perkins's influential work—compendious treatises, sprawling expositions, and the comparatively short pamphlets on conscience and consolation—looked to William Haller something like "a descriptive psychology of sin and regeneration." The parts that most interest me blend late Elizabethan psychology, such as it was, with Calvinist soteriology. Patched together, those parts compose a virtual anthem to what Perkins once called "holy desperation." Let us start with the decree of election and the doctrine of predestination, with the assertion that "before all times [God] purposed in himself to shew mercy on some . . . and to pass by others," for this soteriological proposition lay at the foundation of pietist practical divinity.[39]

Perkins was the most prolific Calvinist at Cambridge. He lectured at Christ College and preached at St. Andrews just as the doctrine of predestination was coming under fire from several other Cambridge fellows in the 1590s. The critics claimed that predestination "hamstrings all industry and cuts off the sinews of men's endeavours." They said that Perkins, "ascribing all to the wind of God's spirit, leaveth nothing to the oars of men's diligence." Perkins never flinched. He asserted that the Bible categorically supported the predestinarian position. God chose Jacob and condemned Esau before they were born, that is, before the oars of their diligence hit the water. Moreover, the choice ("as regards election") was irrevocable. God's choices were as "unchangeable" as God's nature. Nearly obsessed with practical applications, with practical divinity, Perkins looked there as well to defend predestination. He knew the elect were already troubled by their unworthiness. They would have been burdened beyond endurance, he said, if they suspected that God acted on impulse or that, once selected, they might be rejected. To calm such fears, he often reiterated that the elect simply could not fall from grace.[40]

But how could it be held that God acted or chose justly, if neither human diligence nor indolence affected divine action or choice? Perkins replied by questioning the question's assumption that what passed for justice in this world was somehow comparable to "the absolute rule of justice." He hastened to point out that "the absolute rule" was vastly different from temporal rules and statutes that prescribed punishment for the justly accused and assured acquittal of the innocent. Divine rule and justice were so different that they could not be compassed by this world's sense of fairness, which was not to say, Perkins went on, that divine decrees were "bare and naked . . . without reason or cause."[41]

Efforts had been made to "save" both humanity's sense of fairness and God's justice without clipping divine sovereignty. Perhaps God elected the faithful on the basis of foreseen faith and merit. John Calvin, however, suggested that such a conflation of predestination and divine foreknowledge untenably made faith its own cause. In early reformed orthodoxy, Christ was the sole "foundation for election"; the faithful "are elect in Christ." Only the savior merited the grace of God's forgiveness, and he merited it for all the faithful. He was predestined to suffer, then to die for the elect who were predestined to benefit from his atonement.[42]

Perkins elaborated. Making divine foresight something of a cause was "nothing els but a device of man's braine." It was "plausible to reason," perhaps, but wholly incapable of demystifying divine election and, he added, terribly contemptuous of divine will. "To say that forseene faith or unbeleefe are the moving cause whereby God was induced to ordaine men either to salvation or damnation is to undoe the divine order of causes." It makes God's will "a secondary or middle cause subordinate to other causes." Numbers of colleagues, however, had canvassed alternatives, finding none acceptable. They said their "device" was all that prohibited the imputation of injustice or arbitrariness to God. Perkins already had disallowed such imputations, yet he also had calculated the "device's" cost to divine sovereignty and refused to pay it. Instead he maintained that divine causality as well as the divine rule of justice were incomparable and incomprehensible. Analogies to human causality, just as those to justice in this world, were best left untried. Rather than launch analogies and speculations skyward, reformed Christians, according to Perkins, should "descend into [their] owne hearts."[43]

Technically, this was no solution to the problem of predestination, no explanation why God chose some and rejected others. Mysteries so profound were more than a match for "our little dish of wit," Eusebius Paget once observed, and Perkins agreed. It was wiser to descend to get what reformed Christians can possess, a surer conviction of their election, than to climb the heavens in search of what they cannot, a full justification of God's ways with the world.[44]

Perkins vigorously commended descents and sometimes set the consequences of neglect in conditional clauses incompatible with his predestinarian position: "if thou runne on in thy wickednesse . . . it is a thousand
to one at length [that God] wil destroy thee." This "if" and others could
definitely be taken as damaging testimony against Perkins's commitment
to the doctrine of election or, at the very least, as proof that the language
of exhortation from the pulpit played havoc with doctrines defended at
the desk. Or, possibly, Perkins wrote here about the signs of election and
reprobation, wanting only to imply that if ostensibly reformed Christians
"runne on in wickednesse," smart money would wager on their damnation. If they descend, look for the sin within, admit their wretchedness,
and appeal for divine clemency, then "it is a thousand to one" that God
decreed their salvation beforehand and that God is gratified, one might
even say vindicated—but not at all surprised—by their conformity with
divine will.[45]

John Calvin was known to have frowned on frequent descents. He
feared demoralization, worrying that Christians would tend to forget
the legacy of the cross if they too often emphasized their unworthiness for grace and too assiduously dredged up evidence of same. But
Perkins pressed for self-analysis, for full disclosure of "the uglinesse of
our natures." He figured that pietists profitted from experiencing their
wretchedness, from learning "what [they] are without all colours of de-
ceit." After they knew the extent of their corruption, once they had been
humbled by self-assessments, the elect, Perkins presumed, would take
their humiliation as a mark of divine favor. Of course, he had to address
the objection that pietists were merely making virtues of their vices and
were inflating the importance of their remorse. In his short *Dialogue containing the Conflict betweene Sathan and the Christian*, he had the devil raise
that objection and a Christian answer it with the contention, now familiar to us, that only the regenerate could be profoundly dissatisfied with
themselves. How absurd and, in this instance, how diabolical to suggest
that "holy desperation" could "proceed from the flesh"! What Winthrop
would call "discomforts of anguish and unquietnesse" directed attention
to the "reliques of sinne *in the righteous*." They, the discomforts, that is,
not the "reliques," were God's gifts, so, notwithstanding Satan's skepticism, distressed pietists could justifiably assert they were "assured inwardly."[46]

If "assured inwardly," why were pietists so "much in prayer"? Why did they pray for assurances they already had? Perkins ascribed questions of this sort to the Catholic critics of Calvinism whose experience of inward assurance, he said, had been limited. "We pray for the pardon of our sinnes," he told them,

> not because we have no assurance thereof, but because assurance is weake and small: we grow from grace to grace in Christ, as children do to man's estate by little and little. The heart of every beleever is like a vessel with a narrow necke, which being cast into the sea is not filled at the first, but by reason of the straite passage receiveth water drop by drop. God giveth unto us in Christ, even a sea of mercie, but the same on our parts is apprehended and received onely by little and little, a faith groweth from age to age: and this is . . . why men having assurance pray for more.[47]

What Perkins called "full perswasion of God's mercy" and considered "the highest degree of faith" possible awaited the results of those descents undertaken with grave doubts anything of that kind would be found but also with some faith it would. "Doubtings abound," Perkins conceded, but that only meant "we must labour to be assured."[48]

If their descents were successful, reformed Christians discovered the sin within, rebelled against its rule over their conduct, made "serious invocation for pardon," and made headway "against our manifold doubtings." But "full perswasion," like perfection, was beyond their reach. "Certentie we ascribe to all faith," Perkins explained, "but not fulness of certenty." Christians could hope for "unfallible certentie," substantive rather than skeletal assurances, he continued, if they dispel those doubts that tended to thwart pious initiatives. The words around Cambridge for such debilitating distrust were "utter" or "final" despair and "slavish feare." Whereas other fears led to self-scourging, repentance, and piety, "slavish feare" kept the reformed Christians "trembl[ing] at the judgements of God" and preyed on their hopelessness. Catholic priests were thought to have been masters at instilling "slavish feare." Convinced he was exposing the underside of the old church, William Fulke charged that sacramental confession had been cooked up to keep the laity dependent on the clergy's expensive absolutions and indulgences.[49]

Catholics argued that reformed Christians could not possibly know all their sins—however deep they descended, whatever shoals they discovered—and that sins had to be known and confessed to be forgiven.

Did they indeed, Perkins asked? Or could it be the case that "when God pardons the knowne sinnes of men whereof they do in particular repent, [God] doth withall pardon the rest that are unknowne"? Much as Fulke, shuffling along the same Cambridge streets, Perkins thought effective confession a matter of effort rather than absolute efficiency. It seemed to him "that the ignorance of some hidden sinnes, after a man with diligence hath searched himselfe, cannot prejudice an unfallible assurance of the pardon of them all." [50]

Yet Perkins admitted that admirable "diligence" was also dangerous. Industrious searches for hidden and half-hidden sins might well edge pietists perilously close to "utter" and "final" despair. The Catholics were alert to this problem; their solution was the same as that to the problem of unknown and unrepented sins. Priests, as confessors, they said, assisted Christians to make a complete reckoning and, should that fall short, confessors relieved anxieties about unmentioned sins with plenary pardons. But pietists thought the solution worse than the problem. They claimed that the Catholics' idealizing conception of sacrament and ministry was as bad or worse than their flawed practice.

From the pietists' perspective, Catholic confessors eliminated the need for Christians to descend and search themselves. Absolutions abridged what ought to have been soterially advantageous bouts with doubt and discouragement. Perkins scanned scripture and found no authorization for sacramental confession. In the earliest communities, he concluded, the faithful gave their reckoning and expressed their repentance directly to God. Occasionally, for the edification of their congregations, officials recommended public disclosure, but priestly interventions, according to Perkins, were unscriptural, medieval, and unwise. He contended that Pope Leo I never meant to empower priests to hear private confessions and to pardon sins in the fifth century. The pope had only urged consultation with the clergy when a specific sin perplexed the sinner. "Universall law enjoyning to confession as to a necessarie act of salvation" was something Pope Innocent III invented much later and contrary to the canon law that, Perkins maintained, stipulated that "wee may obtaine pardon though our mouthes bee silent." No "precept of old" and no precedent, save for that of Innocent and his Lateran Council in the thirteenth century, braced the current Catholic practice. The scripture and Christian antiquity drove Perkins, Fulke, and their Cambridge colleagues to resolve that "a sinner is not clensed by the judgement of a priest but by the bounty of divine grace." [51]

Walter Travers registered a curious complaint about Catholic confession in England. Best known for his quarrels with Richard Hooker, with whom he shared a pulpit in London, Travers took aim at religious formalism wherever he found it and was particularly alarmed by "new confessors, shrivers, and absolvers" smuggled from the continent during the early 1580s. He thought that the priests were preparing for an imminent invasion, recruiting a fifth column, and trading solace for the realm's secrets in the confessional. They were the pope's spies and the devil's agents, Travers said, and they were doubly dangerous. They gathered up information on England's defenses and retailed a false sense of security that compromised Christians' salvation by quieting their anxieties. They silenced the critical "compunction of the hart" that might otherwise have precipitated intrapsychic struggles, "that conflict . . . we find and feel in our selves." Down the road, as a result of the priests' presence, Elizabethan pietists would lose their freedoms from "Romish" ways and "slavish feare," but Travers was certain that his coreligionists daily lost what Richard Greenham had identified as the very best "amongst [the] many testimonies of our estate in grace and favour of God."[52]

Later, John Donne summed up conventional complaints about the confessional: priests "make merchandize of our souls." Yet pietists also shifted blame to laymen, who willingly sold their souls for bogus reprieves and consolations. For the dissemblers hoodwinked the unsophisticated priests sent to confess and save them. They contrived incomplete or inaccurate accounts of their sins, and they feigned contrition. The thrill at having duped a confessor, however, and then having gotten a pretend pardon was no compensation for the genuine assurance of election. Pietists were aware that duplicity was not an exclusively Catholic affair. Feigners and contrivers were among those to whom they preached as well, and the descents and self-analysis they prescribed would not get very far unless analyst and analysand worked honorably. To assure as much, Edward Topsell urged that the two become one, that reformed Christians become their own confessors. The premise was that sinners among the elect could not long fool themselves. God gave them an accusing conscience. Sermons effectively primed it; only a matter of time, then, before Christians' hearts would become "both priest and sacrifice."[53]

Joseph Hall had an idea of how punishment and pardon worked internally, and he advised that "when . . . thy conscience like a stern sergeant shall catch thee by the throat and arrest thee upon God's debt, let thy onely plea be that thou hast already paid it. . . . Bring forth that bloody acquittance sealed to thee from heaven upon thy true faith, straight way thou shalt see the fierce and terrible look of thy conscience changed into friendly smiles and that rough and violent hand that was ready to drag thee to prison shall now lovingly embrace thee."[54] Hall's narrative speeds from seizure and arrest to acquittal and deliverance ("straight way thou shalt see"). At any turn in the pietists' "interchangeable course" the change might have been this quick, but we now know that conscience and sermon gradually "worke[d] hearts to hearty sorrow," as John Downhame noted, and that the way was seldom "straight" or rapidly run.[55]

Conscience was not an arresting officer for William Perkins, although Perkins was partial to images of detection, detainment, and conviction. Conscience, he argued, was a warden or "keeper" that God had deputized "to follow [a Christian] alwaies at his heeles and to dogge him . . . and to prie into his actions." Conscience was also a judge, "a little God sitting in the middle of men['s] hearts and arraigning them in this life as they shal be arraigned for their offences . . . in the day of judgement." Moreover, due to the tenacity of sin, conscience became a tyrant or tormentor, "a little hell within us." Word around Cambridge was that Christians typically and recklessly ran from that little hell headquartered within them to a more terrifying and everlasting one when they hastened to acquit themselves and to consort with confessors sent from Rome and Rouen. Yet they were going to need more counseling if they were to understand how their consciences could be both "a little God" and "a little hell."[56]

Perkins often obliged. Hellish torment, he explained, was a "holy desperation" — "holy," because it was God's doing. Only if God abetted the effort could Christians refuse consent to their "unregenerate parts." Only with God's help could descents lead to scalding self-inquiry or, as Perkins preferred, "inquisition." Only God could bring those who "partly will and partly abhorre that which is evil" to greater righteousness and to a greater assurance of their election.[57]

"Holy desperation" was one kind of wretchedness. It always augured well for the salvation of the desperate subjects, but it subsisted only under certain conditions: divine election, God's instigation and cooperation, the subjects' awareness that they could not "runne on" their records and win salvation as a reward, the despair that followed from that awareness, and their growing confidence in God's mercy. To a considerable extent, however, "holy desperation" created some of those conditions. Perkins called it a "hammer" applied to Christians' "stony hearts," which "must be bruised in pieces" before they can be pieced together as penitent prodigals.[58]

Readers may be reminded of John Donne's *Holy Sonnets* that memorably invite God to batter the poet's heart but that also, "on this lowly ground," equate battering, bruising, and "holy discontent" with instruction and assurance: "teach mee how to repent; for that's as / good as if thou hads't deal'd my pardon with thy blood." Perkins is now reprinted, circulated, and read far less frequently than Donne, yet in his time he enjoyed an enviable reputation while Donne was fitfully promoting himself and experiencing dreadful difficulties. Perkins was celebrated for "mak[ing] his hearers' hearts fall down." He shamed them by depicting their captivity to sin, but he also consoled them with promises of emancipation. When he spoke of the wretchedness that self-accusation generated, he inflected captivity and underscored condemnation. "He would pronounce the word *damne* with such emphasis as left a doleful echo in his auditors' ears a good while after"; an excellent omen for reformed Christians who valued re-preaching. But he was also known to have described a second kind of wretchedness that came upon everyone. "The most righteous man that is" goes through a bad patch. The apostle Peter walked on water until misgivings sent him under. It was only "naturall" for Christians to suspect, even "confidentially avouch that God hath forsaken them and cast them off." And the consolation for disturbing thoughts about God's desertion was similar to that for "holy desperation"—those thoughts about one's own desertion or apostasy, wickedness, and impotence—because the two kinds of wretchedness were parts of the same "interchangeable course." Consolation in both cases came with a rearticulation of the predestinarian position, specifically its cardinal principle that the decree of election was irrevocable. Doubt and despair provisionally "lessen" the reformed Christians' "communion with Christ" or, as Winthrop said, their chances "to close with Christ," but God's will was "unchangeable." Among the elect, therefore, "the bond of conjunction is never dissolved." Despair only seems to undo what can never be undone, and the seeming, Perkins insisted, with reference to the apt coincidence of faith and doubt in Mark 9:24 ("I believe; help my unbelief"), was part of the bond's strengthening.[59]

"A Grieved Spirit": Hooker and Dent

One anticipates something quite different from Richard Hooker, if only because he disliked emotional, impromptu, "indigested" prayers. Yet the first sermon in his series on Habakkuk composed during the 1580s dealt with the dialectic between faith and doubt and concentrated on issues resembling those that preoccupied Greenham and Perkins. The sermon allows that memories of God's mercies ought to confirm faith. They should make it sturdy enough to withstand all tremors of doubt, even to survive misfortune. But Hooker saw that a small setback often induced reformed Christians to swap faith for fear. All the signs of divine favor "together have not such force to confirm our faith as the loss, and sometimes the only fear of losing a little transitory good, credit, honour, and favour of men." Sometimes it took only "a small calamity," Hooker sighed, "to breed a conceit . . . that we are clean crost out of God's book." At those times the elect supposed that God's promises were meant for others. They convinced themselves that they were "cast into corners like the sherds of a broken pot." [60]

Nonetheless, when a yearning for righteousness survived the conviction that it had been lost, Richard Hooker could tell that the wretchedness also signaled the survival of the yearned-for righteousness. The yearning, which made the apparent loss all the more weighty a burden, was itself a sure indication of election. "The desire of mercy in the want of mercy," Perkins proclaimed, "is the obtaining of mercy." Likewise, Hooker said that a desire to believe in God's pardon and favor itself betokened belief and, what should have been equally heartening, betokened the "secret love and liking . . . of those things that are believed." God's plans for the faithful included fear, disappointment, and doubt. "God will have them that shall walk in the light to feel now and then what it is to sit in the shadow of death. A grieved spirit, therefore, is no argument of a faithless mind." [61]

Hooker disapproved of discussions and definitions meant to flatter the faithful with exaggerated estimates of the strength of their assurances. Babble of that sort inclined inexperienced Christians to expect of themselves and of others a perfectly steadfast faith, "neither doubting nor shrinking at all," though it was utterly unrealistic to look for total control. They forgot that "a foggy damp of original corruption" settled on all hearts and minds. Hooker insisted that his brand of Christian realism, his insistence on the necessary imperfection of faith, did not cheapen it or make it worthless. God "worketh that certainty in all which sufficeth abundantly to their salvation," not promptly but "abundantly." After all, biblical stories mixed doubt with faith, Hooker noted, featuring the often-repeated passage in Mark: "I believe; help my unbelief" (9:24). And when the apostle wrote about Abraham's faith, namely, that "no distrust made him waver" (Romans 4:20), it was not to identify and commend some unattainable confidence, Hooker explained, but to discriminate between doubts deriving from infidelity—from which patriarch, apostle, and the elect of every generation were free—and doubts deriving from infirmity that weakened the strongest faith and to which all were susceptible.[62]

Occasionally, pietists must have been astonished by "the frailty of our nature." They were just incapable of sustaining faith in their election, no matter how well stocked that faith might be with scriptural assurances of pardon and with "as many evident, clear, undoubted signs of God's reconciled love toward us as there are years, yea days, yea hours past over our heads." Faith, then, was unsustained at times but never forfeit; among the elect, "the utter subversion of faith" was impossible. The elect lose their nerve and, like all humans, they are easily beguiled by the devil. Hooker knew that they were "apt, prone, and ready to forsake God" but that God was not apt, prone, or ready to forsake them. To themselves and to would-be consolers, the faithful sometimes seemed "stone-dead" spiritually, but such appearances were misleading and would pass. "Infidelity, extreme despair, hatred of God and all godliness, and obduration in sin, cannot stand where there is the least spark of faith, hope, love, or sanctity, even as cold in the lowest degree cannot be where heat in the first degree is found." Hooker would not let the subject drop. He was sure wretchedness stirred regeneration. It certainly stirred humility, and "the enemy that waiteth for all occasions to work our ruin hath ever found it harder to overthrow an humble sinner than a proud saint." Yet humility did little good when it too swiftly forgot how wretchedness spawned it. For modesty with no memory tempted Christians to summon their divine judge and savior "to a reckoning, as if [they] had him in [their] debt-books." They barrelled into trouble without ever realizing they had crossed from modesty to pride. They must be told, Hooker insisted, why humility that demanded recognition and reward would never be the source of lasting happiness; "happier a great deal is that man's case, whose soul by inward desolation is humbled, than he whose heart is through abundance of spiritual delight lifted up and exalted above measure." [63]

Compilers of handbooks printed to improve self-discipline could hardly have ignored what Hooker called "inward desolation" and Perkins "holy desperation." The handbooks were itineraries or guides that combined the language of exhortation from sermons and letters of consolation with that of explanations from learned treatises on predestination, election, and assurance. Arthur Dent's *Plaine Man's Path-Way to Heaven* is a fine specimen. Its widespread circulation in several impressions during the first decade of the seventeenth century attests to its popularity. Dent acknowledged debts to his fellow Essex preacher, George Gifford, and to Perkins, drawing on their spadework on "the grounds of religion" to answer laymen's practical questions. One character, Philagathus, accepts that "godly men cannot escape thorow this world without blowes" but wonders how the elect will persevere during their ordeals without losing the assurance of election. Impatient and contemptuous, another interlocutor on the *Path-Way*, Asunetus, favors the wrong response: "tush, what needs all this ado? If a man say his Lord's prayer, his tenne commaundements, and his beleefe, and keepe them, and say no body no harme, and doo as he woulde bee done to . . . no doubt he shall be saved," and saved "without all this running to sermons and pratling of the scriptures." Dent's imperturbable referee, Theologus, calls and corrects Asunetus's flagrant fouls with plenty of instruction on the value of accusing sermons. He also addresses Philagathus's inquiry with scriptural assurances that "the Lord knows how to rescue the godly from trial" (2 Peter 2:9) and that "many are the afflictions of the righteous but the Lord delivers him out of all of them" (Psalms 34:19).[64]

The Bible, for Dent and his Theologus, did not "prattle" about pardon. But textual assurances had to be supplemented with experiences of despair, that is, with dread that God would issue no amnesty. At first, sinners were to read their desolation and dread as signs that God had forsaken them. Dent and his pietist colleagues read those signs differently, more favorably, and would have others come around to their opinion. For they thought despair a good omen. Of course, if Christians who were oppressed by doubt and despair stubbornly assumed they were cursed by God, they probably were. But if they ran to the very sermons Asunetus thought profitless, if they began to curse their wickedness, if they took oppression as an occasion to learn about the sin within and, as far as possible, to correct what had been crooked, they might then derive formidable assurance of election from their frightening struggles with uncertainty.

Smith and Greenham had announced the obvious: censorious sermons were generally unwelcome. The comfortable and complacent wish to keep the lid on their iniquity. The afflicted yearn for consolation, not accusation. Dent's *Path-Way*, however, reiterated that pulpit accusations and self-accusation were rehabilitating, that "inward desolation" and "holy desperation" were therapeutic. "Trembling" and "quaking" were symptoms of recovery, if not of health. Unruffled Christians who seemed to draw on a limitless reservoir of self-assurance were in the greatest danger. "Rockt aslepe in the cradle of security," they resembled Asunetus. They trusted that doctrinal conformity, ritualized recitations of the creed—their "beleefe"—and basic morality would serve them well and save them. Dent presumed that the realm was filled with these composed and conspicuously careless Christians.

> If we did certainly know that the Spaniard should invade our nation, overrunne it, and make a conquest of it; that he should shead our blood, destroy us, and make a massacre among us; yea that wee should see our wives, our children, our kindred and deare friends slaine before our faces, so as their blood should streame in the streets, what a wonderfull feare and terrour would it strike into us. We would quake to thinke of it. Shall we not then be much more afraide of the damnation of our soules? Shall we not quake to think that Christ shall com to take vengeance. . . . But alas we are so hard hearted, and so rockt aslepe in the cradle of security that nothing can moove us, nothing can awake us.[65]

The righteous, then, are not unruffled. Dent proposed that they will know intuitively that calm connotes reprobation and that they "shalbe crushed in peeces in feeling." But feeling their burden and putting together their "peeces," they will have their assurance of election.[66]

Asunetus will hear nothing of assurance. He imagines that Christians can only hope for the best. Theologus again corrects him: "nay, we must goe further than hope wel," for the elect can "fetch the warrant of our salvation from within our selves." And the "warrant" is precisely the wretchedness that comes with and from a lively feeling of one's misery and corruption. "Wee feele not corruption by corruption, but we feele corruption by grace," Theologus alleges, "and the more grace we have the more quickly we are in the feeling of corruption." "Your sad condition," he says elsewhere to the wretched *and* redeemed, "is a special mercy of God to you."[67]

Another of Dent's roguish characters, Antilegon, has an understandably appealing yet really scandalous plan. He confides that he will delay asking forgiveness until he is at death's door and can sin no more. Then, and only then, he will orient himself appropriately, sorrowfully, and worshipfully, and obtain pardon. To Dent, the premeditation proved clearly that Antilegon was not to be counted among the elect. For Christians could no more will their ways into and out of despair than plot the right times for sin and repentance, and to assume otherwise was reprehensible. Repentance "is no ordinarie three hours matter" but rather an enduring struggle. It was Greenham's "interchangeable course," Dent's sinuous "pathway," charted by God, who had arranged when and how reformed Christians would place their doubts and despair in the proper soterial perspective. From their vantage, the elect can only look to be "crushed in peeces in feeling" so they may discover God's sufficiency, ubiquity, and grace in their insufficiency, contingency, and suffering.[68]

Dent knew something about that second kind of wretchedness described by Perkins. "Even in the very elect and in those which are grown to the greatest persuasion," which is something less than "full persuasion," doubts recur. Possibly because the elect, aided by grace, so effectively sifted their shortcomings and so completely exposed "the leaven of sin" within, they found it hard to imagine a patience and love vast enough to cover the multitude of their sins. Their predicaments reminded Dent of the difficulties that would have attended persons "set in the top of the highest steeple." Dent's hypothetical climbers, however, were really more suspended than "set," for when they "looketh upward and perceiveth [themselves] fast bound and out of all danger," they rejoice in the remarkable powers that hold them aloft. And just as those "grown to the greatest persuasion," they may feel "cock-sure." Yet when they look down, Dent continues, "because man's nature is not acquainted nor accustomed to mount so high," they will be terrified and prey to despair. They will doubt their ability to hold their positions, "behold[ing] the earth so far beneath."

But Dent did not warn the faithful against looking down. Quite the contrary, he urged them to "looke downeward to our selves," to confront their doubts and fears. For their "grieved spirit[s]" would then comprehend "experimentally" the anguish of David, Job, St. Paul, and Jesus Christ. Once they understood that "the most excellent servants of God may fal into fits and pangs of despair," they would realize that the elect who descended or "fell" rose again with greater confidence in their election and assurance of divine mercy. Their "fits" and "pangs" could well have been the devil's doing, but even that disturbing possibility could console: "if they were not of God," Dent speculated, "the divell would never be so busie with them."[69]

Tracking therapeutic despair through devotional literature—through the pietists' prayers, sermons, and consolations—one may ask whether it was a relatively isolated, occult, or underground phenomenon. If we selectively review the literature of the late Tudor Renaissance, we may end up with a response that says much about Elizabethan religion and culture and that affords a fresh perspective on Elizabethan introspection.

Spenser: "Why Shouldst Thou Then Despeire"

"A man of hell that cals himselfe Despaire" dwells in a cave in the ninth canto of the first book of Edmund Spenser's extended allegory, *The Faerie Queene.* By the time he decided to visit the dreadful place and its resident, Spenser's protagonist, a knight named Redcross, had survived several ordeals, though none brought him closer to death than the one awaiting him in the cave. While he and his companion Una were traveling to her homeland (where he was destined to render her family noble service), they met a frightful and frightened stranger who was racing in the opposite direction with a noose around his neck. The poor soul paused long enough to tell them a terrifying tale.[70]

The stranger and a lovesick friend had chanced upon Despaire a short time before. Their meeting was disastrous, for the friend was seduced to suicide, and Despaire very nearly persuaded the stranger as well (1.9.23–32). After hearing of the heinous crime, Redcross gallantly resolved to punish the seducer. He proceeded to the cave where he found Despaire, an unimposing figure, "his garment nought but many ragged clouts, with thornes together pind and patched" (1.9.36). Within sight of the suicide's corpse, he prepared to dispatch the shabby scoundrel, but as he reared to strike, the noble knight made an almost fatal mistake. Redcross asked a rhetorical question: "what justice can but judge against thee right?" Despaire took the opening and answered with a brief for suicide that justified his former seductions and came close to claiming Redcross as his

next victim. The would-be avenger "was much enmoved. . . . [H]ellish
anguish did his soule assaile" (1.9.48–49).

Despaire argued that all were sinners. The longer they lived, the more
they sinned. As sins multiplied, the punishment at life's end would be
more severe.

> Then do no further goe, no further stray,
> But here lie downe, and to thy rest betake,
> Th'ill to prevent, that life ensewen may.
> For what hath life, that may it loved make,
> And gives not rather cause it to forsake?
> Feare, sicknesse, age, losse, labour, sorrow, strife,
> Paine, hunger, cold, that makes the hart to quake;
> And ever fickle fortune rageth rife,
> All which, and thousands mo do make a loathsome life.
> Thou wretched man, of death hast greatest need,
> If in true ballance thou wilt weigh thy state. . . .
>
> (1.9.44–45)

By prolonging life, Despaire contends, Redcross only funds or feeds his
desire to sin. The determination "to draw thy dayes forth to their last
degree" becomes, in Despaire's slick story, "the measure of thy sinfull
hire." Gesturing to "highest heaven," the speaker takes a stab at calculat-
ing the cost. God, he says, sees all. The knight's tenacious hold on life
will count against him as surely as the sins that such a life is bound to
spawn. Death, of course is inescapable, and with death comes judgment,
which presumably would go easier on any deceased who carries fewer
sins and less guilt into the next life.

> Is not his law, let every sinner die:
> Die shall all flesh? what then must needs be donne,
> Is it not better to die willinglie
> Then linger, till the glasse be all out ronne?
> Death is the end of woes: die soon, O Faeries' son.
>
> (1.9.47)

Despaire was cunning. He cleverly turned the predestinarian position
against objections to suicide that might otherwise have been drawn from
it. Granting that the wages of sin were death and that Redcross, as a Prot-

estant Everyman, had sinned, Despaire put the point that suicides, for all they could know, did not violate God's will but submitted to it. Perhaps God arranged the knight's encounter in the cave. Maybe Redcross would not preempt God's judgment by dying then and there, but rather would conform to God's will and fulfill his destiny (1.9.42).[71]

Una watched Redcross turn suddenly suicidal, but she was not taken in. Snatching the knife from his hand, she inquired of him, "why shouldst thou then despeire, that chosen art?" (1.9.53). Her question is critical, although it had no immediate effect on her companion. He had been saved but was in no condition to accompany her much farther on their journey, so she booked her knight into the House of Holiness in the next canto to convalesce and grow more assured of his election. We follow them shortly, but it is important first to look briefly at what preceded Despaire's near fatal intervention to discover how Redcross, though "chosen," struggled with doubts and experienced the "inward desolation" defined by the pietists.

When we meet Redcross in Spenser's first stanza, he is a riddle in armor, full of "soveraine hope" yet "too solemn sad." Una had already appealed to his probity and chivalry, persuading him "to avenge" and liberate her people. He is "right faithfull" from the start yet swarmed by doubts, hopeful yet dismayed, the internal strife hauntingly suggested by battles and "jeopardies" as he strides, then regularly stumbles, through *The Faerie Queene*'s first book.

Much of the stumbling is due to Duessa, who replaces Una after a sorcerer separates her from the knight. To win Duessa, Redcross slays her lover, Sansfoy, but learns immediately from Fradubio that the conquest of faithlessness is never a lasting one. What the hero learns only later is that Duessa, disguised falsehood, is a dubious trophy. As long as she impersonates and substitutes for Una, she sees to it that he stays bewitched and bewildered. For instance, as luck and Spenser would have it, Duessa and Redcross are spotted by Sansjoy who recognizes his hapless brother's shield and former mistress. Sansjoy is bent on revenge, and Duessa runs no risk cheering for him, for Redcross is so beguiled by now that he misapprehends nearly everything. At the very moment of victory, he is confused and frustrated when Duessa rescues his adversary.

> Therewith [Redcross's] heavie hand he high gan reare,
> [Sansjoy] to have slaine; when loe a darksome clowd

Upon him fell: he no where doth appeare,
But vanisht is. The Elfe [Redcross] him cals alowd,
But answer none receives: the darknes him does shrowd.

(1.5.13)

Duessa sweeps Sansjoy to safety, keeping Redcross, despite his win over faithlessness and near total conquest of joylessness, shrouded in gloom. The knight has stanzas and cantos to cross, many indiscretions to repent, before his captivity to Duessa, doubts, and despair are more completely understood and thus more readily overcome.[72]

Redcross sinks to his very lowest point in the dungeons of Orgoglio, or Pride, yet another of Duessa's consorts. But intrepid Una learns his whereabouts and, anticipating treachery, recruits Arthur to redeem her one-time champion. After having dispatched Orgoglio, Arthur searches frantically for Redcross until he hears a "hollow, dreary, murmuring voyce" and "piteous plaints and dolours" behind an iron door. The conditions of incarceration reduced Redcross to a whimper. The ill-used knight mistakes Arthur and his deliverance for death, welcoming it (1.8.38).

Arthur was shocked by what he found, a "ruefull spectacle of death and ghastly drere" (1.8.40). The poem's first protagonist, humbled by pride, was utterly demoralized; "the chearelesse man, whom sorrow did dismay had no delight to treaten of his griefe," no delight, that is, until he is re-united with Una (1.8.43). It has been said that Orgoglio's brief triumph and partnership with Duessa represented to Spenser and late sixteenth-century readers the unholy alliance between European tyrants and the church of Rome. Plenty of room in such political allegory was left for Arthur, Una, and Redcross, then, to play as Tudor policy, God's grace, and English Calvinist Christianity respectively. Yet, at the moment of rescue, foreground is ceded to the psychological effects of captivity, to the fall that comes with and after pride. From that alone, but also from this quick, selective review of the plot, one may conclude that desolation and despair were nothing new to the knight when he met Despaire in the ninth canto. In fact, it would appear that Redcross's brush with suicide and Una's saving intervention were the culmination of previous trials and distress.[73]

The culmination, but by no means the conclusion, for his narrow escape from the cave of Despaire left Redcross almost as desperately dejected as his detention in Orgoglio's "care" and dungeon. Una is candid about his fitness and his prospects.

Come, come away, fraile, feeble, fleshly wight,
Ne let vaine words bewitch thy manly hart,
Ne divelish thoughts of dismay thy constant spright.
In heavenly mercies hast thou not a part?
Why shouldst thou then despeire, that chosen art?

(1.9.53)

Why indeed? The answer might be found in the ongoing duel between God and the devil—in this instance, between Una, who personifies God's grace or Christians' hope, and Despaire, the devil's henchman, if ever there was one. Yet we now know that pietists thought despair therapeutic, part of each sinner's remorse, repentance, and rehabilitation. So sides may not be drawn quite so confidently, and Una's question, "why despeire," requires further consideration. To be sure, the devil drives despair-unto-death, from which the elect, "that chosen art," should hastily push off. Yet there is no question that desires for death are part of the pietist Everyman's "holy desperation" and "inward desolation." While Redcross recuperates in the House of Holiness, the "anguish of his sinnes [was] so sore that he desirde to end his wretched dayes" (1.10.21). His convalescence is no picnic; "distressed doubtfull agonie" awaits him at every turn (1.10.22). For example, he obviously valued scripture before he entered the near fatal cave in the ninth canto. He gave Arthur a copy of the Bible as a token of his gratitude. Nonetheless, his inability to counter Despaire's exegetical sleights of hand tells against his understanding of sacred texts. Redcross stays at the House of Holiness to learn that the Bible is an indictment. Even his first "taste" of heavenly instruction compels the prodigal knight to face the magnitude of his offenses and intensifies his bout with despair. Guilt and grief produce anxiety, and purgation requires pain: "and bitter Penance with an yron whip"; "sharpe Remorse his hart did pricke and nip"; "and sad Repentance." All the while, he had the sun in his pocket, "that chosen art," but "his torment often was so great that like a Lyon he would cry and rore" (1.10.27–28).[74]

No wonder, then, that a vision of the celestial city tempts Redcross to leap from the House of Holiness to heaven as his time at the asylum draws to a close. It is not wholly unlike his other suicidal impulses, and it is thwarted just as they were, for his pathway to heaven is that of the pietist "plaine man," the route through setback, doubt, and despair, as subsequent performance shows (1.10.63).

Redcross was never readier to confront the fiendish dragon enslaving Una's people than when he left the House of Holiness in her company, enlightened and inspired. But his three-day battle with the demon goes badly at times. The wounds he inflicts on his enemy increase its fury (1.11.22). Flames from its breath nearly compel him to take off his helmet—according to well-schooled commentators, an unmistakeable reference to 1 Thessalonians 5:8 and an indication that Redcross just about gives up his hope for salvation (1.11.26). Indeed, several stanzas later, he desires death, as he had in Orgoglio's dungeon and in Despaire's cave (1.11.28). So backsliding is very much a part of Redcross's battle and apparently was part of Spenser's battle plan. God pushed the protagonist forward, but God also forced him to retire "a little backward for his best defense" and then let him slip, fall, and come to rest where he could refresh himself for another assault (1.11.45–46). Despaire, therefore, was right about one thing when he pressed his case for suicide: "the further he doth goe, the further he doth stray." He was right, that is, if the second "further" refers to recurrence rather than distance and if the "he" refers to every reformed Christian (1.9.43).

Now that we are nearly finished with him, Redcross looks like an excellent candidate for Greenham's "interchangeable course" and Dent's pathway. But is it permissible to park the dialectic of faith and doubt or the dialectic of assurance and despair on Spenser's capacious lot without seeming to trade on secrets about the poet's intentions?

On one count, the poem's Protestantism is universally acknowledged. Interpreters may disagree about the Catholic pedigree of the first book's wicked characters, Duessa, of course, prominent among them, but none deny *The Faerie Queene*'s antipapal prejudice. But the preeminence of faith or fideism is somewhat controversial. In the House of Holiness, Charity is kept pregnant with good works, surpassing in fertility her elder yet unmarried sisters, Fidelia and Speranza. "A multitude of babes about her hung" (1.10.31), making Charity the largest or, as the apostle Paul would have said, the "chiefest" theological virtue. But seniority is Fidelia's card, and Spenser played it impeccably to indicate that all who would be saved must pass through faith. Hence, it is hard to see how the first book is "deliberately ambiguous" and harder still to endorse the observation that "Spenser's stand is with the Catholics in the current faith-versus-works controversy." Confidence in works and willpower, which was customarily ascribed to Catholics in the sixteenth century, can hardly be said to survive *The Faerie Queene*'s overwhelming sentiments to the contrary:

> What man is he that boasts of fleshly might,
> And vaine assurance of mortality,
> Which all so soone, as it doth come to fight,
> Against spirituall foes, yeelds by and by,
> Or from the field most cowardly doth fly?
> Ne let the man ascribe it to his skill,
> That thorough grace hath gained victory.
> If any strength we have, it is to ill,
> But all the good is God's, both power and eke will.
>
> (1.10.1)[75]

Harold Skulsky does not question the poem's Protestantism, but what bothers him is that assurance of election in the first book is no more to Redcross, and usually is less, than his trust in valor and armor. It appears that Una "has failed in . . . her peculiar mission," Skulsky says in his suggestive discussion of despair, though he singles out no specific incident. She failed "to give [Redcross], by her very presence, a ground for thinking he is elect."[76]

Skulsky is appropriately skeptical. If Una is grace or divine favor, it should surprise us at first that "fiduciary certainty," as he calls it, was incessantly undermined. Grace, after all, was thought to be invincible. Yet, from the pietists' perspective, undermining certainty was exactly what grace and despair were supposed to do. The elect would not finally lose favor, but their confidence could and should have been shaken. Skulsky, then, ought to have been warned off before asserting that predestination in the first book was, at best, parenthetical and, at worst, a lunatic notion. For one must not leave out of account the therapeutic functions of recurrent doubt and despair, which, in measured doses, were precious antidotes against both complacence and arrogance. The returns of uncertainty signaled to pietists their divine apothecary's benevolence, even as those returns gave rise to expressions of misgiving and mistrust with respect to that benevolence. Skulsky seems to have expected the "full persuasion" that William Perkins deliberately cut from the predestinarian position, a faith that precluded faults and errors and left the faithful altogether unflappable, rather than that "unfallible certantie" that Perkins defined as an accumulation of fallible assurances. George Gifford's censure of separatists during the late sixteenth century may well apply to Skulsky and other literary historians who nowadays pay the pietists little or no heed and who expect too much of Elizabethans' promises and assurances: "yee run upon the rocke of an hereticall opinion of perfection."[77]

Assurances were constantly forged from imperfections and uncertainties, from the "continual disquietnes" that they had occasioned and that pietists came curiously to treasure as they invested interiority with tremendous significance. Consolation derived from desolation, but, understandably, the Christians to be consoled balked at the prospect of inward journeys alerting them to their unworthiness and wretchedness. And that could be why the journeys were urged on them so often, in prayer, preaching, and perhaps poetry.

Of course, the first book of *The Faerie Queene* does not so much commend the journey as contemplate it, and there is far more to Spenser's grand achievement than the "descents" prescribed by the pietists. No trawler could possibly haul the catch, or, as an admirer puts it, "no single reading is likely to follow through, or even alight on, all the possibilities of response which this typically multivalent Spenserian text invites." An invitation to any reader acquainted with the requirements of pietist practical divinity, however, seems clearly part of the package. It begs the reader to fix on the protagonist's diehard vulnerability and on a dialectic between despair and assurance.[78]

There can be no question that Spenser frequented the old haunts of the romantic quest narrative and that he rerigged the genre's conventions, complicating the relationships between good and evil, between wretchedness and redemption. Impishly, perhaps, he arranged it so the protagonist or pilgrim reflected the vices he conquered, joylessness and infidelity, to select the obvious. He kept Redcross teetering on the verge of defection and fiddled with the romantic quest in other ways as well. He defined heroic action in the terms of Christian spirituality. Most of Spenser's sources—Malory, Hawes, Ariosto, and Tasso—prospered alongside unreformed religion, but the Elizabethan Calvinists disapproved of quests that contained conspicuous traces of superstition and idolatry, boasted an explicit sensuality, and appeared to condone or celebrate homicide. The more severe Calvinists discouraged the cult of St. George, although that intrepid dragonslayer was too familiar a figure to disappear completely. The hero in Spenser's "Protestant allegorical romance" consequently was a hybrid. He was something of St. George grafted on St. Paul, the latter, as we have seen, widely celebrated by pietists. No pietist *militia Christi* could have been cast without a nod to that apostle of interiority.[79]

But this is not to say that Spenser was casting his hero in precisely that way. Poets' purposes, of course, require guesswork to reconstruct, no matter how much personal history they leave us and no matter what they have written about their writing. In the end, even the most timid students of authorial intent must play hunches. Conjecture may orbit around the question of reliability or sincerity when poets have said something about their poetry. It may soar from silence and supply reasons and meanings when none are given. As scholars turn from poetry to drama, they must often call on conjecture to supply the dramatist, because scripts from the late Renaissance, as they have survived, are commonly products of collaborative effort. Playwrights frequently adapted the work of peers and predecessors. Published scripts, in places, are patchwork. Prompt-books, company improvisations, the players' imprecise recollections, not to mention the interpolations and deletions dictated by playgoers' initial "reviews," all left tracks that are not easily identifiable. Hence the uncertainty of authorship—irregularly, but often enough—turns interpretation into risky business. It would do so increasingly in what follows, had this entire interpretive enterprise, at its start, not veered from the intelligence behind its texts to cultural practices and preoccupations.

I think of those preoccupations as atmospheric conditions that make a specific range of responses elicited by the texts or performances conceivable, even plausible. We have been isolating one preoccupation of the late Elizabethan age. We began with the suspicion that it shaped the intelligences and intentions of some prolific Calvinists and pietists, notably but not exclusively, Greenham, Perkins, Hooker, and Dent. That the preoccupation was part of Edmund Spenser's project is less easily determined, but less important than the possibility that it made a distinctive reading of the first book of *The Faerie Queene* more likely and more edifying than others. Now we shall see what playgoers might have made of the age's great drama of despair if they were at all influenced by the pietists "much in prayer."[80]

Marlowe's Faustus, "Destitute of All Helpe"

Drawn from legend onto the Elizabethan stage by playwright Christopher Marlowe, Dr. John Faustus is devastated by despair. He believes his sins are unpardonable, and to a well-wisher who coaxes him, a scholar-turned-conjurer, to "remember God's mercies are infinite," he replies that "the serpent that tempted Eve may be saved, but not Faustus" (A.1401–4; B.1935–39).[81]

Confidence in his corruption and in the inescapability of its dreaded consequences colors Faustus's character soon after the play gets under way. He borrows Christ's last words from the cross in the fourth gospel to seal his own bargain with the devil (and maybe also to shock biblically informed playgoers):

> *Consummatum est:* thys bill is ended
> And Faustus hath bequeathed his soule to Lucifer
> But what is this inscription on mine arm?
> *Homo fuge,* whither should I flie?
> If unto God, hee'le throw me downe to hell.
>
> (A.515–19; B.462–66)

From that moment, the evil powers in the play lobby against hope. A wicked angel seconds the protagonist's assessment of his predicament and prospects: "if thou repent, divels shall teare thee in peeces" (A.709; B.650). And later, Mephostophilis, who negotiated the bargain for Lucifer, intervenes in both the early versions of the play to keep Faustus from contemplating reprieve, advising the bedevilled doctor in the longer text, "thou hast no hope of heaven, therefore despaire [and] thinke onely upon hell" (B.1983–84). Lucifer's deputies see to it that despair quickly douses Faustus's tentative expressions of remorse, that "dispaire doth drive distrust" into his thoughts (A.1171).

Some critics of the play have decided that despair also drives suspense from the drama. However much Faustus thrashes about, they say, playgoers had to assume then—and they should assume now—that he could not, therefore would not, repent. Even the extended middle of the script, with its conjurer's tricks and horseplay, failed to lift the gloom and doom that descended on late Tudor audiences, Arieh Sachs alleges, when Faustus made his fateful contract. "The diabolical pranks obliquely underscore Faustus's reprobation . . . by indicating the forgetfulness and the obliteration of his sense of sin by his desperation.[82]

On this reading, there were no surprises, nothing puzzled playgoers, and Faustus himself offered the best plot summary: "dispaire and die" (A.1315). But it is one thing to say that Faustus perceived the inevitability of his damnation and quite another to presume that playgoers understood it that way. For, unlike Faustus, pietists held that self-accusation and intense feelings of dissatisfaction were principal ingredients in the popular recipe for personal regeneration. Despair, maybe even that despair afflicting Faustus, was not necessarily seen as symptomatic of defeat. William Perkins, we know, explained that it was a precondition for entering heaven through God's "mercie gate"; the faithful, he said, must be "touched inwardly with a lively feeling of [their] owne misery."[83]

Faustus, however, illustrates the Elizabethan intuition that such feeling and misery were as perilous as they were potentially helpful and therapeutic. "Immoderate fear," Richard Greenham implied, could throw reformed Christians into confusion. Their wretchedness might persuade them that God's "mercie gate" was closed against them. Apparently that was why the pietists were quick with their consolations, one of which, Edward Dering's, seems particularly relevant to Faustus's predicament. "Care not for hell," Dering urged, "for the nearer we feele it, the further we are from it." Can we determine on the basis of what we know about pietist practical divinity and what we find in the script how Faustus's despair played among playgoers acquainted with the consolations associated with pious Elizabethan introspection? In other words, can we discover what interpretive leverage pietism afforded Marlowe's sixteenth-century patrons?[84]

The playwright, as noted, is at some remove from these questions. But no sooner have we stripped Marlowe of celebrity status and decline to defer to him as absolute arbiter of his play's meanings, than we discover him brushing against the pietist consensus I have tried to reconstruct. For during the 1580s Marlowe studied for the ministry at Cambridge. Scholars propose, though without much evidence, that he grew contemptuous of the "painefull preachers" there, whose squabbles annoyed Canterbury and the court. William Cecil, the chancellor, ordinarily "a brake on the severity of others," often intervened to prevent disorder from spreading through the colleges. The statutes in effect at St. John's College from 1580 gave the master impressive power to silence any feuding factions, but when William Whitaker summarily dismissed a troublesome colleague, Archbishop Whitgift protested the dismissal. As master of Trinity College years before, John Whitgift earned a reputation for exacerbating rather than ending theological controversy. In all, there was a steady downpour of criticism at, and of, the university, an oddly irreverent place at times, for the training of reverend gentlemen. While pietists preached sheer cruelty to oneself and great kindness to others, in each Cambridge camp, in every quarrel, excitable partisans were quick with invective and energetically unkind.[85]

The desire to number Christopher Marlowe among those partisans has proven just about irrepressible. The Cambridge controversy on which most Marlowe watchers have concentrated pitted predestinarian Calvinists against defenders of free will. Too little is known about Marlowe's career at the university to say anything with certainty—and that particular controversy reached crisis proportions only after he left for London—but Marlowe's *Faustus* seems to many watchers to have taken some forceful stand on the question of God's sovereignty and human autonomy. The difficulty, from an umpire's perch, is that efforts to identify that stand and then to associate it with one or another of the Cambridge factions have produced contrary and equally compelling opinions.

Wilbur Sanders claims that Marlowe echoed ultra-Calvinist positions on the unconditional character of God's decrees of election and reprobation, and he designates *Faustus* "the final consummation of the puritan imagination." Others salute the play as a vindication of human freedom and responsibility, as if they were unfurling the ancestry of their politically and religiously liberal traditions. Douglas Cole points out that Mephostophilis and lesser tempters could not desist, even after Faustus made his deal with the devil; fresh incentives had to be shuffled on stage because the protagonist was free at any time to disavow. "His choices had been made, not once but many times; and each time it had been his own." One can only and safely conclude that *Faustus* kennels packs of problems for theological interpretation. One or another passage may seem to warrant flat assertions about the playwright's position on predestination, or at least the play's position, but contrary assertions appear plausible after a careful look at neighboring passages and phrases. Neither the ultra-Calvinist predestinarians nor the proto-Arminians at Cambridge could have formulated partisan and unassailable explanations of the play, had they wished to do so.[86]

I do not mean to imply here that Elizabethan Calvinists were drama critics in the ordinary and contemporary sense of the term. Most Calvinist criticism, in fact, amounted to a nervous concern about Christians' addictions to staged entertainments. Pietists commonly reviled players and companies that seemed to them intent on graphically describing crimes of passion and sympathetically portraying passionately ambitious protagonists. Edward Topsell referred to theaters as "houses of sinne . . . which gaine more persons to the devil then the churches can soules to the Lord." Ironically, however, the play that fetched playgoers right to the devil's door exploited a relatively uncontroversial pietist paradigm and was more faithful than most other entertainments to time-honored and theologically preferred stage traditions.[87]

Marlowe's *Faustus* makes no secret of its debts to medieval morality plays: temptations accost an Everyman figure, good and wicked counselors compete for his attention and gratitude, and salvation is very much at stake. Faustus is Marlowe's knight or pilgrim, searching at first, it would seem, for immortality with honor, but wholly disconcerted by a syllogism: the reward of sin is death; all sin; so all must die (A.69–76; B.66–73). Whereas death's approach compelled Tamburlaine, another Marlovian hero, to ponder what he had left unconquered, the prospects of death and damnation drive Faustus to conquest: "all things that moove betweene the quiet poles shalbe at my commaund." To become a princely conqueror like the redoubtable Tamburlaine, however, would not be enough. The mightiest wartime monarchs, after all, could not "raise the winde or rende the cloudes." If Faustus must sin and, sinning, must die, he will sin boldly and sell his soul for powers worth the price: "A sound Magician is a mighty god: / Heere Faustus trie thy braines to gaine a deitie" (A.86–93; B.83–89).

But once the purchase of a sorcerer's power is arranged, Faustus is tormented, first by omens and voices ("abjure this magicke"), then by the appeals of the play's good angel, and finally by its well-meaning old man. Despair repeatedly filled the protagonist's soul and filled the theater as well, drawing crowds for two years after the first performance. Declining receipts forced the company to cancel in 1597, but five years later, the play was revived.

Popularity possibly derived, in part, from the dramatic possibilities afforded by scripted struggles for and within the protagonist's soul. Faustus's consciousness was an occupied and embattled territory on display, but display of that sort was not uncommon. Thomas Wright, a self-styled expert on passion, advised orators to learn from Tudor stageplayers how to feign affliction "in soule and hart." Had his students attended some productions, though, they would have been disappointed. Actors playing Apius in an Elizabethan adaptation of Chaucer's *Physician's Tale* had little opportunity to teach them anything. "How am I devided," the script reads, yet lust and shame compete for only an instant. Apius wantonly misbehaves, "car[ing] not for Conscience the worth of a fable," so Conscience dies for want of influence and leaves Apius half the play to intrigue without compunction. By contrast, if Nathaniel Woodes's *Conflict of Conscience* had been performed, Wright's orators could have feasted on feigned affliction and dramatically "wofull exclamations." At first, the protagonist, Philologus, is stiff and steadfast, undivided; he successfully resists Avarice and lectures a papal legate sent to persuade him to give up the reformed faith. His courage is exemplary, and he is sure that martyrdom is God's reward rather than his punishment (1222–28). Division, anxiety, unbearable tension, wretchedness, and woe come only after Sensual Suggestion disposes him to think a bit further ahead. And then come the exclamations and the torment "in soule and hart," and they come in great gusts.[88]

Foreboding causes Philologus to fall. At the prompting of Sensual Suggestion, he imagines the fate of his bereaved family, its property confiscated by authorities after his conviction for heresy. Conscience implores him to reconsider, but his tempter sweetens the pot with promises of pleasure and wealth. Philologus has only a few lines, however, to enjoy his family's security and his ill-gotten gain. Horror visits him with Deadly Desperation in tow, and Woodes's protagonist thereupon believes he is irrevocably damned. "I shall no pardon get" (1735); "I feel [God's] justice towards me, his mercy is all gone" (1760). Two friends undertake to improve his spirits. They tell him to repudiate his apostasy, reminding him of God's boundless compassion. Philologus has a ready reply: those in the past, pitied and pardoned, were "always elect . . . [but] I am reprobate" (1995–97).

In the first version of Woodes's script, Philologus commits suicide; in a second, he renounces his apostasy—"oh joyful news"—and dies of hunger in prison. In both, he dies offstage, far more quietly than Marlowe's Faustus. Woodes announced rather than dramatized his endings, so one is left with the impression of unresolved conflict. The protagonist intellectually assents to standard propositions about the limitlessness of God's mercy, yet he resists the suggestion that God would be merciful to him.[89]

Marlowe probably seeded his *Faustus* with ideas from *Conflict* or from its sources, commentaries on the life and death of an infamous Italian Calvinist who defected to the old church. But theme and character in *Faustus* were definitely drawn from *The History of the Damnable Life and Deserved Death of Doctor John Faustus*, a late Tudor translation of the legends about a pensive renegade professor, given occasionally to regret his "haughty mind, proud aspiring stomach, and filthy flesh," "never falling to repentance truly," yet becoming "so woeful and sorrowful in his cogitations." Whatever else Marlowe got from one or several of his sources, however, he found and implanted a conscience that accused and cursed rather than excused and consoled. It resembles the conscience about which the Cambridge pietists preached, that "little hell" for which they were grateful. They believed it was good to feel inexcusably wicked and wretched. Might theatergoers have been inclined to view Faustus's doubts and despair in light of what their preachers were saying about self-accusation, conscience, and misery?[90]

Or, as Richard Waswo and John Stachniewski strenuously insist, did the late Tudor theatergoers normally perceive the protagonist's course as "a rapid and varied downward plunge"? Might they have found Faustus destitute from the start? Was he thought to be in hell the very moment he turned from God to the lure of magic? If so, theatergoers experienced no suspense and, according to Waswo, had no sympathy. They saw only Faustus's "mounting desperation and hysteria." Regret and sorrow, on this reading, were not taken as signs of recovery but as infernal shocks that further convulsed the hopeless protagonist. Everyone knew from the beginning how the ordeal would end, because they realized that hell had invaded time, that the playwright's purpose was "to dramatize damnation as a moral reality."[91]

Interpretations of this kind amount to an infernalization of all five acts of *Faustus* and either assume or appear to document a corresponding infernalization of despair, which, of course, is altogether incompatible with Calvinist depictions of wretchedness and regeneration. For when Edward Topsell confirmed that despair "finished" faith, he did not mean that "discomforts of anguish" put an end to otherwise resilient hopes and prayers among the elect. Despair "finished" faith by refining it, by keeping the faithful from growing "overproude." What seemed to be a lost cause might only be a lost battle, and wars within (and for) Christians' souls could not be won without some lost battles, without the Christian losing some ground to despair.[92]

But would a merciful God subject the elect to the kind of misery experienced by Faustus or, for that matter, by Redcross? How many battles must be lost, so to speak, before a desperate Christian may take the losses as evidence of divine retribution rather than as therapeutic reproaches?

The pietists were unwilling to count, it seems; they would not calculate how much suffering was sufficient in specific cases or in general terms. Nonetheless, an "apt similitude" occurred to Thomas Wilcox while he was contemplating consolation and watching parents walk with their children on the banks of a river, "nowe and then making sembleance as if they would throw or thrust them into [the water]. The more nigh they are to danger, whether it arise from the negligence . . . of the children themselves or seeme to be layd uppon them from the very loving and naturall parentes, the more sure and fast hold they take of them." [93]

What was most to be feared in a Christian's life, then, was the absence of fear. "Peace I leave with you," Jesus said in the gospel of John (14:27), "let not your hearts be troubled, neither let them be afraid." But pietists maintained that Jesus had not dispelled every "distress of mind." William Fulke, the master of Pembroke College while Marlowe was at Cambridge, explained that an untroubled heart was terribly troubling because repentance must be "continuall." The elect, God's children, should hope to feel no more secure than the children of the "very loving parentes" whom Wilcox observed. The results of their apparent brushes with danger were earnest desires to hold fast to God and "continuall repentance." Panic by the river, "now and then," was the high price reformed Christians paid for their independence from the confessional. [94]

James Calderwood suggests that Elizabethans "lost the comforts of authority—the sense of place in a fixed hierarchy, the certainty of truth, the psychological protection of the Roman patriarchy—and discovered that they were alone and borne down by feelings of insignificance and helplessness." But we have learned that the pietists gave those feelings a good name. What looks to Waswo like Faustus's "downward plunge" presumably looked to them like a promising descent, a bloodletting of sorts. Although Tudor playgoers probably knew the legend's end, to the extent that they were familiar with their preachers' sanctification of desolation ("holy desperation"), they may nonetheless have been waiting for Faustus to break and mend, much as sentimental audiences today harbor hope for the rehabilitation of a doomed though endearing hoodlum on screen. But Faustus did not mend; he did not even break, as we shall see. He struggled to no avail for the resolve to condemn himself and beg forgiveness. [95]

For Faustus was trapped, confounded, one could say, by a disorienting circularity in the Calvinist hermeneutic: Christians must know them-

selves as sinful and saved to understand scripture, yet they must understand scripture (as an indictment, summons, and reprieve addressed to
them) to acquire knowledge of their sin and salvation. From the start,
Faustus comprehends neither scripture nor himself. He concentrates on
biblical phrases about sin and divine retribution, overlooking the ad-
joining passages on divine clemency. His first soliloquy samples possible vocations with such abandon that he is shaken with every dis-
carded future. One question, what will Faustus become? manifestly begs
another, who is Faustus? Arthur Lindley memorably describes the impression left by the rapid rehearsal of plausible professions when he writes
of the Marlovian hero as "a kind of subatomic particle: energy moving
swiftly enough to create the illusion of substantiality." Faustus possesses
himself, one discovers, only when he is demonically possessed, and then
the self that he and the devil possess is painfully and desperately divided.[96]

Pietist practical divinity offered several ways around the aforesaid circularity, to live within it, though, not to dodge it. Calvinist consolers
were known to propose one way or tactic that figures prominently, if
profitlessly, in *Faustus*. Sometimes they recommended conversations and
cooperation with a conferee who could be trusted to judge the authenticity and sufficiency of one's remorse and repentance. In the *Damnable
Life*, a kindly old man occupies some lines to impart wise counsel. The
conferee was a neighbor whose unlooked-for intervention nudged the
protagonist to reassess promises made to the devil and, "in a manner," to
repent. Predictably, Mephostophilis would have none of this and hastily
returned to outgun his rival.[97]

In both versions of *Faustus* the episode develops more or less as it did
in the *Damnable Life*. The old man insists that "accursed Faustus" may yet
be redeemed. He spies a good angel hovering over Faustus's head "with
a violl full of precious grace, offer[ing] to powre the same into thy soul."
God only requires "teares falling from repentant heavinesse." "Call for
mercy," the old man pleads with Faustus, "and avoyd dispaire" (A.1307,
1320-24; B.1835-38). Unlike Marlowe's old man, though, some critics
are certain that the protagonist has no chance. Skeptics point out that
there is no stage direction to indicate the angel's presence and they dismiss the old man's apparition and optimism. But if the old meddler were
deluded, the delusion was contagious. Faustus grows hopeful: "I feele
thy words to comfort my distressed soule," he tells the old man; "leave
me a while to ponder my sins" (A.1324-25; B.1839-40). And pondering

elicits some regret—not enough to dispel despair but enough to summon Mephostophilis to protect his investment. The resourceful demon, alas, prods Faustus to repent his repentance, to grovel and beg the devil's pardon (A.1336-39; B.1850-54).[98]

This brief but beautifully crafted episode is one of Faustus's several flirtations with repentance, none of which confirmed the protagonist as one of God's elect. Once the old conferee is put to pasture, for example, Faustus unreservedly turns to "heavenly Helen," obligingly supplied by Mephostophilis, the Helen who made Troy forget its safety and now makes Faustus forget heaven. Yet two things about the encounter with the old man arrest our attention after Faustus lavishes his on the temptress: the conferee's appeal and the first of Faustus's replies.

"Stay thy desperate steps," the old man urges; "call for mercy and avoyd dispaire." What should we make of this oracle's juxtaposition of "desperate steps" and some purportedly avoidable "dispaire"? The latter seems to refer to something more sinister than that provisional and therapeutic misery prescribed by the pietists. It looks like the despair that Hooker called "extreme" and that Dent called "finall and total." Lawrence Tomson also wrote about an "utter desperation," and William Willymat decried "the wicked kind of desperation," whereby Christians "despaireth utterly" of their salvation. Therapeutic despair escorted deeply divided souls to the brink of this second, final, fatal despair, only to keep the elect from crossing over. The devil, according to Thomas Wilcox, would have shoved the soul of every reformed Christian across, encouraging them to doubt the extent of God's mercy, had the pietists not beat him at his diabolical game. To win, they had only and unequivocally to underline the obvious: Christians who despaired of pardon must yearn to have it, and the yearning is as much God's work as the giving of grace and the forgiving of sins. So "the desire of mercy in the want of mercy is the obtaining of mercy." The decent old man in *Faustus* would have had good cause for hope had he known this, although, with a single, deceptively acquiescent line, the protagonist dashed his conferee's hopes. "Leave me a while," he tells the old man, "to ponder my sins."[99]

Faustus will *ponder* his sins. Whatever we may think of his thinking, sifting, or weighing, pietists would have found the pondering insufficient without that "lively feeling" of misery. Angelo, in Shakespeare's *Measure for Measure* (2.4), and Claudius, in *Hamlet* (3.3), when they thought about repentance and tried to repent, discovered a world of difference between weighing their sins and being weighed down by them, between thinking about their sorrow and feeling wretched and sorrowful. Pietists were told as much by their preachers and would-be consolers. Faustus's reply to the old man promises an inquiry rather than one of William Perkins's inquisitions. He will "ponder [his] sins," not pummel his heart and conscience.

Moreover, Faustus will ponder *his sins*, not contemplate Christ and pardon. Apparently he has not advanced one inch from positions occupied earlier in the play when he came across the syllogism of sin (the reward of sin is death) and, later, as he resigned himself to the truth of Lucifer's underhand opinion that "Christ cannot save thy soule, for he is just" (A.714; B.655). Calvinists, of course, knew that the devil maliciously misled Christians by harping on justice and on their unworthiness for mercy. In the last analysis, though, they minded less than one would have thought, for the devil's malice, just as the human misery or wretchedness it caused, augured well for regeneration. One of the pamphlets collected by Samuel Pepys and bound with others as *Penny Godlinesses* advises that "no man ought to draw such a sad conclusion in reference to himself, as that the season for grace is quite expired. . . . When Sathan pesters you with thoughts that there is no help remaining, but that the acceptable time is all slipt away, rather hope to the contrary, for Sathan is a lyer, and because he is so busie about you, is a sign he is afraid to lose you." [100] But to ponder sins and forget the "sweet comfort" of Christ's cross was to forfeit hope and to play directly into the devil's hands. Faustus did not crave Christ's comfort and was heading for disaster. The old man read the signals correctly when he departed "with heavy cheare, fearing the ruine of [Faustus's] hopelesse soule."

Initially, the play's wicked powers prohibited Faustus from confronting the pietists' paradox, kept him from considering that his wretchedness betokened election and redemption. "Scarce can I name salvation, faith, or heaven," he confides and seems, if only for a moment, to lament, "but fearful echoes thunder . . . in mine eares" (A.648–49). But then he chases after distractions, diligently giving remorse and repentance the widest possible berth. Ostensibly learned conversations with Mephostophilis ("come . . . let us dispute again") and his flirtations with heavenly Helen spare Faustus the grim yet soterially necessary inventory of his offenses. He simply will not face the magnitude of his sins or the amplitude of God's grace.

But no distractions are available during Faustus's final hour. He cannot keep from discovering and descending into the terrible war within himself. Conflict intensifies as fortune's wheel or God's unalterable will or maybe Faustus's willful and incorrigible disobedience—or some combination of the these—brings player and playgoer to the end.

> O I'le lepe up to my God: who pulles me down?
> See, see where Christ's blood streames in the firmament,
> One drop would save my soule, half a drop, ah my Christ,
> Ah rend not my heart for naming my Christ,
> Yet wil I call on him, oh spare me Lucifer!
>
> (A.1462–66; B.2048–51)

The final soliloquy in *Faustus* goes well beyond the ending of the *Damnable Life*, in which the protagonist simply explains to students and friends why he could not adequately repent. He said that "the tyrannous threatenings of [his] enemy" unnerved him, and that explanation was the closest he came to protesting his fate. Alongside *Faustus*'s histrionics, this is a shallow well. Marlowe's Faustus blames and curses fate, others, himself. He begs for time and, it could be argued, for mercy just before serpents and adders dismember his body and transport his soul into deathless pain.

Stephen Greenblatt's boast on Marlowe's behalf seems apt: anxiety is "heightened and individuated . . . to an unprecedented degree" as the play draws to a close. Pietists, of course, would have objected that God set the precedent. They could have cited paradigmatic deathbed dramas to which their devotional literature often alluded, texts that chronicled how God cast the godly into hellish despair ("down to hell") during their last hours of life, so they might "rebound the higher into heaven." There would be no "rebound" in *Faustus*, nothing like Prospero's pardons in the last act of *The Tempest* or like the good duke's amnesty in *Measure for Measure*. For all the conjuring, cursing, bragging, and begging at the end of Marlowe's play, neither mountains nor mist hide Faustus from "the heavy wrath of God."[101]

The only comfort available to the playgoer during and after the player's final rending and writhing is the knowledge that "I am not Faustus," a conjectural comfort that is at the center of Martha Tuck Rozett's presentation of audience attitudes in late Elizabethan London. "For a society that sought everywhere for signs of election," she suggests that "Faustus was the ultimate 'Other,' deliberately embracing damnation in a blasphemous parody of Christ's sacrifice for man." "An undercurrent of despair," ran through "even the most confident members of the elect," according to Rozett, yet they were sure to find their despair quite unlike Faustus's and to derive some assurance of their election from the difference — "I am not Faustus." The protagonist's "resoluteness" would have impressed them, Rozett says, stressing how rapidly he rejected good counsel and closed ranks with the wicked. Speed and "resoluteness" would have made playgoers' plodding seem harmless, if not virtuous. They could rest assured; as dreadful as their doubts and distress happened to be, they were far less ferocious than those played out before them. But what we have seen of the pietists' prayers, preaching, and consolations may incline us to suspect that some Calvinist patrons were equally, if not more, attentive to Faustus's irresoluteness, to his admittedly fitful resistance. After all, they were counseled to take the slightest signs of resistance, regret, and despair as "sufficient argument of the work of grace begun in us," "contrary grace," as it was called, because it crossed the grain of a sinner's behavior and unbelief. The grain or pattern of Faustus's character was indeed conspicuously marked. About that, Rozett was quite right: sudden appeals for divine help were swiftly silenced, self-imprecation was cut short, his pondering now looks like an empty gesture when measured against the self-scourging commended by pietists. But if playgoers kept in mind that the first moves of "contrary grace" were relatively feeble, hesitant, and indecisive and if they remembered that despair was expected to work therapeutically, they might bullishly have presumed that bearish Faustus could or would be saved.[102]

But he was not saved, and the play's end was not scripted for the squeamish. The outcome of Faustus's ordeal makes it clear that he was not among the elect and that he was too terrified of divine justice to accept divine mercy. Read back into the drama, that statement acquires the authority of a foregone conclusion, and despair will seem to lead inexorably to damnation, an idea that Arieh Sachs thinks "traditional and conventional." Sachs makes his case by drawing extensively on medieval sources, on Chaucer, Caesarius of Heisterbach, and the medallions displayed at Amiens. Marlowe might easily have missed Caesarius, a thirteenth-century Cistercian, but it is hard to imagine he would not have heard at Cambridge something like Perkins's rejoinder, "the church of Rome erreth in this, that shee teacheth desperation to be a sinne against the Holy Ghost." More to the point here, Elizabethans who never traveled to Amiens and lingered long at the cathedral—and there must have been many—were likely to have been familiar with the English pietist "tradition" or "convention" summarized by Richard Greenham: "it is the nature of all men never to come to God wholly till they be destitute of all helpe." Calvinists could consider themselves lucky, under some circumstances, to be destitute and wretched in England.[103]

Obviously, there is nothing peculiarly English or Calvinist or pietist about despair. Throughout the history of the Christian traditions, unsettling self-inquiry, self-accusation, and doubts about God's exceptional goodness and the unconditional character of divine reprieve complicated believers' faith and contrition. The apostle Paul and especially Augustine of Hippo enigmatically acknowledged how difficult it was for the elect to return to God, who graciously never withdrew from them (*nusquam recedis et vix redimus ad te*). Elizabethan pietism elaborated the difficulty, marking the cost of despair yet confirming the incontestable, soterial advantages of "holy desperation." Despair shocked the impenitent and precipitated crises of conscience and crises of faith, thus assuring that election did not issue in long spells of complacence and arrogance. So what Spenser called "distressed doubtful agony" was always in season. And, as the good angel in *Faustus* insists, it is "never too late" for despair.[104]

The angel's phrase, "never too late," is commonly overlooked by contemporary critics of the play's theology. Ordinarily they quarrel over the conditional clauses that follow it: "never too late, if Faustus can repent" (A.708); "never too late, if Faustus will repent" (B.649). The quarrels are quite similar to the ones occasioned by Augustine's enigmatic admission. Did Augustine and Marlowe argue for divine sovereignty and predestination (*nusquam recedis;* "can repent") or for human freedom and responsibility (*redimus;* "will repent")? As promised, I have nothing to add or contribute to the study of authorial intent. I am also unprepared to say what Elizabethan playgoers may have made of the auxiliary verbs. Nonetheless, enough has been said about late Tudor pietism to tease us with the possibility that Elizabethan playgoers would have noted that part of the angel's encouragement that critics now pack away with the play's ephemera, "never too late."

"Therefore despair."

Notes

1. Abraham Fleming, *The Diamond of Devotion* (London, 1602), 96; Laurence Chaderton, *An Excellent and Godly Sermon most needful for the time wherein we live in all Securitie and Sinne* (London, 1610) C2v-C7r; and Robert Wilson, *A Right Excellent and Famous Comoedy called the Three Ladies of London* (London, 1584).

2. See Edward Topsell, *Time's Lamentation* (London, 1599), 190-91.

3. Norman Fiering, *Moral Philosophy at Seventeenth-Century Harvard* (Chapel Hill: University of North Carolina Press, 1981), 181-89. Also consult Patricia Caldwell, *The Puritan Conversion Narrative: The Beginnings of American Expressionism* (Cambridge: Cambridge University Press, 1983); the introductory remarks in *God's Plot: The Paradoxes of Puritan Piety, being the Autobiography and Journal of Thomas Shepard*, ed. Michael McGiffert (Amherst: University of Massachusetts Press, 1972); and, for "the poetics of empathetic conversion," Karl F. Morrison, *Understanding Conversion* (Charlottesville: University Press of Virginia, 1992), particularly 44-49. John Geree records the exemplary pietist's "first care" in *The Character of an Old English Puritane or Non-conformist* (London, 1646) A3r.

4. For continuities, see Charles Lloyd Cohen, *God's Caress: The Psychology of Puritan Religious Experience* (Oxford: Oxford University Press, 1986), and Charles E. Hambrick-Stowe, *The Practice of Piety: Puritan Devotional Disciplines in Seventeenth-Century New England* (Chapel Hill: University of North Carolina Press, 1982).

5. John Downhame, *Guide to Godlynesse* (London, 1629), 64, 186.

6. William Perkins, *Discourse of Conscience*, reprinted in *William Perkins, Pioneer Works on Casuistry*, ed. Thomas Merrill (Nieuwkoop: B. de Graaf, 1966), 71.

7. Stephen Egerton, *A Lecture Preached by Maister Egerton* (London, 1589) B6v; Thomas Becon, *The Resurrection of Christ*, reprinted in *The Writings of the Reverend Thomas Becon*, ed. William M. Engels (Philadelphia: Presbyterian Board of Publication, 1843), 481; William Fulke, *The Text of the New Testament* (London, 1589) 426r; and Downhame, *Guide*, 299. For Egerton's popularity, see *The Diary of John Manningham*, ed. John Bruce (Westminster: J. B. Nichols and Sons, 1868), 74-75, 101.

8. Nicholas Bownde, *The Doctrine of the Sabbath plainely layde forth and soundly proved by Testimonies both of Holy Scripture and also of the olde and new Ecclesiasticall Writers* (London, 1595), 183-87, 201-8; Bownde, *The Unbeleefe of S. Thomas the Apostle laid open for the comfort of all that desire to beleeve* (Cambridge, 1608), 68-72, 136-41, 189; George Gifford, *Foure Sermons upon severall partes of Scripture* (London, 1598), 131-34, citing Romans 8:12; Nicholas Hemmingsen, *The Epistle of the Blessed Apostle Saint Paul to the Ephesians*, trans. Abraham Fleming (London, 1581), 149-52; and Richard Hooker, *Of the Laws of Ecclesiastical Polity* (Cambridge: Harvard University Press, 1977-82) 1.8.11.

9. Arthur Dent, *The Plaine Man's Pathe-way to Heaven* (London, 1601), 14-16;

Downhame, *Guide*, 786–87. John Morgan quite correctly emphasizes "the greater importance of experiential faith over rationalism" among late Tudor Calvinists, occasionally italicizing "experiential" and "lively" to underscore the preeminence of feeling. But he is chiefly interested in the expanding "sphere of competence" awarded reason in its regenerate state, for which, see Morgan, *Godly Learning: Puritan Attitudes towards Reason, Learning, and Education, 1560–1640* (Cambridge: Cambridge University Press, 1986), especially 56–59.

10. Leonard Wright, *A Summons for Sleepers* (London, 1589), 19–20; and Pierre de la Primaudaye, *The French Academie*, trans. Thomas Bowes (London, 1589), 12–17, for *l'âme enveloppée d'infinies perturbations vicieuses.*

11. See Calvin's *Commentarius in epistolam Pauli ad Romanos*, ed. T. H. L. Parker (Leiden: E. J. Brill, 1981), 151; Calvin *Institutes of the Christian Religion*, 2 vols., trans. Ford Lewis Battles, ed. John T. McNeil (London: SCM Press, 1960) 2.2.20; and Fiering, *Moral Philosophy*, 150–57.

12. Calvin, *Institutes* 2.2.27 and 4.5.11–12. For "spectacle," see Andrew Delbanco, *The Puritan Ordeal* (Cambridge: Harvard University Press, 1989), 180, referring to the introspection of New England pietists.

13. Consult David Steinmetz, "Calvin and the Divided Self of Romans 7," in Kenneth Hagen, ed., *Augustine, the Harvest, and Theology (1300–1650)* (Leiden: E. J. Brill, 1990), 309.

14. For Perkins's influence, see *Winthrop Papers*, vol. 1 (Boston: Massachusetts Historical Society, 1929), 169, 199, 211. For the composition of Winthrop's *Journal*, see Cohen, *God's Caress*, 244–45.

15. *Winthrop Papers*, vol. 1, 156–58, 194.

16. Ibid., 205.

17. Wilcox, *Large Letters, Three in Number, For the Instruction of such as are Distressed in Conscience* (London, 1589), 43–44.

18. Dudley Fenner, *An Answere unto the Confutation of John Nichols, his Recantation* (London, 1583) 57r. For lecturers, see Irvonwy Morgan, *The Godly Preachers of the Elizabethan Church* (London: Epworth Press, 1965), 33–60; and Paul Seaver, *The Puritan Lectureships: The Politics of Religious Dissent, 1560–1662* (Stanford: Stanford University Press, 1970). For pietist insistence, see Patrick Collinson, *The Elizabethan Puritan Movement* (London: Cape, 1967), 226–27, 426.

19. John Penry, *A Treatise wherein is manifestlie proved that Reformation and those that sincerely favor the same are unjustly charged to be Enemies unto Her Majestie and the State* (Edinburgh, 1590) C4v.

20. Ibid. A2v, C3r, D1r.

21. Topsell, *Time's Lamentation*, 14, 22, 213–14; and, for "snevill," Wright, *Summons*, 46–47.

22. Henry Smith, *The Works of Henry Smith*, 2 vols. (Edinburgh: J. Nichol, 1866–67) 1:499; 2:59–61, 84–86.

23. See, *inter alia*, Smith, *Works* 2:233–42; Nicholas Bownde, *A Sermon contain-ing many Comforts for the Afflicted in their Trouble*, appended to John More, *Three Godly and Fruitfull Sermons* (Cambridge, 1594), 8–10; Bownde, *Unbeleefe*, 46–50; and John Downhame, *A Treatise of Securitie* (London, 1622), 69–70. For Cotton and other "converts" at Cambridge, consult Seaver, *Lectureships*, 173, 182–83; and Larzer Ziff, *The Career of John Cotton: Puritanism and the American Experience* (Princeton: Princeton University Press, 1962), 14–35. For "affective preaching" in seventeenth-century New England, see Hambrick-Stowe, *Practice of Piety*, 117–23.

24. Thomas Fuller, *The Church History of Britain*, vol. 5, ed. J. S. Brewer (Oxford: Oxford University Press, 1845), 191–92. Margaret Spufford echoes this evaluation by detailing Greenham's massive and marathon efforts, preaching and catechesis, and then surveying the "lukewarm" phrasing of wills filed during his pastorate. "There is less feeling," she says, "in the wills of Dry Drayton than [in those of] any other parish I have examined." Maybe so, but it is difficult to endorse Spufford's verdict on the villagers' intractability and Greenham's ineffectiveness ("the saddest example of the lack of influence"), which seems suspended from a chance remi-niscence and four slender threads: of the eight wills composed during Greenham's incumbency, four, she says, were "completely neutral." This must be measured against the many early editions of Greenham's collected works and against the tell-ing tributes and eulogies inscribed by Joseph Hall. Compare Spufford's *Contrasting Communities: English Villages in the Sixteenth and Seventeenth Centuries* (Cambridge: Cambridge University Press, 1974), 327–28, with *The Collected Poems of Jospeh Hall*, ed. Arnold Davenport (Liverpool: Liverpool University Press, 1942), 102–3.

25. Richard Greenham, *A Short Direction*, in *The Works of the Reverend and Faith-full Servant of Jesus Christ, M. Richard Greenham*, ed. Henry Holland (London, 1605), 605–6.

26. Richard Greenham, *Very Godly Meditations on the 119. Psalm*, in *Works* (1605), 652–53; and Greenham, *Sermon on Hebrews 13:17*, in *Works* (1605), 779–80.

27. Richard Greenham, *Godly Instructions*, in *Works* (1605), 277, citing Leviticus 19:17 and Jude 33.

28. Richard Greenham, *Of Prophecie and Preaching*, in *Works*, (1605), 419; Green-ham, *Grave Counsels and Divine Directions*, in *Works* (1605), 736; and, in this con-nection, Egerton, *Lecture* C4v.

29. Greenham, *Godly Instructions*, 391–92.

30. Greenham, *119. Psalm*, 575; Greenham, *Godly Instructions*, 395–98; and Greenham, *Of the Sending of the Holy Ghost*, in *Works* (1605), 844.

31. William Harrison, *The Difference of Hearers or an Exposition of the Parable of the Sower* (London, 1614), 40–41, 194–98.

32. Richard Greenham, *Quench not thy Spirit*, in *Works* (1605), 243–44; Green-ham, *119. Psalm*, 676–77; and Downhame, *Guide*, 73–77.

33. Richard Greenham, *Sweet Comfort for an Afflicted Conscience*, in *The Works of*

the Reverend and Faithfull Servant of Jesus Christ, M. Richard Greenham, ed. Henry Holland (London, 1612), 103; and Greenham, *Sermon on Proverbs 28:15,* in *Works* (1605), 797–801.

34. See Greenham, *Sweet Comfort,* 98; Greenham, *Grave Counsels,* 11; Greenham, *A Short Form of Catechising,* in *Works* (1605), 251; Greenham, *Godly Observations,* in *Works* (1605), 823–24; and Greenham, *A Letter Consolatorie,* in *Works* (1605), 260–63.

35. Greenham, *A Godly Exposition of the XVI. Psalm,* in *Works* (1605), 757.

36. Greenham, *Sweet Comfort,* 110; Greenham, *Letter Consolatorie,* 269; and Nicholas Bownde, *Medicines for the Plague* (London, 1604), 142–43.

37. Greenham, *Letter Consolatorie,* 265; and Greenham, *119. Psalm,* 590–91.

38. Cf. Lake, *Moderate Puritans and the Elizabethan Church* (Cambridge: Cambridge University Press, 1982), 155–59.

39. William Perkins, *An Exposition of the Symbole or Creed of the Apostles,* in *Works,* vol. 1, (London, 1616), 278; and William Haller, *The Rise of Puritanism* (New York: Harper, 1957), 82, 91–92.

40. Perkins, *Exposition,* 281–82, citing Romans 9:10–13 and Romans 11:28–29. For the critics' charges, see Thomas Fuller, *The Holy State and the Profane State,* ed. Maximilian Graff Walten (New York: Columbia University Press, 1938), 91–92.

41. Perkins, *Exposition,* 288.

42. Calvin, *Institutes* 3.22.2, citing Acts 4:28. For reformed orthodoxy, see Richard A. Muller, *Christ and the Decree: Christology and Predestination in Reformed Theology from Calvin to Perkins* (Durham, N.C.: Labyrinth Press, 1986), 92–93, 140, 165–66.

43. Perkins, *Exposition,* 284, 293–94.

44. Eusebius Paget, *A Verie Fruitful Sermon necessary to be read of all Christians concerning God's Everlasting Predestination, Election, and Reprobation* (London, 1583) A8r.

45. Perkins, *Exposition,* 137; and Perkins, *Exhortation to Repentance,* in *Works,* vol. 3 (London, 1631), 412–13, 422–23.

46. William Perkins, *A Dialogue containing the Conflicts betweene Sathan and the Christian,* in *Works,* vol. 1 (London, 1616), 406. Also compare Calvin, *Institutes* 3.2.24 with Perkins, *Exhortation to Repentance,* 416.

47. William Perkins, *A Reformed Catholike,* in *Works,* vol. 1 (London, 1616), 564.

48. William Perkins, *A Treatise of Man's Imaginations,* in *Works,* vol. 2 (London, 1617), 478; Perkins, *A Treatise tending unto a Declaration whether a man be in the Estate of Damnation or in the Estate of Grace,* in *Works,* vol. 1 (London, 1616), 367–68; and Perkins, *A Commentarie or Exposition upon the first five chapters of the Epistle to the Galatians* (London, 1617; facsimile repr., New York: Pilgrim Press, 1989), 108–11.

49. Fulke, *Text* 434r; and Perkins, *Galatians,* 102.

50. Perkins, *Discourse of Conscience,* 57–60.

51. William Perkins, *Probleme of the Forged Catholicism or Universalitie of the*

Romish Religion, in *Works*, vol. 2 (London, 1617), 570–71. Also consult Thomas Becon's dedication to the Duchess of Richmond (1549), in Becon, *Writings*, 181–82; H. D., *A Godlie and Fruitfull Treatise of Faith and Workes* (London, 1583) D3r–v; and Dudley Fenner, *Certaine Godly and Learned Treatises*, (Edinburgh, 1592), 140, 149–50.

52. Walter Travers, *An Answere to a Supplicatorie Epistle of G.T. for the Pretended Catholiques* (London, 1583), 263–68, 283–85; and Greenham, *Letter Consolatorie*, 879.

53. Topsell, *Time's Lamentation*, 250–51. Also consult Perkins, *Forged Catholicism*, 266; William Willymat, *Physicke to Cure the most Dangerous Disease of Despair* (London, 1605), 55–56; and, for "merchandize," *The Sermons of John Donne*, vol. 10, ed. Evelyn M. Simpson and George R. Potter (Berkeley: University of California Press, 1962), 157–58.

54. Joseph Hall, *Heaven upon Earth or Of the True Peace and Tranquillity of Mind*, in *A Recollection of such treatises as have been heretofore severally published* (London, 1615), 115.

55. Downhame, *Guide*, 611.

56. Perkins, *Discourse of Conscience*, 9, 72.

57. Perkins, *Treatise tending unto a Declaration*, 372–73.

58. William Perkins, *The Foundation of the Christian Religion*, in *Works*, vol. 1 (London, 1616), 78–79.

59. See Perkins, *Treatise of Man's Imaginations*, 466–67; Perkins, *Treatise tending unto a Declaration*, 409–10; and Perkins, *Reformed Catholicke*, 566. For the "doleful echo," consult Fuller, *Holy State*, 90. For Donne's Sonnets, *The Complete Poetry of John Donne*, ed. John Shawcrosse (Garden City, N.Y.: New York University Press, 1967), 338–51, and the discussion of Donne in this book's conclusion. And, for the persistence of doubts during repentance, see the next chapter's comments on Thomas Wilcox's *Discourse on Doubting*.

60. Richard Hooker, *A Learned and Comfortable Sermon of the Certainty and Perpetuity of Faith in the Elect*, in *The Works of Mr. Richard Hooker*, vol. 3, ed. John Keble (Oxford: Clarendon Press, 1888), 479.

61. William Perkins, *A grain of Mustard Seed*, reprinted in *The Work of William Perkins*, ed. Ian Breward (Abingdon: Sutton Courtenay Press, 1970), 398–402; and Hooker, *Learned and Comfortable Sermon*, 475.

62. Hooker, *Learned and Comfortable Sermon*, 471–72.

63. Richard Hooker, *Answer to the Supplication that Mr. Travers Made to the Council*, in *Works*, 577; Hooker, *A Learned Discourse of Justification, Works, and how the Foundation of Faith is Overthrown*, in *Works*, 492–94, 517–19; and Hooker, *Learned and Comfortable Sermon*, 472–74. Also see Debora Kuller Shuger, *Habits of Thought in the English Renaissance* (Berkeley: University of California Press, 1990), 80–81; and Collinson, *Elizabethan Puritan Movement*, 294–95.

64. Dent, *Path-Way*, 27, 93–95, 124–29, 365.

65. Ibid., 357.

66. Ibid., 403; and Dent, *A Sermon of Repentance* (London, 1630), 27.

67. Dent, *Path-Way*, 263-68, 408-11.

68. Ibid., 276-77.

69. Ibid., 242-44.

70. References to *The Faerie Queene*, ed. A. C. Hamilton (London: Longman Press, 1977), are given in parentheses, citing book, canto, and stanza. For Spenser's caves, see John Erskine Hankins, *Source and Meaning in Spenser's Allegory* (Oxford: Clarendon Press, 1971), 74-80.

71. For Despaire's theology, see Ann E. Imbrie, "Playing Legerdemaine with the Scripture: Parodic Sermons in *The Faerie Queene*," *English Literary Renaissance* 17 (1987): 142-49. For Redcross as Everyman, see John N. King, *English Reformation Literature: The Tudor Origins of the Protestant Tradition* (Princeton: Princeton University Press, 1982), 158; but also consult King, *Spenser's Poetry and the Reformation Tradition* (Princeton: Princeton University Press, 1990), 189, 193.

72. See Judith H. Anderson, *The Growth of a Personal Voice: Piers Plowman and 'The Faerie Queene'* (New Haven: Yale University Press, 1976), 34-35, 209-10, for the combat with Sansjoy, joylessness, "far more exclusively psychological" than Redcross's other contests.

73. Michael O'Connell, *Mirror and Veil: The Historical Dimensions of Spenser's 'Faerie Queene'* (Chapel Hill: University of North Carolina Press, 1977), 54-57, for Pride and political allegory.

74. Cf. Michael MacDonald and Terence R. Murphy, *Sleepless Souls: Suicide in Early Modern England* (Oxford: Clarendon Press, 1990), 36-37.

75. On Spenser's "ambiguity" and Catholic "stand," see Carol V. Kaske, "Spenser's Pluralistic Universe: The View from the Mount of Contemplation (*The Faerie Queene* 1.10)," in *Contemporary Thought on Edmund Spenser*, ed. Richard C. Frushness and Bernard J. Vondersmith (Carbondale: Southern Illinois University Press, 1975), 134, 143, 146-47. For the poem's Protestantism, see King, *Spenser's Poetry*, 58-65; and Anthea Hume, *Edmund Spenser: Protestant Poet* (Cambridge: Cambridge University Press, 1984), 72-106.

76. Harold Skulsky, "Spenser's Despair Episode and the Theology of Doubt," *Modern Philology* 78 (1981): 233-34. Skulsky concludes that the first book is "an unsparing dismissal of certainty" (240).

77. George Gifford, *A Short Treatise against the Donatists of England* (London, 1590), 23.

78. Consult, in this connection, Darryl Gless, *Theology and Interpretation in Spenser* (Cambridge: Cambridge University Press, 1994), which has been immensely helpful here, although the invitations that he suspects were addressed to the "theologically astute reader" are not quite those extended, I think, to the pietists.

79. See King, *Spenser's Poetry*, 188-202; King, *English Reformation Literature*, 132; James D. Boulgar, *The Calvinist Temper in English Poetry* (The Hague: Mouton,

1980), 153–55; and Patrick Cullen, *Infernal Triad: The Flesh, the World, and the Devil in Spenser and Milton* (Princeton: Princeton University Press, 1974), 24–25, 39.

80. Marjorie Keniston McIntosh, *A Community Transformed: The Manor and Liberty of Havering, 1500–1620* (Cambridge: Cambridge University Press, 1991), 191–93, notes the "strongly Protestant" tenor of wills after 1560, mentioning that testators who held power in parish and manor emphasized the doctrine of election. For the presence of those like them at the theater, see Ann Jenalie Cook, *The Privileged Playgoers of Shakespeare's London, 1576–1642* (Princeton: Princeton University Press, 1981). And, to combat "the persisting impression that Calvinists in Renaissance England were unanimously opposed to the stage," see Margot Heinemann, *Puritans and Theater: Thomas Middleton and Opposition Drama under the Early Stuarts* (Cambridge: Cambridge University Press, 1980); and Paul Whitfield White, "Calvinists and Puritan Attitudes under the Early Stuarts," *Explorations in Renaissance Culture* 14 (1988): 41–55.

81. I quote from the A text (1604) republished by W. W. Greg with a longer version of the play first printed in 1616, cited as B. Parallel passages are cited parenthetically, and variations go unmarked, with few exceptions, because I find that relatively few discrepancies influence the argument of my presentation. Although I quote from A, I do not mean to signal a vigorous dissent from Greg's conclusion that B more adequately represents the play's original structure, yet I subscribe to the consensus that A is more aesthetically effective and, notwithstanding that collaboration in A was likely, relatively free from obvious interpolations by Marlowe's successors. Conveniently, as Leah Markus notes, the A text also throws into greater relief Faustus's "introspective conflict." See Greg's *Marlowe's 'Doctor Faustus': 1604–1616* (Oxford: Clarendon Press, 1950); and Leah S. Markus, "Textual Indeterminacy and Ideological Difference: The Case of *Doctor Faustus*," *Renaissance Drama* 20 (1989): 7, 23. In addition, consult *The Complete Works of Christopher Marlowe*, vol. 2, ed. Fredson Bowers (Cambridge: Cambridge University Press, 1974), 123–59; Constance Brown Kuriyama, "Dr. Greg and *Doctor Faustus:* The Supposed Originality of the 1616 Text," *English Literary Renaissance* 5 (1975): 171–97; and Michael J. Warren, "*Doctor Faustus:* The Old Man and the Text," *English Literary Renaissance* 11 (1981): 111–47. To sample several interpretive possibilities, see Max Bluestone's review of the literature, "*Libido Speculandi:* Doctrine and Dramaturgy in Contemporary Interpretations of Marlowe's *Doctor Faustus*," in *Reinterpretations of Renaissance Drama: Selected Papers from the English Institute*, ed. Norman Rabkin (New York: Columbia University Press, 1969); and Roy T. Ericksen, '*The Forme of Faustus Fortunes': A Study of 'The Tragedie of Doctor Faustus' (1616)* (Oslo: Solum, 1987).

82. Arieh Sachs, "The Religious Despair of *Doctor Faustus*," *Journal of English and German Philology* 63 (1964): 639; although, on the sympathy elicited by the protagonist's antics, see Roger Sales, *Christopher Marlowe* (New York: St. Martin's, 1991), 152, 158. For amplifications of Sachs's contentions about inevitability and suspense, see Richard Waswo, "Damnation Protestant Style: *Macbeth, Faustus*, and

Christian Tragedy," *Journal of Medieval and Renaissance Studies* 4 (1974): 84-85; and John Stachniewski, *The Persecutory Imagination: English Puritanism and the Literature of Religious Despair* (Oxford: Clarendon Press, 1991), 292-331, 341-42.

83. Perkins, *Treatise tending unto a Declaration*, 403.

84. Edward Dering, *Certaine Godly and verie Comfortable Letters full of Christian Consolation* (London, 1590) B3r; and Greenham, *Grave Counsels*, 13-14.

85. H. C. Porter, *Reformation and Reaction in Tudor Cambridge* (Cambridge: Cambridge University Press, 1958), 126-29, 185-86. William Urry, *Christopher Marlowe and Canterbury*, ed. Andrew Bucher (London: Faber, 1988), collects the very little detail Marlowe's life left biographers, but also review Frederick S. Boas, *Christopher Marlowe: A Biographical and Critical Study* (Oxford: Clarendon Press, 1940); Paul Kocher, *Christopher Marlowe: A Study of his Thought, Learning, and Character* (Chapel Hill: University of North Carolina Press, 1964); and Judith Weil, *Christopher Marlowe, Merlin's Prophet* (Cambridge: Cambridge University Press, 1977).

86. See Douglas Cole, *Suffering and Evil in the Plays of Christopher Marlowe* (Princeton: Princeton University Press, 1962), 204-6, 210, 235-36; and Wilbur Sanders, *The Dramatist and the Received Idea* (Cambridge: Cambridge University Press, 1968), 223, 235, 244-45, 251.

87. Topsell, *Time's Lamentation*, 60. Also see Perkins, *Galatians*, 177; and Phillip Stubbes, *The Anatomy of Abuses* (London, 1583) L5r-M1v ("Of Stage-playes and Enterluds with their Wickednes").

88. Parenthetical citations refer to lines in the often anthologized 1581 edition of Woodes's *Conflict of Conscience*. See also Thomas Wright, *The Passions of the Mind in Generall* (London, 1601), 179-81, for orators and feigned affliction; and Bernard Spivack, *Shakespeare and the Allegory of Evil* (New York: Columbia University Press, 1958), 78-79, for "the psychological and histrionic opportunities in temptation and seduction." John S. Wilks, *The Idea of Conscience in Renaissance Tragedy* (London: Routledge, 1990), 42-43, 61-65, 153, 269, comments usefully on that issue as well but overstates, I think, the "psychological realism" of *Apius and Virginia*. Nonetheless, compare Andrew Gurr, *The Shakespearean Stage, 1574-1642*, 2d ed. (Cambridge: Cambridge University Press, 1980), 101, which argues that actors "in a packed repertory . . . [had] little chance for deeply studied portrayals of emotions at work."

89. For an analysis of *Conflict*'s two endings, see David Bevington, *From 'Mankind' to Marlowe: Growth of Structure in the Popular Drama of Tudor England* (Cambridge: Harvard University Press, 1962), 246-51.

90. The extant edition of the English translation of *Damnable Life* was published in 1592, but an earlier edition may have followed more immediately the publication of the *Faustbuch* in 1587. For the characterization given here, see *The History of the Damnable Life and Deserved Death of Doctor John Faustus*, ed. William Rose (London: University of Notre Dame Press, 1925), 89-90, 104-5. For Marlowe's other sources, see Lily B. Campbell, *"Dr. Faustus: A Case of Conscience," PMLA* 67 (1952): 219-39.

91. Waswo, "Damnation," 86, 93–94, 99; and Stachniewski, *Persecutory Imagination*, 330–35. William Empson, *Faustus and the Censor: The English Faust-book and Marlowe's 'Doctor Faustus,'* ed. John Henry Jones (Oxford: Basil Blackwell, 1987), 171, attributes to an enterprising censor the manipulation of the playgoers' "craving[s]" to see a wicked person tortured.

92. Edward Topsell, *The Reward of Religion* (London, 1597), 26–27. Also see, in this connection, Bownde, *Sermon containing many Comforts*, 16–17; Bownde, *Medicines for the Plague*, 77; Thomas Wilcox, *A Discourse touching the Doctrine of Doubting* (Cambridge, 1598), 105, 113–16; Anthony Cade, *Saint Paules Agonie* (London, 1618), 19–22; Dering, *Comfortable Letters* C7v–C8r; and Stephen Egerton's translation of Matthew Virell's *A Learned and Excellent Treatise containing the Principall Grounds of the Christian Religion* (London, 1594), 36, 81–82, 169–70. For psychomachia and "homiletic tragedy," see Bevington, *'Mankind' to Marlowe*, 196–97; and Horton Davies, *Worship and Theology in England from Cranmer to Hooker, 1534–1603* (Princeton: Princeton University Press, 1970), 68.

93. Wilcox, *Large Letters*, 8–9. Also see Topsell, *Time's Lamentation*, 241; William Perkins, *The Whole Treatise of Cases of Conscience*, reprinted in *Pioneer Works on Casuistry*, 125–26 ("God hath the greatest stroke in these distresses of mind"); and John Phillip, *A Sommon to Repentance given unto Christians for a Loking Glasse* (London, 1586) D4r.

94. Fulke, *Text* 444r. Also see Richard Hooker, *A Remedie against Sorrow and Fere* (London, 1612), 11–12.

95. Cf. James L. Calderwood, *Shakespeare and the Denial of Death* (Amherst: University of Massachusetts Press, 1987), 12; John Carey, *John Donne: Life, Mind, and Art*, 2d ed. (London: Faber and Faber, 1990), 43; and Garry Waller, *English Poetry of the Sixteenth Century* (London: Longman, 1986), 99–101.

96. Arthur Lindley, "The Unbeing of the Overreacher: Proteanism and the Marlovian Hero," *Modern Language Review* 84 (1989): 7.

97. *Damnable Life*, 183–86. For the Calvinist conferees, see Greenham, *Letter Consolatorie*, 877–78; and Fenner, *Answere unto Nichols* 52r–53r, 57r.

98. The A text makes the old man more militant, but Greg is unconvincing when he argues that the militancy "was the work of a robustious actor who excusably found the original [B] version too tame" and that the old man's interventions ought not be ascribed to Marlowe. Compare Greg, *Faustus*, 122–23, 384–87; and, for stage directions and the alleged apparition, see Stachniewski, *Persecutory Imagination*, 298.

99. Wilcox, *Doctrine of Doubting*, 273. Also see Perkins, *Grain of Mustard Seed*, 398–402. For utter or final despair and the like, see Hooker, *Learned Discourse*, 517–19; Dent, *Path-Way*, 244; Laurence Tomson, *The New Testament of our Lord Jesus Christ* (London, 1576) 324v; and Willymat, *Physicke*, 2–3.

100. Quoted in Margaret Spufford, *Small Books and Pleasant Histories: Popular Fiction and its Readership in Seventeenth-Century England* (Athens: University of Georgia Press, 1981), 209. Also see Perkins, *Treatise tending unto a Declaration*, 409–

10 ("not to be troubled of Sathan is to be possessed of him"); and John Freeman, *The Comforter* (London, 1621), 229-30, first printed in 1591.

101. For the late Renaissance "strategy of salutary anxiety," see Stephen Greenblatt, *Shakespearean Negotiations* (Berkeley: University of California Press, 1988), 133-47; and G. M. Pinciss, "The 'Heavenly Comforts of Despair' and *Measure for Measure*," *Studies in English Literature* 30 (1990): 303-13. For "rebound[ing]" see Fuller, *Holy State*, 91.

102. Martha Tuck Rozett, *The Doctrine of Election and the Emergence of Elizabethan Tragedy* (Princeton: Princeton University Press, 1984), 12, 27, 38-39, 209, 220-21, 242, 246. Alan Sinfield, *Literature in Protestant England, 1560-1660* (London: Croom Helm, 1983), 81-105, anticipates Rozett's arguments, specifically with his appraisals of "heroic assertion" and late Renaissance tragedy. Also consult King-Kok Cheung, "The Dialectic of Despair in *Doctor Faustus*," in *'A Poet and a Filthy Playmaker': New Essays on Christopher Marlowe*, ed. Kenneth Friedenreich, Roma Gill, and Constance Brown Kuriyama (New York: AMS Press, 1988), 193-201. Cheung understands that despair "implicates [Faustus] in the very [Calvinist] context from which he tries to extricate himself," but she is indifferent to Rozett's contextual concerns, largely unaware of late Tudor pietism, and struck instead by Marlowe's affinities with Kierkegaard.

103. Greenham, *Godly Instructions*, 775; Greenham, *Letter Consolatorie*, 873, 879; Greenham, *Grave Counsels*, 11; and Perkins, *Treatise tending unto a Declaration*, 377-78. To this, compare Sachs, "Religious Despair," 626-27, 632, 643-44.

104. Compare Augustine's *Confessiones* 8.8 and *De libero arbitrio voluntatis* 2.20.54 with Henry Smith, *Jacob's Ladder*, in *Works* 2:84-86.

3

Hamlet's "Kind of Fighting"

Things happened very quickly at Elsinore, too quickly for Prince Hamlet. His mother's remarriage was celebrated "a little month" after his father's death. "The funeral baked meats / Did coldly furnish forth the marriage tables" (1.2.180–81). Claudius, the deceased king's brother and assassin, is the beneficiary of such haste. In a wink, he becomes both king and husband to his brother's wife. When playgoers meet him, he is also Hamlet's chief critic: "to persever / In obstinate condolement is a course / Of impious stubbornness. 'Tis unmanly grief" (1.2.92–94). Hamlet, however, will take his time mourning his father and then avenging him. He contemplates, deliberates, and delays. Claudius strikes or has others strike for him. He drafts plans then implements them, with relatively little time intervening. With phrases that bear on Hamlet's truancy, he urges Laertes to avenge his father, Polonius, whom Hamlet had killed:

> That we would do
> We should do when we would, for this 'would' changes,
> And hath abatements and delays as many
> As there are tongues, are hands, are accidents,
> And then this 'should' is like a spendthrift sigh,
> That hurts by easing. But to thee quick o' th' ulcer—
> Hamlet comes back; what would you undertake
> To show yourself your father's son in deed
> More than in words?
>
> (4.7.117–25)

The irony is that had Hamlet been expeditious and "shown" himself "in deed," Claudius would not have ruled through four acts. He would not have lived to urge Laertes to rid the kingdom of his dilatory but, by then, menacing stepson. Still, the requirements of the stage must be served; the featured deed in revenge drama must be deferred. Obstacles of all sorts usually fill the bill and delay the coup de grace. Conspiracies are the inconveniences of choice in late Tudor revenge, yet words get in Hamlet's way. He speaks at considerable length about his distress. He broods over the identity of his father's ghost and over its appalling story of fratricide. He broods over his mother's indecency, her hasty remarriage. Most of all, he broods about his brooding.

In scene after scene, playgoers and readers are treated to a genuinely mesmerizing anatomy of resolve. Abhorrent changes—from father to ghost, from widow to wife, and from nephew to stepson—prompt Hamlet to inquire what it might mean to act decisively in times so "out of joint." It is often said that the attractiveness of Hamlet's character derives from an enduring fascination with this question, but Hamlet's answer is very much of the sixteenth century. He finally adopts a transcendent perspective, confessing that "there's a divinity that shapes our ends, / rough-hew them how we will."

> Sir, in my heart there was a kind of fighting
> That would not let me sleep. Methought I lay
> Worse than the mutinies in the bilboes. Rashly,
> And praised be rashness for it—let us know,
> Our indiscretion sometimes serves us well
> When our deep plots do pall, and that should learn us
> There's a divinity that shapes our ends,
> Rough-hew them how we will.
>
> (5.2.4–11)

By the last act Hamlet learns how to keep his resolve and his character uncontaminated by Elsinore's outrages, injustices, and opportunism. Ostensibly he submits to that shaping divinity, the "special providence in the fall of a sparrow," exhibited as well in the rise and fall of tyrants and tyrannicides. Previously he showed initiative, but he also harbored and displayed an oddly unproductive indignation and insolence. By the fifth act he is poised to "let be." "If it be now, 'tis not to come; if it be not to come, it will be now; if it be not now, yet it will come. The readiness is all. . . . Let be" (5.2.209–13).

James Calderwood is intrigued by the wordiness that preceded readiness. With all his wordplay, Hamlet seems to him "like the subject of an as yet unpredicated sentence. He had drawn about him a wealth of self-modifying adjectives, phrases, and clauses that enrich his being and subtilize his character." He remains in a "pre-actional state," and Calderwood suspects that Shakespeare deliberately keeps him there as long as the conventions of drama permit. "In Shakespeare's imagination, fullness and vividness of individual being seem to be associated . . . with characters who are contemplating, but not yet committed to action, like Brutus or Macbeth, or perhaps with characters whose style of life constitutes a deferment of responsible action." [1]

But what of the playgoers? Were they content to watch Hamlet unsystematically poke through his grief, misery, and irresolution? Were they as impatient as Claudius with his "unprevailing woe"? Did they have any difficulty conceiving of introspection as a legitimate "abatement"? Did they think deferral was delinquency? Did they dismiss Hamlet as a malingering malcontent whose few noble sentiments were submerged in a self-pity that kept him from what he would and should have done? Were they bothered by the protagonist's ineffectual belligerence? Hamlet, after all, seems to be playing to someone's discontent, to dissatisfaction with the play's "action" or, to be precise, with his own inaction. The protagonist volunteers wry assessments of his character and scolds himself as "a dull and muddy-mettled rascal," a "John-a-dreams" or dawdler (2.2.552–53), who "prompted to my revenge by heaven and hell, / Must like a whore unpack my heart with words / and fall a-cursing like a very drab" (2.2.570–72).

Hamlet's delays invite critics to speculate about chemical imbalances and character flaws. They guess about family secrets at Elsinore, personal crises, and philosophical dispositions. Some find Hamlet a bookish, gloomy, even cadaverous adolescent. Others think him a virtuous, circumspect, courageously self-probing prince. By proclaiming (though not enacting) Hamlet's popularity among citizens and schoolfellows, Shakespeare would appear to have overruled the first. Delay and nearly ceaseless self-scolding stand somewhat against the second, unless delay can be construed as tactical rather than pathological. Precisely that possibility accords well with Calderwood's Hamlet, who intuitively senses that act inhibits freedom and who refuses to allow himself to become the deed's creature. He refuses to subordinate identity to role, and, as Calderwood sees it, "the compulsion to act" and the "preclusive" nature of revenge reward actor and avenger with a social role that sadly confines, as it defines, character.[2]

Maurice Charney explains the tactical nature and purpose of Hamlet's delay more simply. He suggests that the protagonist is playing for time to position himself and his uncle, his intended victim, so that he can "take action without becoming tainted by his own violence." Without setting aside important pragmatic aims and the advantages gained with time, I am convinced that Hamlet suspends revenge chiefly for self-analysis, which, as Calderwood says, "graduates" and turns into ambitious explorations of both the meaning of social roles and the significance of any action in a vulgar world.[3]

The exploratory meditations occasionally start toward more abstract subjects but unfailingly reconverge on the question of identity and on Hamlet's resistance to roles, a resistance that begins with the play. Even before he learns of his uncle's crime, Hamlet will not play his part, will not, that is, accept his duty and assignment to celebrate with his new family. "How is it that the clouds still hang on you," Claudius asks, only partially perceiving the cause of his nephew's grief. "Not so, my lord," Hamlet replies, "I am too much in the sun" (1.2.66–67): too much a son in mourning to make haste from funeral to wedding and, very possibly, too much in the role of son to resume his relatively carefree and enviable life.

Hamlet is increasingly overwrought, a hive of questions and curses after he hears the ghost's tale. He cannot keep still. As Calderwood notices, "the roaming and irresolute self takes priority over the revenge-minded son," although irresolution, in this instance, did not mean inaction. Hamlet censures his mother, mystifies and murders Polonius, feigns madness, maddens Ophelia, and turns playmaker "to catch the conscience of the king." The episodes punctuate delay and complicate Hamlet's reflections on identity and action. Shakespeare's anatomy of resolve, then, is set in a story of irresolution that is really a blend of fitful action and contemplation. In the final analysis, however, the script's memorable soliloquies suggest that contemplation and self-study are more important than action, and they also hint that resistance to roles is Hamlet's role. Hamlet promises he will be silent (1.2.159), but *Hamlet* becomes a five-act battle against silence.

The play, of course, could go no other way. Hamlet cannot keep his word and hold his tongue. He artfully struggles to get himself said. Widely read and respected commentators insist that he was woefully unsuccessful, that his struggles and soliloquies only seem to foreground and inventory subjectivity or identity while they actually undermine them. I want to take a quick look at those assessments and then offer an alternative to them by continuing on the course already charted in the preceding chapters, namely, by reconstructing, as much as one can, the "kind of fighting" familiar to Elizabethan pietists and returning to a set of personal struggles that were strangely similar to those of Shakespeare's unfathomable yet unforgettable Dane.

The struggles chronicled in John Donne's *Holy Sonnets* strike John Carey as symptoms of "ceaseless agonized introspection." The devotional literature composed to inspire such struggles—some of it compressed into the two previous chapters—seems to have shared the same discursive field as Hamlet's wordiness and readiness. To test that observation, we will return to the pietists' objectives, which, I think, were expressed with admirable candor and clarity. Pietists scolded parishioners for "so much stupor and . . . want of sence and feeling," and they wanted them to become their own confessors and "erect an inquisition over [their] hearts." They wanted the consciousness of corruption to "pierce to the heart and take . . . holde of the affections," producing displeasure, agony, but also consolation and assurance. Did *Hamlet* obliquely address late Tudor playgoers with similar intent when Hamlet schemed against his uncle?

> I have heard that guilty creatures sitting at a play
> Have by the very cunning of the scene
> Been struck so to the soul that presently
> They have proclaimed their malefactions
> (2.2.575–78)

Probably not. *Hamlet* is not camouflaged Calvinism. No amount of interpretive acrobatics will make either Hamlet or Shakespeare a pietist. Even so, if we glance behind the scenes to restore the cultural practice of which sermon and soliloquy were parts, maybe we can advance our understanding of prayer, despair, and drama, deepening our appreciation for late Elizabethan introspection.[4]

Hamlet, Lost

Generations of theatergoers have grown fond of a heroic Hamlet. Admittedly, he was not the man of action his uncle was. His heroism was quite unlike that of the colorless Fortinbras; Hamlet led with his head, not with his strong arm. Nonetheless, his headwork seemed to many, if not most, theatergoers to have built character. This Hamlet was thoughtful, wary perhaps, but not timid. His soliloquies could never have been mistaken for what James Calderwood calls "noise" at Elsinore, "the tautologies of Polonius, the airy ostentation of Osric, the vacuities of Rosencrantz and Guildenstern, and other forms of verbal inflation around Claudius." Calderwood's epithets for "noise" and "court speech" suggest that the distinction was to Hamlet's credit. Yet that creditable Hamlet has gotten lost, and the loss has recently been blamed on the victim, specifically on his "lengthy speeches of self-erasure," which "problematize subjectivity," "subvert" or "sabotage" rather than build character. This arraignment is a medley to which Catherine Belsey, Jonathan Dollimore, Francis Barker, and, at times, Calderwood himself contribute, yet to Barker belongs the honor of having "erased" the familiar Hamlet most thoroughly.[5]

Barker claims that Hamlet only seems to be "excavat[ing] a hidden level of reality," "an inner reality of the subject" that is distinct from Elsinore's "inauthentic exterior." Hamlet digs, drills, and descends all right, but onlookers deceive themselves, Barker says, if they think he finds anything, for "at the center of Hamlet, in the interior of his mystery, there is, in short, nothing." Substantive depth, integrated identity, and nobility are read into the script, not from it. Barker's Hamlet sounds bewildered, generally incoherent, but the incoherence invites "bourgeois critics" to superimpose "the deadly subjectivity of the modern" and "a system of presence" on drama that actually documents "the impossibility of presence" and simultaneously celebrates spectacle and semblance. So the Hamlet discovered by bourgeois critics—"liberal humanists," for Belsey; "idealist critics," for Dollimore—is one they made in their own image.[6]

Catherine Belsey says in a tone of mild condescension that "liberal humanism" "finds its own reflection, its own imaginary fulness everywhere." The origins of "the unified subject" in the late seventeenth century, she says, are undervalued and commonly overlooked, because Hamlet's soliloquies tempt humanists to dart back to Elizabethan tragedy. The soliloquies seem to indicate or even to insist that their speaker is more than show or spectacle (1.2.85) and to encourage critics to find an "imaginary fulness" behind his antics and masks. But Belsey finds more *and* less than wishful humanists had; she finds two selves in the soliloquies, and neither of the two conforms to bourgeois, liberal, idealist expectations. One self condemns the other. "The subject of the utterance" is "a rogue and peasant slave," to himself and others in the theater, a damnable procrastinator. "The subject of the enunciation" is his implacable critic. Belsey is not surprised that her "humanists" have missed this: the first hardly appeals to those hunting for individual dignity in the late Renaissance. The second subject, whose sole function seems to be to frown on the indolence and irrationality of the first, is a sour and sorry self. Yet things get worse for "the unified subject" in Hamlet's soliloquies. "The subject of the utterance," under fire, breaks apart into many selves, and "the subject of the enunciation" is utterly lost among them. Belsey, then, thinks that Hamlet plays not two, but too many parts, and that the result is pathetic, not heroic. "Hamlet is, after all, the most discontinuous of Shakespeare's heroes."[7]

Belsey, Barker, and Dollimore agree that an "impression of interiority" presides over Renaissance scholarship. Dollimore thinks he knows why bourgeois, humanist, idealist predecessors flocked to the sixteenth century to locate the origins of their flattering sense of identity or subjectivity. Since at least the nineteenth century, he notes, historians tirelessly promoted the view that the Renaissance was irreligious, unabashedly secular. They prevailed upon students of literature to accept both their interpretations of the "subversion of providentialist orthodoxy" and their expectations that a decline in God's power and prestige would have prompted positive assertions about human autonomy and sovereignty. Dollimore commences to correct all this, echoing the now standard reply that Renaissance hostility to metaphysics has been overstated. But then he changes course; he allows incipient secularism and skepticism considerable influence, albeit not the kind that previous interpreters ascribed to them. Borrowing from Montaigne, who "perhaps . . . does more to decenter man" than any other late Renaissance author, Dollimore recalls that individuals had long been shadows to God's sun. Once the sun set, the shadows disappeared. They did not grow into "substantial autonomous sel[ves]."[8]

Another of Montaigne's metaphors bears more directly on Hamlet's purported vanishing act or self-erasure: *"nous sommes par tout vent"*; "we are all wind. And even the wind, more wisely than we, loves to make a noise and move about, and is content with its functions, without wishing for stability and solidity, qualities that do not belong to it." But, alas, those are the favorite qualities of the so-called bourgeois, humanist, idealist critics, who never quite forgave Montaigne for so mellifluously passing from inconsistencies in human behavior ("impossible that they have come from the same shop") to the incoherence of human character. "*Nous sommes tout de lopins*"; "we are all patchwork, and so shapeless and diverse in composition that each bit, each moment, plays its own game. And there is as much difference between us and ourselves as between us and others."[9]

It may be too much to claim, as Harry Levin did, that "in introspection, [Hamlet's] mentor is Montaigne," for there is a dearth of evidence for direct dependence. Still, Levin is right about the resemblances: "the soliloquies are like [Montaigne's] *Essays* in balancing arguments with counter-arguments, in pursuing wayward ideas and unmasking stubborn illusions." They are also similar in another important way. The soliloquies and the *Essays* are asides, ostensibly private exercises or explorations. Indeed, that may explain why many recent critics, Dollimore in the lead, regularly revisit them to document disintegration and the alleged "annihilation" of the self in the late Renaissance. For Dollimore and other "conventionalists" are supremely confident that custom or convention constructs character, although Hamlet and Montaigne were not. Hamlet, in effect, resists social roles underwritten by the conventions of court life (and by those of revenge drama). Montaigne withdrew to his study to examine himself, possibly, as has been said, because he feared "disconfirmation," because, that is, he anticipated that companions in direct conversation would refuse his demands for recognition. Conventionalists' assumptions are substantiated if the retirees come undone; so, instead of Montaigne's self-affirming curiosity, which excelled in finding alternatives to beaten paths, they discover in his discourse a series of forfeitures that "decenter" character. They decide that Montaigne's digressions were crises of identity. As he and Hamlet searched for some lost thread, the two unraveled and, according to conventionalists, they proved how difficult it was (and is) for personality to come together and cohere in solitude.[10]

Hamlet's alienation can hardly be overstated. He insolently distinguishes himself from the dissembling at court; he is "less than kind," and he "know[s] not seems" (1.2.65, 76). These early expressions of hostility toward conventions and courtesies come before the first soliloquy, but one could still argue that Hamlet is something of a conventionalist: he is angry because the court does not observe the conventions for mourning; he decides not to withdraw and return to the university but stays at Elsinore; his antisocial gestures and asides were discernible, surface traces of his internal, contested efforts to stay responsibly engaged, to persevere and "set things right" (1.5.188–89). So before we declare Hamlet lost and then attempt to find him, we might ask ever so briefly why the conventionalists' Hamlet and not a more conventional Hamlet gets all the play these days.

My hunch is that conventionalist critics are persuaded that the special function of many of the arts is "to break the spell of individuated existence." The phrase, *Bann der Individuation*, and the persuasion belong to Friedrich Nietzsche. They appeared early in his exceptionally generative *Birth of Tragedy*, recently and, I believe, justifiably described as "practically the hinge between Romanticism and everything that is post-Romantic." *Birth* does not dignify self-assertion as heroism, for such assertion produces and perpetuates highly individuated character. Genuine heroism overcomes, "break[s] the spell of," individuation, and attribution of authenticity, in select circles, honors heroism by proclaiming it a species of self-overcoming, an optimistic self-annihilation (*Vernichtung der Individuums*). Few conventionalists travel far without citing Nietzsche or one of his latter-day apprentices, so I think it can be argued that some perception or conviction of this kind breeds much of the conventionalists' work that either submerges character in circumstance or dissolves it into discursive practice.

To be sure, in some respects, Nietzsche's almost apocalyptic enthusiasms are remote from conventionalists' propensity to lose Hamlet. For one thing, Nietzsche's solvent is more encompassing and far more sublime than cultural praxis. He wrote rhapsodically about undifferentiated, primordial being, about some "Dionysian universality" achieved through intimacy with an *Ursein* or *Ur-Eine*. So self-cancellation was tantamount to reabsorption and self-transcendence, a maneuver (and equation) familiar to all students of asceticism and the history of Christian traditions. We will want to keep that familiarity (and similarity) in mind when we reposition *Hamlet* and Hamlet in the religious culture of late Tudor England; yet by attending to the play, to the prince, and—once again—to the pietists, we may find that Nietzsche's discussion of "self-annihilation" and several conventionalists' comparable conjectures about self-erasure are postscripts, in this application, slightly out of place.[11]

Conformity, Interiority, and Melancholy

To find the Hamlet Elizabethan playgoers were likely to have found in *Hamlet*, we reconceive, as best we can, the therapeutic value the pietists ascribed to self-scourging and to ostensible, provisional self-cancellation. The first two chapters here have taken us some distance. Ideally, the first chapter's presentation of prayerful inventories and the second's repossession of pietist despair yielded more of the context, more of what is sometimes called "the horizon of expectations" than we had before. But it bears repeating that repossession here should not be associated with "ideas-of-the-time approaches" to intellectual, cultural, and literary history, most of which trade on purportedly dominant and uncontested ideas and on the authors' intentions. Things are seldom, if ever, as neat as those efforts to bind author, text, and context presume. In the Elizabethan age, uncertainties and controversies about the significance of despair complicated perceptions of character (and the acquisition of assurance of election). Those complications, though, have not prohibited us from retrieving a plausible Elizabethan Faustus. In fact, they are very much a part of the story I have been telling and have wanted to tell, because the pietists performed and fashioned complicated rather than neatly circumscribed characters when they performed and fashioned prayerful, wretched, prodigal selves. The argument of this chapter is that the pietists' complications help us find a compellingly Elizabethan Hamlet.[12]

At a very basic level, Hamlet is easy to find. He stands out from the crowd at Elsinore. Even before he hears the ghost's tale of regicide, fratricide, and double usurpation (seizure of bed and throne), he rules out any reconciliation; Hamlet is "less than kind" and more than contrary. Most other Danes pass swiftly from mourning to marriage feast. He cannot or will not shed his grief. His mother urges him to remove his "inky cloak," a dark, hooded mourning garment that must have made him seem the somber monk at a generally festive court. Hamlet responds that more than seeming is at stake.

> 'Tis not alone my inky cloak, good mother,
> Nor customary suits of solemn black,
> Nor windy suspiration of forced breath,
> No, nor the fruitful river in the eye,

> Nor the dejected havior of the visage,
> Together with all forms, moods, shapes of grief,
> That can denote one truly. These indeed seem,
> For they are actions that a man might play,
> But I have that within which passeth show—
> These but the trappings and the suits of woe.
>
> (1.2.77–86)

"That within which passeth show" gets scripted and shown, orienting players and alerting playgoers to the labored way that leads to resolve. To be precise, Hamlet's is the labored way. The court at Elsinore makes haste ("but two months dead, nay, not so much, not two"); Hamlet, as we know, hesitates and deliberates, and one could say that his deliberations overtake the play. They arrest attention as well as the play's action. As the playgoers eavesdrop on the prince plotting, they can hardly underestimate how much the plot depends on his lacerating self-inventories. Elsinore's inhabitants come to think Hamlet mad and place his madness at the center of their concerns. So Claudius appears to speak for players and playgoers: "madness in great ones must not unwatched go" (3.1.189).

Critics agree. David Pirie, for one, concludes that madness enables Hamlet to step away from "monster custom" (3.4.162), from what Pirie calls "the earnest lunacies" at Elsinore. Hamlet's, by contrast, is a feigned lunacy, a calculated insubordination, much as the wise foolishness of the court jester. For Hamlet discovers that "real life" is "heartlessly fraudulent," and his "most frequent response to the play is not an attempt to rewrite it into a moral work concerned with sin and conscience . . . [but] an often disconcertingly humorous rejection."[13]

Perhaps so, but Claudius is not amused. He sees his nephew's antics as subversive, and one virtue of Karin Coddon's recent essay on madness and treason is that it underscores the king's perception and suggests how Hamlet's antic disposition "enacts the faltering of ideological prescriptions designed to define, order, and constrain subjectivity." "Disordered subjectivity," Coddon says, irrefutably foregrounds the prospects for, and the problems attending, self-government. Interiority is constructed as "a consistent reluctance to privilege any generic or hierarchic discourse of authority."[14]

The assessments of Pirie and Coddon survive the flip from soliloquy to sermon. "Disconcertingly humorous rejection" (Pirie) applies well to pamphlet literature generated by the religious controversies of the late sixteenth century, especially to the Marprelate satires. "Reluctance to privilege" and subversion of authority (Coddon) apply widely and well to pietist critics of papacy, episcopacy, and conformity. The pietists asserted they were champions of conscience battling "subjects of custom," and combat imagery was quite appropriate. Religious dissidents were almost eager for a quarrel. Sermons anticipated and tore apart counterarguments. Pamphlets returned insults on the half volley. English Calvinists rarely turned down the opportunity to vilify "popish" conformity, yet the pietists among them were equally interested in Christians' self-vilification, interested in the conflict that restaged on a personal level the contest between conscience and custom that characterized their efforts to reform polity and worship. It is said they unwittingly led the retreat in religion to some realm of "private sentiment" and that their emphasis on "devotional privacy" amounted to "asocial mysticism" that shattered the communitarian spirit and mutual care in late medieval Catholicism. Recent observations of this kind capture the substance, though not the urgency, of some late Elizabethan injunctions. For example, in 1600, Thomas Wright counted among the pietists' "palpable absurdities" the idea that everyone should ponder the meaning of scripture privately and that anyone could do so profitably. But Wright objected: "whosoever buildeth his faith upon his owne private and singular exposition . . . is an infidell."[15]

At just about the time Wright pressed Protestants to give up their "palpable absurdities" and infidelity, Richard Bristow also sprang to the defense of the "subjects of [Catholic] custom." "Our church it is and our church onlie which hath by the spirit of wisedom and discretion so sorted and severed from the corps of truth al blemishes, corruptions, [and] uncertaine or singular opinions." Institutional piety coupled nostalgia ("it was never so good world with us priestes since everie souldier and servingman could talk so much of scripture") with disdain for the reformed Christians who defiantly deliberated over issues that *the* church had settled centuries before. Bristow was shocked that reformers contemptuous of Catholic custom and conformity were "so foolish to think [they] can . . . leape at one jumpe from Luther to the apostles." Their acrobatics were an affront to common sense.[16]

For their part, the pietists appealed to uncommon sense, an appeal that critics like Wright and Bristow dismissed as insanely self-important and as the source of those unwanted "blemishes" or "singular opinions." Introspective, hyper-reflective pietists saw themselves attacked from two sides, and they saw little to choose between the defenders of common sense and Catholic custom on one flank and the "luke-warme gospellers" and "drowsie" Calvinists on the other—all the above preferred conformity to interiority and trusted churches not just to steer them toward salvation but to take each step with or, *horribile dictu*, for them. William Fulke admitted that churches were indispensable and remembered that the venerable bishop of Hippo, Augustine, had conceded he would never have believed the Bible had it not been for the church. But Fulke assumed Augustine only meant he owed his reverence for the sacred texts to the church's instruction and valued inward journeys more than his church's rituals. Fulke supplied what he thought Augustine plainly intended but may occasionally have left unsaid: Christians owed their remorse and regeneration to the subtle subsurface work of God's spirit and to the ministry of God's word, known exclusively through private and self-probing deliberation.[17]

Pietists' deliberations passed through despair en route to assurance, and the late Tudor remarks about the passage that have survived leave the distinct impression that faith in election and salvation was not easily sustained. For that very reason, if for no other, faith was a favorite subject for analysis, for pietist self-analysis. Nicholas Bownde, like his stepfather, Fulke, held that the church could assist Christians to get and guard their faith. Intelligent persons, he argued, hardly hesitated to take their questions and complaints to the appropriate professionals in law and medicine. The same ought to apply in divinity, Bownde continued, but, on that count, the intelligence too often posted high hurdles, and "there is nothing in us more to hinder us from beleeving than to harken to our owne reason." A statement such as this, of course, could be taken to handicap self-inquiry, but we know the nature of Bownde's bias against reason. We have already encountered his preference for billowing sentiment and spiritual discernment ("a supernaturall inlightening"). In this instance, he hoped only that the church might save Calvinists from missteps that attended the wrong kinds of self-help.[18]

Bownde, then, agreed with Fulke: there could be no solid substitute for intuition, deliberation, and catharsis, all of which were largely, if not wholly, unmediated affairs between pietists and their God. And the two agreed with other pietists that the faithful would grow capable of

judging the church and its reasoning as well as themselves. In his Lan-
cashire sermons, William Harrison distinguished challenges confronting
pietists from the acquiescence reportedly required by the Catholics. He
often echoed the apostle's imperative to "test everything," and he sent
his condolences to the "subjects of custom": "I know the popish seminaries will not suffer you to trye their seed; you must trust them and take
it upon theyre word, but we allowe and require you to trye ours." Reformed Christians "tried" and tested and "look[ed] inside for a way out"
of "redemptive institutions" that Stephen Collins thinks were "fragile
at best." [19]

Ardent "subjects of [Catholic] custom" would have had a hard time
making any sense of Collins's talk of fragility. As befitted apologists for
tradition, Wright and Bristow remained convinced that apostolic succession assured their "redemptive institution" nothing, if not "an unshake-
able base." They would have said—in different words, they did say—that
"fragility" characterized whatever momentary consensus emerged from
the "singular opinions" of their heretically self-indulgent opponents,
dedicated pietist outsiders whose prayers and narratives of self-discovery
made a show of turning their insides out.

Thomas Spark answered the Catholic critics. He targeted the myth
of Catholic calm, conformity, and consensus, reveling in his expositions
of the terrible "disagreements" and ferocious factions that disturbed the
peace of the medieval church. Spark stressed the contentiousness of anti-
popes and the petulance of popes, who seemed strident even when no
rival incited rebellion. "Your good ones," he said, referring to the highest
of Catholic hierocrats, "have been as hard to find as cole-black swans."
He knew that the likes of Wright and Bristow would stay with the one
interpretation of apostolic succession that fit the official line on church
consensus and authority. He flirted with another, with a second interpretation that defined succession and continuity in terms of disposition.
It was a mistake, Spark held, to identify continuity with custom and to
identify apostolic succession with the orderly (or, if truth be told, not-
so-orderly) succession of generations and of church leaders. "Al this kind
of rhetorick of yours," he told the Catholics in 1591, "is grounded upon
a false principle, namely, that the church and the ministers thereof have
been and alwais must be so visible that in al times demonstration may be
made thereof." The apostles taught, and pietists of every age learned, that
conscience corrected custom. So while it seemed to "subjects of custom,"

Wright and Bristow, that Calvinists were leaping from the late sixteenth century back to the apostolic age in an ungainly manner, to say the least ("having not one place to rest . . . in all that long space of fifteen hundred years which is betweene"), pietists among them argued that they needed "not one place to rest." In fact, their restlessness assured them that they were the apostles' authentic heirs. Spark was certain that he "carried" within him an apostolic "minde and purpose." Outward conformity and calm were no guarantees of continuity; continuity depended on conscience, interiority, and unrest.[20]

Few would deny that custom had advantages over conscience. It must have been easier to measure, if not also to make, headway when one's assurance of election was predicated on conformity, on something demonstrable. Ordinarily, a restless conscience affords more suspense than assurance, but there was nothing ordinary about pietists' equations of suspense and restlessness with assurance.

To recall that suspense was a staple of Elizabethan drama is surely not to suggest that dramatists and actors took their cues from the pietists. Playwrights were well provided with theatrical models. Protagonists in revenge tragedies conventionally scaled obstacles and set their courses around and through a collection of court intrigues, the obstacles and intrigues keeping up the suspense even though outcomes were certain. Yet Roland Frye is right: had Shakespeare done no more than draw from the catalog of conventional suspense mechanisms, "his *Hamlet* would have been no more noteworthy than other blood and horror shows." Obviously, Shakespeare did more. He vastly improved on what he inherited. He "varied the form so that the audience was often kept wondering whether [Hamlet] ever would achieve revenge at all." What Frye finds "of far more lasting interest," however, was how shrewdly the playwright layered in "the suspense of probing the ultimate mysteries of human nature and destiny." I will not argue that the "suspense of probing" owed anything to the religious culture this book has been describing, yet some similarities seem to warrant further investigation. We may find that Elizabethan soliloquies and pietist sermons share, if not a common source, a climate of opinion about brooding, prayer, despair, and drama.[21]

Suspense in *Hamlet* is sometimes attributed to—and Hamlet's delay blamed on—the ghost's questionable character. The ghost's credibility, that is, had to be checked and rechecked before the protagonist could get his act together. But I think too much has been made of this. The conflict between conformity ("I know not seems") and interiority ("that within which passeth show") is apparent even before Hamlet is informed of the ghost's existence.

An alternative explanation for "the suspense of probing" in *Hamlet* casts the protagonist as a typical late Tudor melancholic, a specimen of the moody, indecisive student with whom, some say, Elizabethan playgoers would have been all too familiar. Kristian Smidt's is the simplest recent statement of the possibility that Shakespeare, wanting to transform revenge drama, exploited what was known about melancholy to make "inner motivation" (rather than circumstance) Hamlet's chief impediment. Smidt maintains that the playwright capitalized on the common perception that late adolescents "by overmuch study" were peculiarly susceptible to fits of self-analysis. *Hamlet* explicitly calls attention to Hamlet's studies: just "when we might reasonably expect to see him rush on stage, sword in hand," Smidt says, he arrives reading a book. On this reading of his reading, however, Hamlet is little more than a morose malcontent, sulking while groping for some scintilla of sense in a sordid world.[22]

Elizabethans may well have thought students conspicuously susceptible and depressible, as Smidt claims, but early modern religious psychology was more complicated than that and seldom stopped analyzing maddening self-analysis. Of special concern here are the suggestions that thoughtful, troubled, and self-probing pietists were mentally unbalanced. Predictably, that diagnosis did not go unchallenged, and the fortunate consequence of objections and challenges is that we have several discussions of distinctions, as well as connections, between melancholy and therapeutic despair.

As Hamlet was making his debut, Richard Rogers was trying to understand why some Christians found it impossible to get a sure hold of comforting doctrine. They were listless and ill-at-ease. They brooded about their brooding, much as Hamlet would on stage. Rogers wanted to distinguish the melancholics among them, those whose wretchedness and misery were caused by chemical imbalance, from the self-absorbed pietists whose distress was *un*natural, soterial, and therapeutic. He turned to the standard source at the time, to "Doctor Bright, Physition."[23]

Timothy Bright's *Treatise of Melancholie* was first published in London in 1586. It analyzed experiences of "darknes, perill, doubt, [and] fright" that afflicted the reprobate and the elect alike. Others before Bright gathered that the "natural" cause of melancholy was a surplus of black bile — the grossest part of the blood, "juice or excrement," "this muddie humour." It settled in the spleen and sent vapors to the brain. The vapors then clouded judgment so that "large monstrous fictions" were mistaken for grim, menacing facts. The melancholics' dreams seemed haunted and surreal. "Exceeding sadness" filled their waking hours. Vapors so disabled the senses that they knew no friends and found the world unfriendly and incomprehensible. Relationships, routines, and all their certainties seemed to them to have been somehow dismantled and to lay in unfamiliar pieces, so melancholics could not match response to stimulus. They fled from "society," suffered "the lamentable effects" of their apparent misanthropy, withdrew "into those extremities of heavy moode," and utterly perplexed those around them. Perplexity gradually turned into animosity, and animosity increased the melancholics' isolation and sense of alienation. Bright was struck by the similarities between "those extremities of heavy moode" and the solemnity (or "heavy moode") of the pietists who ripped and ransacked their consciences while struggling through despair and desolation to some assurance of their election. All the more reason, Bright figured, to lecture his colleagues on the distinction between melancholy and "the soul's proper anguish": "when anie conceit troubleth you that *hath no sufficient grounde of reason* but riseth onely upon the frame of your brayne which is subject . . . unto the humour, that is right melancholicke."[24]

The italics are mine. According to Bright, bile and vapors were natural causes but not rational causes. "Holy desperation" might make the afflicted seem as dejected, or even as demented, as melancholics, but Bright concluded that desperation, and not melancholy, was the soul's "proper" and reasonable anguish. It was "proper" and reasonable because sinners should feel sorrow and disorienting remorse for their sins. They should be anxious about the prospects for pardon, if they understood the magnitude of their offenses and infidelity. Bright implied that the "meere fancy" of melancholics was commonly and deliberately confused with pietists' "proper anguish" by persons prone to deprecate religious sentiment; so contagious was the confusion, he said, and so convincing the misperception, that deeply (but properly and reasonably) disturbed Christians were likely to latch on to the physiological explanation of their dis-ease, although their "humors in quantitie and quality [were] not exceeding nor wanting . . . naturall proportion." Rather than be overcome by shame, the depressed "labor by al meanes to benumme the sense of that stinge which sinne ever carrieth in the tayle." They understood the real reasons for their anguish and misery, yet they tried to suppress their knowledge of wrongdoing and of the sin within, preferring a natural to the rational cause of wretchedness. Feeling wretched and irredeemable, the elect often lost sight of the consolations available to them, but Bright was ready to help them refocus.

> You say you feele small strength of faith and no support of that hope which maketh so ashamed. Beware least you judge unjustly of the wayes of God and esteeme that for small which is great, and vile which in the sight of God is most pretious. For herein the enemie may take encouragement to your great disadvauntage. You feele not that taste thereof you sometimes felt and do you judge therefore you are bereved utterlie thereof? What? Consider the soule is nowe sicke and distasteth much wholesome meate of consolation and loatheth many pleasaunt and fragrant cuppes of comfort and counsell, and yet the indevours of God's children in this behalfe are not therefore of themselves bitter or unsavory, so you are not to measure the absence of this grace by that you presently [feel] but by that in times past (while the soule stoode free from this disease of temptation and trial) you have felt of comfort in the spirite through an acceptable measure of faith according to the dispensation of God's grace and not according to our fancy, but as he shal think meete to be ministered unto us. Neither is the tryall of faith to be taken according as the soule feeleth it in it self but also . . . by the course and trade of life which hath passed before and those fruits which are are evident to the eyes of others who can judge more sincerely than the afflicted whose understandings are somewhat altered through Sathan's terrors.[25]

The afflicted, then, should look to "the course and trade of life," discover evidence of God's abiding care and mercy, consult "others who can judge more sincerely." To those "others," Bright addressed many of his remarks, training "spiritual physicians" to tease assurance from "small strength of faith." He was supremely confident that reformed Christians could "receave comfort of the least sparke of faith." Pastors as spiritual counselors must fan that spark, not to cure "the soul's proper anguish" once and for all, but to bring the faithful to "a more advised consideration" of their predicaments. They must, in other words, be reminded that God never gave grief intending the aggrieved to make short work of it. Faith proves and strengthens itself only when the faithful are "discouraged and entangled with spiritual cares." Discouragement—"inward desolation" or "holy desperation"—does not "argueth want of faith, not so, but the place for farther increase of faith and the fruits thereof."[26]

We are accustomed to hearing as much, and it must seem that contraries in the pietists' presentations of practical divinity constantly pulled English Calvinism in two opposite directions. Discouragement is commended, for "the soul's proper anguish" is prevenient to regeneration; encouragement is commended, for the suspense might otherwise drive the faithful to distraction. The danger, though, is that the faithful may become so discouraged that they forget the transcendent reasons for their misery—a "kind of fighting" that strikingly resembled Hamlet's—and misapply medical diagnoses to their dis-ease.

Battle imagery occurred to Bright as he coaxed discouraged and therapeutically desperate pietists to be ever more confident in the outcomes of their ordeals. For more than a millennium, Christian theorists had written about spiritual warfare, finding discouragement both *casus belli* and battleground. Understandably, each Christian was said to go into battle with some anxiety. One needed no extra sense to see that a legacy of wrongdoing and some sense of the sin within weighed down the good Christian soldier, the pietist *miles Christi*. Yet "you must not be discouraged like a milk soppe or a fresh souldier untrained and unacquainted with warfare," Bright coached, recognizing that winning depended on a compelling articulation of the threat of losing. He ascertained as well that winning also depended on maintaining suspense, for suspense produced "proper anguish." Both the suspense and anguish subsided only when a Christian's "sparke of faith" developed into an assurance of victory and of irreversible election. "There is no feare of overthrowe" once each pietist's "kind of fighting" or campaign gathers momentum; "if the strugling tayle of the enemie annoye, they may shew their malice and hostilitie but their force is fayled."[27]

Those who composed the pietists' "pathways" and guides to godliness echoed Bright's concern that reformed Christians, who were bereft of confessors' counsel, might rely instead on medical advice. Emancipation from alleged Catholic superstitions could lead, then, to credulity of another, equally pernicious, kind. When John Downhame spurred

readers to "mortify melancholike discontent," he urged them forego
the standard medical remedies and think of their discontent, their "inward desolation," as a divine therapy. Their brooding was not a disease
but a divinely, therefore wisely, arranged dis-ease, signaling their spiritual well-being. Downhame's position was Bright's, expressed later in
seventeenth-century journals and diaries, later still, in an odd assortment
of confessional autobiographies. But arguably no one raised wretchedness to the rank of poetry more effectively than Søren Kierkegaard, not
just in his elegant reflections on despair but in his journal entries as well:
"only those persons who, brought to this point of life-weariness, are able
to maintain that God does it out of love and [who] do not conceal in their
souls, in the remotest corner, any doubt about God as love—only those
persons are matured for eternity." [28]

"Spiritual physicians" were principally interested in the dis-ease that
"matured" the elect "for eternity," but they did not rule out the possibility that pietists suffered both from natural causes (bile and vapors)
and for good reason ("proper anguish"). The same person could very
well be afflicted with "large monstrous fictions" and with the therapeutic
accusations of an indignant conscience, accurate to the point of infal-
libility. Causes, then, might coexist, even coalesce, but the cures were
distinct. "Melancholike discontent" might be eased by music, medicine,
or diet. The resourceful patient could turn to William Langham's *Garden of Health*, a popular pharmacopoeia, procure figs and lemons, and
follow the instructions for ingestion. To master sorrow and despair, to
take soterial advantage of desolation and desperation, to reanimate what
Greenham called "lumpish . . . and dead spirits," however, Christians
must "common with [their] owne hearts" and flock to their pastors for
"comfortable speeches, exhortations, arguments, [and] advice." [29]

Robert Burton esteemed those "comfortable" words so highly that he
transcribed some and paraphrased others in his vast *Anatomy of Melancholy*, netting many of the sentiments we have recorded thus far. John
Stachniewski makes an intriguing case for the *Anatomy*'s Pyrrhonism,
claiming its rehearsal of "the Calvinist position" lacked conviction, but
Burton cited Bright, Perkins, and Greenham deferentially and often.
He unreservedly declared their supremacy to Catholic consolers, the supremacy of the pietist conscience to Catholic custom. He cursed "popish" consolations and absolutions because the customs of unreformed
religion purportedly inhibited the development of an accusing con-

science. "Strange forgeries, fopperies, fooleries, unrighteous subtilties, impostures, and illusion[s]" had been devised by the priests, he charged, "to enthrall, circumvent, and subjugate" "the gullish commonality." "'Tis familiar with our papists," Burton continued, "to terrify men's souls with purgatory, tales, visions, apparitions, to daunt even the most generous spirits."[30]

But such "cruel tyranny" was not just a matter of priests gulling the "gullish." Nor was it simply a matter of tellers of customary yet unlikely "tales" palming off penances and purgatory on fairly intelligent though trusting ("generous") souls. Burton declared that Catholic priests were without rivals at terrorizing souls, but he scolded some pastors of his reformed religion for following rather close behind them. "We are some of us too stern, too rigid, too precise," he complained, mentioning the "tyranny" of the "indiscreet" who preach too much about reprobation *ab aeterno*, "intempestively rail" at the faithful yet timid, and "thunder out God's judgments." He feared that they "so rent, tear, and wound men's consciences" to inspire self-accusation that the intended accusers are struck dumb, "almost mad and at their wits' ends." The *Anatomy* nears saying that excess, grief, and guilt drive the pious mad, but it retains the distinction between disease and the spiritual dis-ease that the late Tudor "spiritual physicians" urged on their patients. Burton saw that "there is much difference" between the melancholic and the mad who "fear without a cause" and the godly who sorrow and tremble "upon great occasion." And his prognosis for the latter was good.[31]

The frequent repetition of "comfortable speeches," from the time of Bright to that of Burton, attests to their perceived value. Reformed Christians found them consoling. The apostles of order, Burton prominent among them, took comfort in the comforters' or consolers' containment of grief that might otherwise have caused public disturbance or embarrassment. The *Anatomy* has no kind word for "giddy heads" who preyed on the disconsolate and infected the already desperate with a "preposterous zeal." It scans Europe for examples: "the mad men of Munster," English separatists living in Amsterdam, and spiritualists of all stripes. Yet Burton returned to that trio that had troubled Cosin, Whitgift, and Sutcliffe: "we need not rove so far abroad." Hacket and his two disciples, Copinger and Arthington—"familiar examples at home"— proved the point. In this connection, Burton recalled the charge leveled against "religion in generall" by "the profane Machiavel," the charge that piety makes simple folk simpletons, *simpliciores reddit homines*. Of course, he dared not apply the Florentine's observation too broadly, but he could not resist docking it alongside his contempt for disruptive visionaries "with their private enthusiasms and revelations.[32]

Somewhere apart from the radicals' "preposterous zeal" and the Catholics' alleged craziness and cruelty, Burton left room for his favorites who thundered yet consoled. If he was at all ambivalent about Perkins, Greenham, and the rest, probably the reason was their sense that self-probing never ceased; Burton seems intolerant of the disparity between consolation and cure. He would never have been perfectly at home on the stretches of Calvinist opinion colonized by the pietists who welcomed George Gifford's *Plaine Declaration* that "there is no man so perfect in faith but he hath great remnants in him of dispaire and doubting." [33]

One question that preoccupied the pietists, apparently more than any other, was what to do with those "great remnants." They listened to Thomas Wilcox, as will we before considering Hamlet's "dispaire and doubting." Wilcox is principally known as the ally of Thomas Cartwright and John Field against those Calvinists who resisted the reform of polity during the 1570s, but to pietists who welcomed Gifford's *Declaration* of imperfection Wilcox was a compelling evangelist of insufficiency. His *Discourse touching the Doctrine of Doubting* and related pastoralia prepared them excellently for the "kind of fighting" between faith and doubt commended by accusers and consolers who poured from Cambridge colleges into their pulpits.

Wilcox argued that "remnants of dispaire and doubting" were promising signs. They "promised" or signaled how profoundly the doubters appreciated the persistence of sin within. Nothing very new here, but Wilcox also specified that the "remnants" showed how seriously and aggressively doubters yearned for salvation. They knew God wanted repentance. They also knew that "no man by the gospell can tell whether he have sufficient repentance, yea or no." But if the confessional was not a creditable source for certainty about sufficiency, and if certainty came not "by the gospell," where were they to look? There was the rub, but also the occasion for their "kind of fighting." How might they win? How could reformed Christians ever be assured of their election if they could not be sure they repented sufficiently? How, indeed, for the "remnants of dispaire and doubting" definitely destroyed the assurances derived from faith unless doubt were turned on or against the notion that God required sufficient repentance! To help pietists make that "turn," Wilcox argued that "sufficiencie" suggested a "dignitie" to which none should aspire; "Though we would or could do nothing else all the daies of our lives but repent us of that one [any sin] yet we could not sufficiently perform it." That was true not only because the sin and therefore the satisfaction constituted a debt beyond anyone's means to pay. It was true because the debt had already been paid. Thomas Wilcox notified readers that their creditor was content, wanting only some acknowledgment that the entire transaction had been his, God's, doing. Insufficiency was the problem; a candid, woeful acknowledgment of insufficiency was its redemptive solution.[34]

Wilcox thought Catholics were obsessed with an obscure notion of sufficiency. He imagined their obsessions kept them from conceding that only God could rescue them. If they were among the elect, they eventually came to feel their insufficiency and wretchedness. God would free them, along with the rest of the faithful, from the idea that Christians must do something other than believe that their salvation had been earned for them.

> Though we will not or cannot denie but that repentance is part of the gospell, and joyned with the remission of sinnes, yet it is not therefore annexed thereunto that in the worthiness or sufficiencie of it we might merite assurance, but in the having of it, it might pledge up in our hearts the forgiveness of all our transgressions; and yet not as though it were of our selves, but as it is God's work in us, he giving this glorie of his owne work. . . . Indeede, if repentance were of and from man, it were somewhat that [Catholics] say, but being simplie and onely from God (who if he doe not effectually batter men's stonie and hard hearts, they cannot return to him) [Catholics] cannot speake thus but with great sinne against God. . . . The gospell requireth repentance of us; we confess the truth of the sentence but not in their sense, for . . . he that requireth it, for these ends and purposes that these men imagine, as namely that it should puffe us up in pride and the presumption of merit, that we should thinke we have it of our selves, and so therein assure our hearts, that is most false; but rather because it commeth from God and is the worke of his owne grace in us . . . and therefore may indeed comfort us.[35]

Shorn of its indictment of the Catholics' "great sinne," there was nothing peculiarly Calvinist or pietist about this ascription of all saving work to God. And the same may be said about the idea that self-analysis, which excavated the "remnants of dispaire and doubting," was one way God battered and liberated "men's stonie and hard hearts." Early in the fifth century and against the Pelagians, Augustine of Hippo forecast that unless God took the faithful in tow they could not get safely to port. In his monumental *City of God*, he averred that rough seas would make the journey difficult. And he confided, decades before that, how years of painful self-probing enabled him to discover the towline, to see that God drew him into and pulled him through grief and guilt, as well as sets of disorienting deliberations about death and evil and the meaning of desperation. Efforts to place Shakespeare and Hamlet in some orbit around Augustine seem to me ill-conceived. I think it wiser to keep Wilcox and Perkins and John Calvin himself within Augustine's gravitational field. But, at the moment, it is more important to see how cleverly Wilcox turned the remnants of doubt against the remnants of despair, for then we learn how insufficiency, or to be precise, how doubts about sufficiency, allowed the pietists not only to overcome arrogance but also to locate some limits to despair.[36]

Following the Protestant line, Thomas Wilcox stressed that "our salvation and everie part and peece of it bee ascribed onely and wholie to God's free favour towardes us." Moral success was insufficient, but, by the same token, moral failure or misconduct was insufficient; the elect can neither win nor lose salvation. Whether their conduct earned neighbors' ovations or opprobrium, the elect were regenerated by God's "mighty doings," "provided that no man abuse this doctrine of trueth and comforte to licentiousnesse and carnalitie."[37]

The doubts of the faithful, then, could be good friends to faith and, as such, they were an important part of God's "mighty doings." Arthur Dent confirmed that doubts would not necessarily "impeach" faith; instead, they "argue[d] a perfect soundness and health." Doubts effectively prompted fears about the sufficiency of repentance. They forced Christians to confront their frailty, finally convincing them of insufficiency; therefore, doubts about sufficiency led to a certainty about insufficiency and dependence on God. All the while, Christians sifted their offenses, probed their wretchedness, plunged deeper—but not irretrievably—into despair, "oppose[d] fear to fleshly security." That was Wilcox's plan, and he believed it an obvious extension of the prescription or imperative in 1 Peter 1:17, "conduct yourselves with fear." So when critics objected, touching on the oddity of having doubt and fear serve as handmaidens to faith and assurance, he replied that God arranged it so, that God oversees griefwork and uses doubt, despair, sorrow, and fear to strengthen faith. But Wilcox also admitted that doubt and fear had rightly been counted among the devil's favorite tactics. The admission only seems to undermine the *Doctrine of Doubting*. In fact, it pushed Wilcox to join doubt and fear not simply to the development of faith but also to the discovery of faith. At the risk of resuming the discussion that lodges with Marlowe and Mephostophilis in the previous chapter of this study, we may recall how Wilcox instructed the faithful yet fearful to console themselves. He wrote to reformed Christians experiencing firsthand how the devil thrashes about to pry the faithful from their faith, and he claimed that their experiences should assure them they already have what the devil wants them to forsake. In the throes of "dispaire and doubting," therefore, "he which feeleth and findeth those effects in himself can not but must of necessitie inferre thereupon that he hath faith."[38]

Doubts betokened the presence of faith, if only that "small strength of faith" Bright, Perkins, Greenham, and others thought adequate to take the first leg of a long race against skepticism. Spider-thin at the start, faith grew more robust, competing with doubts and despair. The pietists regretted that stubborn doubts could trip faith in later laps; Wilcox quoted Cyprian of Carthage on that prospect (*debilitent aut frangant fidem*), but he stressed the more optimistic side of his *Doctrine of Doubting*. Doubts and discontent, he said, trained faith, empowering the faithful to "mature to eternity."[39]

Without having stumbled across Wilcox, playgoers have seen *Hamlet* as something of a discourse on doubting. Ivan Turgenev, for example, called the protagonist "skepticism personified." Another called him "the very personification of doubtfulness." And doubts figure significantly in more recent criticism, which, as we have seen, tends to lose or "erase" the prince. I submit that Hamlet loses his place, much as Elizabethan pietists lost theirs; that is, Hamlet loses his sense of belonging, and his desire for conforming, to this world, but he then creates and finds an alternative identity. The desperate, prayerful, prodigal "stretch[es] between contraries," as L. C. Knights says, and the stretching "generates [the] energy of apprehension in which meaning lies." Only in the fifth act do we discover where the "contraries," doubts, discontent, stretching, and "fighting" lead. And what we discover ends the suspense and forecloses on some interpretive possibilities.[40]

Sea Change, Destiny, and Soliloquy

Hamlet confides to Horatio in the last act that "there is a special providence in the fall of a sparrow. If it be now, 'tis not to come; if it be not
to come, it will be now; if it be not now, yet it will come. The readiness
is all" (5.2.208–11). But nothing really prepares us for Hamlet's recourse
to religion. Arthur Kirsch suggests that "what makes [his] acceptance of
Providence finally intelligible and credible to us emotionally, is our sense
as well as his, that the great anguish and struggle of his grief are over. . . .
He speaks to Horatio quietly, almost securely, with an exultant calm that
characterizes the end of a long, inner struggle of grief." Kirsch, to my
mind, nudges his Hamlet a shade too close to sublime tranquility, but
he is right: Hamlet has gained more than just composure. Somewhere,
offstage, he has gotten religion, as some might say today. And Kirsch is
right as well to suggest that he has resolved to "reconstitute" himself.[41]

The fourth act finds Hamlet ready to embark on a voyage to England.
It almost seems that he has grown accustomed to circling around the
singleness of purpose he has long desired. Questions ("what is a man";
"how stand I then") share the script with assertions promising fresh
determination: "from this time forth my thoughts be bloody or be nothing worth" (4.4.33, 56, 65–66). Hamlet's record of stalling and self-
deprecation excuses readers' and playgoers' assumption that "or be nothing worth" carries far greater weight than "bloody thoughts," despite the
fact that he had by then dispatched Polonius with relatively little regret.
But what happens to Hamlet leads to a disposition quite different from
either option flanking the "or."

Hamlet was heading for his execution. His uncle sealed the death warrant and sent it with his nephew's escorts, Rosencrantz and Guildenstern.
But curiosity and a spot of larceny ruined the plan, for Hamlet unsealed
the "grand commission" and substituted orders that the bearers be killed.
He did not witness the deaths of his luckless companions; when pirates
pulled abeam, he landed on the enemy's deck and was left there when the
ships parted. "They have dealt with me like thieves of mercy" (4.16.20–
21), Hamlet reports to Horatio, though he suspects that his salvation
and his return to Denmark were more than matters of curiosity, circumstance, and the kindness of strangers.

> Sir, in my heart there was a kind of fighting
> That would not let me sleep. Methought I lay

Worse than the mutinies in the bilboes. Rashly,
And praised be rashness for it—let us know,
Our indiscretion sometimes serves us well
When our deep plots do pall, and that should learn us
There's a divinity that shapes our ends,
Rough-hew them how we will.

(5.2.4–11)

Maybe, as Lee Jacobus suspects, Hamlet's "sea change" was inspired by his having read the "grand commission" and thereby acquired "absolute evidence" of the treachery at Elsinore. The evidence, then, refortified Hamlet's determination to set things right. As I said before, nothing in the play prepares us for a religious conversion, yet Elizabethan pietists would not have been mystified for a moment. They had learned that God arranged all that seemed, to some, to have been left to chance. They heard as much from their preachers, from Calvinists who quite possibly recalled and rehearsed what John Calvin wrote about mishaps at sea—about gusts, gales, and narrow escapes. Calvin was aware that crude, common sense and "carnal reason ascribes all such happenings . . . to fortune. But anyone who has been taught by Christ's lips that all the hairs of his head are numbered will look farther afield for a cause and will consider all events are governed by God's secret plan." Hamlet's experiences started him looking "farther afield." His rescue and visit to the graveyard immediately upon his return assured that he would thereafter see things differently, see "deep plots" and "readiness" as contours of God's "secret plan."[42]

Graves and gravediggers educate the protagonist, impart a different perspective on the causes and conditions that seem so consequential. Spades turn up (and out of their resting places) lawyers, courtiers, and once prosperous merchants, whose writs, tricks, influence, and affluence no longer give them advantages. Death is the irresistible leveler. An emperor's dust, "that earth which kept the world in awe," may end up corking a beer barrel. "Poor Yorick," when alive, had the court in laughter; after more than twenty years among the worms, however, his skull grinned grotesquely, ineffectually. Even Hamlet's struggles to get himself said seem to come in for humbling comment: "that skull had a tongue in it" (5.1.71).

The playwright appears to have deposited a conventional *ubi est* sermon in the script among the graveyard clods. It must have seemed a likely place; late medieval sermons of that character harped on mortality to debase lofty ambition. The point was to inspire penance for pride and greed, to encourage Christians to consider more gravely what might become of their immortal souls. Still, it is rather fanciful to put playwright and protagonist in the pulpit and far from my purpose to argue that Shakespeare had only Calvin in hand, or even that he had Calvin in hand. Having arrived at Hamlet's sea change, however, I would be irresponsible to drop the line of inquiry extending from prayer and the pulpit to the stage, for the theme that was the very backbone of English Calvinist practical divinity stipulated, as does Hamlet in the final act, that "there's a divinity that shapes our ends" and that "readiness is all." In time, God's "secret plan" repaid wrongdoing. The delays, deliberations, and determination of avengers were parts of the divine plot. To acknowledge as much and to submit to God's direction was to think reverently and act meaningfully rather than preemptively. John Calvin had said that "ignorance of providence is the ultimate of miseries; the highest blessedness lies in the knowledge of it."[43]

"Knowledge of it" was not acquired as was knowledge of all else. Research availed little. Curiosity, according to Laurence Barker, usually did more harm than good. Reformed Christians who were always framing questions were sure to miss the answers, and Barker's long lecture on the "non proficiencye in hearing" blamed that disability almost exclusively on an addiction to asking, not unlike Hamlet's. For the protagonist has a flair for questions. "Hamlet's world," Maynard Mack observes, "is preeminently in the interrogative mood. It reverberates with questions, anguished, meditative, alarmed," he continues. "There are questions that in the play, to an extent . . . unparalleled in any other, mark the phases and even the nuances of the action, helping to establish its peculiar baffled tone."[44]

Barker was typical of pietists who disapproved of piling up questions, pressing for a reckoning, imposing on God. He thought that the pious were best advised to settle for what was revealed and to submit to providence. Impatience to learn its secrets kept the curious in ignorance, in "the ultimate of miseries." Equally to the point, "giddie inquisitions" led not just to ignorance but to arrogance as well. Barker suggested one scenario: there is no end to questioning; fresh questions about God's management of the universe descended on every improvised answer; to intimidate the questioners and critics, theorists paraded the results of their "vain and nicefound" studies pontifically, with undue, unbecoming confidence. Perhaps Barker had an Elizabethan exegete in mind when he preached about the pride of Anaximander, who fussed over his intricate calculations and reported the exact distance, to the furlong, between the sun and the earth as smugly and surely as if he had paced and patrolled it often. Lancelot Andrewes agreed that the prurient were easy prey to pride. He referred mainly to Christians who launched full-scale inquiries before they "enter[ed] into a calling," but he also appears to have included theorists who wanted to know more, say more, and write more than had any predecessor or contemporary about providence, election, and Christian calling. The devil, Andrewes warned, "hath quills to blowe them up as knowledge which puffes up."[45]

Among pietists, knowledge of providence was definitely not "knowledge which puffes up." It was proferred to lay persons low or put them down, proferred, that is, to contrast, as Hamlet does in the graveyard, petty human "plots" with God's "mighty doings." During the 1590s the contrast made Peter Baro and several others at Cambridge uncomfortable. They argued from the pulpit that both election and reprobation were conditional, that human "plots" did have soterial purpose and effect. Church officials responded that salvation was all God's doing and done without consideration for human effort. William Perkins and his admirers grappled with the implications of that official, predestinarian position, coming up with connections between self-analysis and assurance of election. Calvinists were constantly told of the divinity that shaped their ends but also of the value of interior struggles that prove God's providential care for each soul's instruction and that follow, as instruction, a predestined course or pathway to God.[46]

Hieronymus Zanchius, whose *Confession of Christian Religion* was translated in Cambridge in 1599, openly admitted difficulties with a doctrine of absolute divine sovereignty. It was simple: no Christian could just lay aside the urge to see events as "casual" or "chauncable." Resistances were too great, and the flat answer that "nothing can be done or may happen in the world which is not governed by divine providence," Zanchius conceded, raised a crop of questions and controversies about God's authorship of evil and manner of governance. Was God "ceaselessly" active or content to let nature take a divinely charted course? Zanchius was no more fond than Barker of the need to know and the impulse to ask. His *Confession* and Calvin's *Institution* set aside some questions as unanswerable and some answers as incomprehensible. Nonetheless, both Zanchius and Calvin did pronounce on God's relationship to the course of nature at a critical juncture: if justice took its natural course, Christians had every reason to expect their sins would count terribly against them. The knowledge of providence, which Calvin called "the highest blessedness," suppressed those fears. It also protected the faithful from the erosion of faith worked by unremitting inquiry, by "giddie inquisitions." Indeed, it protected them with an incomparable consolation that came from knowing God determined everything and from believing everything worked for the best. When the psalmist asked to be taught God's ordinances (119:108), he was not appealing for precise details, Richard Greenham explained, he was asking for assurance and for comfort. He was asking, as were all pietists in doubt, for faith in absolute divine sovereignty and benevolence.[47]

Nicholas Bownde started with the premise that no hardship came by chance, that God took a "hands-on" or interventionist approach to the work of this world. His conclusion was that God, having ordered up the ordeals and having orchestrated a "kind of fighting" for the introspective pietists, also equipped them to endure and to win. Hence, the elect "neede so much the lesse to feare least [they] should be over-laden." Bownde accounted for wretchedness, doubt, despair, and recovery, layering them into what Niels Hemmingsen called a firm foundation (*immotum*) for assurance of election, "more abundantlie" consoling than any rival to the doctrine of predestination.[48]

To see what life was like without "abundant" consolation, William Fulke looked no further than the regular clergy of the Catholic church, priests who vowed to keep the rules (*regulae*) binding them to the Benedictines, Cistercians, mendicants, and the like. They were sinners, to Fulke's mind, doubly culpable because they covered their insecurities and perhaps infidelity with the presumption that they earned righteousness by making vows and following orders. They made promises they could not possibly honor, for vows and rules (of poverty, chastity, and obedience) did not alter the sad fact that the human will was concupiscent, always and irrepressibly disobedient. When that fact took the field as an army of unruly desires and impulses, the vows and rules only increased the guilt of invariably guilty parties and made more remote the possibility for any meaningful consolation. Clear-headed pietists would be among the last to trust their piety to break their bondage to greed, lust, and pride.[49]

The worthiest aspirations and the grittiest determination to do God's will, without an abiding faith that the doing would be God's, led nowhere worth going. (Hamlet's desire to set things right brought him no closer to his goal through the first four acts.) Of course, it was only human to want to take charge, and John Stockwood discovered human nature at its most assertive, and at its worst, in the hectic activity aimed at improving material conditions—frequently at great cost to spiritual welfare. "Lord, how will we labour, toile, travel, go run, ride, speake, sue, and sue again," he remarked, brooding on the bustling and contentious city of London. And preaching to its citizens in 1578, he slipped from the spectacle of urban life into a pietist manifesto that should surprise no reader of this study.

> There is not therefore anye cause of boasting of our selves, for that we are nothing else indeede but a huge masse and heavy lumpe of sinne. Let us therefore ascribe all the whole glorie of our callyng unto God, that mercifullye hath called us from errour unto trueth, from darkenesse to lighte, from wickednesse to holynesse, from condemnation to salvation, from death to life, yea from hel to heaven: for unto all these and a greate manye moe enormities are we by nature enthralled. Let us therefore enter the deeper into a true consyderation of our selves and into a thorough examination of our owne soules and consciences, and then finding in our selves what indeede wee be of our selves, we shall learne to set lesse by our painted sheathes and to make better accoumptes of God, hys inifinite and endlesse mercie.[50]

In the early scenes of the final act, Hamlet shows that he has learned to "make better accoumptes of God," to set less on his own shoulders. Attentive readers of pietist devotional and didactic literature would have known this meant simply that he submitted to God's will and henceforth desired only and earnestly to make himself useful. Submission and service all but summarized the injunctions in the scriptural letter directing Christians to "confirm [their] call and election" (2 Peter 1:5–10). Pietists often cited the passage to urge virtue and vigilance. Downhame stressed vigilance, hoping that reformed Christians would ward off all temptations that tended to "alienate" them "from God's use." Fenner commended "a continual carefulness . . . in al waies, that is, thoughts, words, and deeds." The objective: to "see [God's] will and approove it." "Mak[ing] better accoumptes of God," then, required restraint, patience, confidence during troubled times, and, at all times, a readiness to please rather than to preempt God ("an earnest desire, a firme resolution, and constant indevour"). This manifesto for restraint and readiness, for "continual carefulness" and "constant indevour," may seem to have been ingredients for a quaint, ingenuous Christian fatalism, but the comforts of predestination and divine providence appear to have been compelling arguments for its frequent restatement and manifold applications to the faithful's predicaments.[51]

Predestination was an "extraordinarily elastic" idea, Keith Thomas declares, alluding to its "self-confirming quality" and versatility. It fed on good fortune and misfortune. Even when good things happened to wicked people, when they were left in peace to enjoy their ill-gotten gain, righteous yet materially unrewarded persons could find some comfort in the doctrine. God apparently no longer cared enough about the wicked to punish and correct them; "the absence of worldly afflictions could sometimes be a dreadful sign of God's lost love." Moreover, bad things that happened to good people were part of divine discipline. Life was a period of probation and recuperation in which short tempers were repaired by long-suffering. Pietists' pulpit explanations of predestination and providence were sometimes that simple. Nearly always, however, they included the provision that submission to God's will must not await comprehensive understanding: curiosity pressed for greater intelligence—for knowledge of the ways God disciplined the elect, the ways God tormented the reprobate, and the differences between the two; piety counseled accommodation. "The readiness is all," Hamlet says, and he could well have been speaking for the Elizabethan Calvinists who subscribed to the cardinal principles of the pietists' practical divinity.[52]

"Readiness" was what Hugh Latimer urged on pastors tempted to leave their villages and flocks during a mid-sixteenth-century epidemic. "Thou canst not shorten thy life with well-doing," he argued, insisting that it made more sense to be ready—faithful and virtuous—in the hour God had appointed as their last rather than to be overly and uselessly cautious and to try to dodge the "appointment." For Latimer, "readiness" was courage and devotion. It described the pastors' willingness to "let be" and to comply with God's mysterious plan for their lives and deaths. Much the same could be said of the "readiness," the resignation and rugged piety of the convicts who submissively climbed the Tudor gallows professing obedience to divine and royal will. Their valedictions and the Calvinists' instructions furnish what could be called "a frame of reference" for Hamlet's utterances, specifically for his adaptation of the doctrine of absolute divine sovereignty. But I want to direct attention for a moment to a piece of that "frame" never before fitted to the others, to a specimen of practical divinity that suggests the relationship between readiness and revenge.[53]

In 1594, George Gifford favored his patron, Robert Devereux, with a *Treatise of True Fortitude*. Gifford sensed how this world regarded fortitude, how naturally the courage of Hannibal or the gallantry of great Alexander—or that of Devereux—how even the legendary steadfastness of coarse common soldiers rushed to mind whenever the word "fortitude" was pronounced. Gifford respected received opinion to an extent, but he protested that "it is out of all doubt that [most popular heroes] had not in them the true fortitude." Persons "hautie, stoute, fierce, and full of revenge" exhibited bravado, stamina, perhaps an admirable seriousness of purpose. Their exploits were *recordabilis*, yet they were "captive unto vanitie and sin." And, Gifford was quick to say, no virtue, definitely not "true fortitude," long survived captivity of that kind. True fortitude belonged to those who set very little stock in the "sturdie and boisterous roughnesse" that passed as fortitude.[54]

It belonged to those who devalued fame and honor, eagerness for which made the zealous so "fierce and full of revenge." For the pious, true fortitude was its own reward, although they were likelier to say it was a gift rather than a reward. For example, Gifford compared it to imputed righteousness. He contended that the reception of faith, fortitude, and righteousness resulted in the displacement of worldly concerns by an incorruptible desire to act as an instrument for God's glory, to act submissively and "passively." It was much easier to detail the displaced concerns than to stipulate what submission, readiness, and passive action might mean; easier, that is, to rehearse tales of unruly passions and of the recklessness the world mistook for valor. For Gifford, stories of revenge were perfect texts, because everything about revenge was "bold and yet ungodly." And everything usually came out wrong. The lesson, then, was that "the right and onelie way unto fortitude should be in lowlines of minde, in meekenes, and in long suffering." To those who clamored for justice, who would settle for no less than speedy retribution, and who assumed that appeals to conscience and patience cloaked cowardliness, Gifford had a ready response. They missed an obvious fact about revenge, he said; they missed or forgot that "the devill hath a great stroke in it."[55]

Gifford's claim about the devil's "stroke in it" referred to avengers' usurpation of God's prerogatives. Decisions about life and death were God's; *"Vindicta mihi."* To trained eyes, history was filled with examples of divine reprisal. Thomas Beard made himself a careful student of God's executive power and learned "how vengeance pursueth malefactours." He took obvious pleasure in raising the curtain on each of the many acts in his *Theater of God's Judgements*, anticipating that readers would find the deity an eminently fair and endlessly fascinating impresario. Sometimes God worked subtly, dropping clues for discerning justices who saw that criminals received "their deserved dewes." But sometimes God suspended due process and fit the punishment to the crime without presenting evidence and preparing justices and juries. Charles of Navarre, "kindler of many great mischiefes," "ever burnt in lust" and burned to death while his servants were warming his bed. Such symmetry, some surprises, even a modicum of suspense found their way into Beard's *Theater*, which composed the theme of retribution into a resounding hymn to divine sovereignty, to which Gifford's *True Fortitude*, one might say, was the marvelously consonant, pietist, didactic refrain: to be "full of revenge" and to force the occasion proved only the avenger's "manhoode" and inveterate attachment to "transitory things," but to await the opportunity to act as God's instrument showed sounder, soterially more mature judgment. Readiness was all.[56]

We will never know for sure what was in Shakespeare's mind as he held Hamlet in a protracted "pre-actional state" or devised Hamlet's "kind of fighting" and then readied him, soon after his sea change and graveyard meditations, for the outcome. So can we say anything about the correspondences between his "fighting" and the pietists' dramatic depictions of theirs? The safest place to start, I think, is the question that has been darting in and out of this chapter and the last: what might Elizabethan playgoers have made of the correspondences between staged self-analyses with their "wofull exclamations" and the wonderful work of "contrary grace"?

Eleanor Prosser argues that Elizabethan playgoers understood why Hamlet's early "surrender to rage" led nowhere and that they expected his fifth-act serenity and submission to God to lead to salvation as well as to revenge. Surely one gets that far without stretching the tether, although doubts about Hamlet's "salvation" survive. Prosser, though, is interested in cataloging late Tudor views on revenge. Her search seems exhaustive, but her conclusion gives the entire enterprise an air of inconsistency. "Is it not likely," she asks with an answer at hand, "that the best way to approach *Hamlet* is to forget all one has ever heard [from her!] about Elizabethan codes and counter-codes . . . to respond as naturally as one would to a modern play?" Contextualizing seems to have inclined Prosser to decontextualize: "our attitude toward revenge is almost the same as the Elizabethan attitude, and it is doubtful that human nature has changed. If we recognize that our intuitions have always been valid . . . we find the tragic issue to be rooted in an ethical dilemma that is universal." Set aside the possibility that Prosser invents rather than "recognize[s]" the validity and universality about which she so suggestively writes, for a road not taken in her book on revenge beckons us. It is a road lined with treatises on practical divinity, a road down which Prosser hardly glances. Having traveled there fairly extensively in this book, we may be able to offer several reasons why the rage and serenity of a revenge drama might have reminded early modern playgoers of more than an ethical dilemma.[57]

In the first place, as George Gifford confirmed, the temptation to vengeance was a standard test for faith. One learned whether faith and true fortitude formed an effective breakwater against waves of sentiment and passions stirred by memories of injury and desires for retaliation. Because delay made for drama and suspense on stage, playwrights occasionally brushed against the issues of patience, faith, and fortitude. They looked to fill the time and to account for protagonists' apparent paralyses. But *Hamlet*, I believe, comes closest during its delays to matching the intensity of pietists' self-concern. Thomas Kyd's *Spanish Tragedy* was busy and bloody with revenge; one murder coiled around the next. Kyd's Hieronimo, it is true, used the interval between strike and counterstrike to raise his few questions about divine destiny and human desperation. Like Hamlet, he delayed, in part, to verify his suspicions about the guilty parties. Unlike Hamlet, however, Hieronimo stewed for just a single act ("I will rest me in unrest," 4.6.197), and his self-probing questions receded as quickly as they were raised, giving way to practical justifications for his "dissembling quiet in unquietness."

> No, no, Hieronimo, thou must enjoin
> Thine eyes to observation, and thy tongue
> To milder speeches than thy spirit affords,

Thy heart to patience and thy hands to rest,
Thy cap to courtesy, and thy knee to bow,
Till to revenge thou know when, where, and how.
(4.6.207–12)

So Shakespeare, not Kyd, was the master of "unquietness," the chief pur-
veyor on the Elizabethan stage of the powerful rhetoric of self-accusation
and self-analysis. For him, disquiet was not just an antechamber but a
capacious "pre-actional state" in which, as Peter Mercer reports, "the
persistent ambiguities of emotion, rhetoric, and acting" were developed
"to their ultimate riddling potential." *Hamlet*, more than any other late
Tudor revenge drama, presents those problems of identity and intention
posed by the brinkmanship of a purportedly benevolent God in an almost
intolerably cruel world.[58]

Perhaps another reason revenge drama reminded playgoers of the
pietists is that several of those directing their spiritual exercises described
the "unquietness" preceding the assurance of election as the soul's revenge on the self. Lawrence Tomson, for one, defined godly sorrow as
revenge. Roger Fenton sent sinners to "work revenge upon [them]selves
for offending such a gracious God." It is hard to imagine that Fenton was
unaware of the place occupied by repentance on the English stage. Man-
kynde was twice contrite in *The Castle of Perseverance*, humbled first by
Penance and later by the prospect of death. Yet "sorrow and woe" of the
kind found in this widely known morality play ("now, alas, my lyf is lak")
and in others quite like it were "small griefe" and "sleight humiliation" to
Fenton who thought that Catholics had no inkling of the seriousness of
self-scourging and such revenge.[59]

Some acquaintance with the ascetics of the old church could have
corrected that impression, had pietists not discredited them for having
missed the mark. According to John Downhame, Catholics retaliating
against the flesh for its incontinence were fighting the wrong enemy with
the wrong tactics.

[God] rejecteth the fast of the Jewes, because therein they onely afflicted their soules with bodily abstinence . . . but did not joyne with
it the spiritual fast. . . . To which purpose one demandeth: what did
it profit that thou afflictest thy body when as thine heart is never the
better? To fast and watch, and not amend thy manners, is all one,
as if a man should take paines to weede and husband the ground

about the vineyard and let the vineyard it selfe grow like a desart, full of thornes and thistles. Now this spirituall and inward exercise is nothing else but a serious humiliation of our soules before God joyned with fervent prayer and unfained repentance. . . . [I]n this humiliation we are to expresse our sorrow and grief of heart by our lamentations and wofull complaints, bewailing our wretched condition both in respect of sinne and punishment and bemoaning our miserie before the Lord as a fit subject whereon hee may exercise his abundant and rich mercies in pardoning our sinnes and removing our punishments.⁶⁰

For all this, though, the chief reason to suspect that the journey from rage to readiness in *Hamlet* evoked memories of those "pathways" charted by preachers, pastors, and would-be consolers is that Shakespeare's most soliloquacious protagonist never let playgoers forget a theme that played in nearly every pietist's parlor, to wit, a self-lacerating admission of one's "miserie" and "wretched condition" makes one "a fit subject whereon [God] may exercise his abundant and rich mercies." This is not to say that *Hamlet* was the drama of every pietist's discontent. Still, before we dismiss the possibility that some late Tudor patrons were alert to the theatrical resonances of sounds and sentiments they heard elsewhere, we may want to take one last look at the contemplative heroics of Hamlet and at the wretched, redeemed, self-absorbed pietists.

Hamlet's soliloquies call to mind the kind of bruising self-exploration pietists came to expect of each other. They resemble the prayers and meditations that comprised a religious rite of passage from despair to assurance of election. Pietists started with rejection. They refused to conform to peers' expectations, that is, to the ways of this world. Their interiority superseded conformity. Conscience rejected custom. Choice was an ordeal that only began with the choosing. Recall only the "painful" preaching, the painstaking self-analysis countenanced by pietists, and then think of the pains scripted for a single soliloquy (3.1.56–90): "the slings and arrows of outrageous fortune," "the heartache," "the whips and scorns of time," to name but a few. The pietists' passageways or pathways led them to a provisional equanimity of sorts. Hamlet's pietist cousins conformed to God's will instead of the world's ways, exchanged discontent and holy desperation for faith that "there's a divinity that shapes our ends," and bent their wills to God's secret plan.

Richard Rogers thought of soliloquies as "intermissions." He referred
to Cicero, who, he claimed, regularly retired from public affairs for quiet
periods of contemplation because swarms of courtiers made it impossible for him to gather his thoughts. Rogers assumed that Cicero learned
he was never "lesse idle or unoccupied then when he was free from busi-
nesse and that he was never less solitary then when he was alone." Retirement resulted in a strange duet, the purposes of which should have been
self-interrogation and self-communion. But Cicero concentrated on the
"momentary and earthly." He may have examined himself, although
Rogers guessed that he principally deliberated about the "morall vertues,
government of commonwealths, and . . . natural causes of things." Christians more intently contemplate the state and fate of their souls, and they
cross from doubt to faith. With so much at stake, more was the shame
and the pity and the penalty when they failed to set time to step aside.[61]

Rogers warned that should Christians start their soliloquies with "only
a cold mislike" of sin and a few fagots of regret for their wickedness,
they were unlikely to be warmed and consoled by God's grace. In fact,
they could be "brought contrarily to like" the very instruments of their
destruction and hence return from their intermissions much worse than
when they set out. Pietists were cautioned to prepare for unpleasantness.
They had to contend with Satan's sophistries and with their own wickedness, yet all that was part of a conversation with God, Rogers assured
them; their anguish was a sign of God's presence. They must not look for
excuses or for acquittal, because God and their consciences were intent
on conviction. Rogers explained that they would be "wounded" but that
the wounds healed during the intermissions that opened them. Only the
unwounded ought to grieve, only the worldly "wise and learned" who
were never bowled over and so never buoyed up. Rogers grieved for them:

And I will not cease to bewaile the unhappiness of the men of our
daies, who in the usuell and daily trifling out of their pretious time,
declare that they are ignorant of their best portion, which is, to have
daily communion with God; but are wise to deceive themselves
in forgoing it for folly and sinne. And therefore it is no marvell,
though of many wise and learned, yet there are so few, which both
finde an heavenly sweetnesse in their owne lives, and are fit to season others therewith, because they are not oft and usuall daily with
the Lord in their soliloquies, that is, in their communing betwixt

God and themselves in their praier and meditation; and in having recourse to him, sequestered from the company of men.[62]

For Rogers, daily soliloquies or intermissions were contemplative heroics within the power of every regenerate Christian to perform. Hamlet has been dubbed Shakespeare's "contemplative hero"—"heroism," in at least one expansively apologetic application, honoring a "furious intellect operating at the most daring and advanced poles of thought" and "calling all into doubt." To be sure, on occasion Hamlet has also been seen as a flop, "well-intentioned but ineffectual, full of talk but unable to achieve anything," at best, a noble failure, but certainly a failure. The latter view dovetails with pietists' notion that self-questioning led to frustration, wretchedness, and "inward desolation." The former, pairing interiority against conformity, corresponds with their elevation of conscience over custom. One may take either view of Hamlet—or, best of all, take them both—without relinquishing the ground gained by comparing Hamlet's "inward researches" and "kind of fighting" with the pietists' prayerful self-inventories and self-incrimination.[63]

But what ground have we really gained? Could it be that the Hamlet we want to find there or to put there is finally no better than a grotesque and a windbag, "operating at the most daring and advanced poles of thought," yet only "ineffectual[ly]," and "full of talk"?

Both *Hamlet* and Hamlet are full of talk. The play wraps Elsinore in intrigue, "seeming," and sin, and the rot in Denmark is only partially the result of regicide. Words play false with sentiment. The problem with common parlance is "conventionality, emptiness, and falsity"; Polonius, that paladin of superficiality and master of misinterpretation, has been called "the cultural prop" at Claudius's court. Hamlet fails to set things right, for he is busy—fluently, soliloquaciously—unsettling and resettling himself. On ground we have gained, pietists familiar with that kind of business, with Hamlet's "kind of fighting," shamelessly promoted it as a creditable preoccupation.

Elizabethan pietists believed that temporary, therapeutic failures were critical to the fashioning and rehabilitation of the prodigal self. And they believed that words, struggling to signify rather than to seem, as well as God's aid or grace, were critical to therapeutic failures and to their ultimate success at personal regeneration. Words begot remorse, elicited assurance of election and submission to God's will, and created and recombined the "vexed contraries" that constituted the inward life. Literary historians are wary of having their favorite Elizabethans share ground with credulous pietists. Anne Ferry, for instance, tries to put miles between the pietists' words and those of her poets and playwrights. Although Calvinists were told to prepare their meditations "with the skill of the apothecary," Ferry finds them endlessly duplicating a conventional compound; she says that the "inward man" of reformed religion was merely "a representative of a generalized self." And to that she contrasts the poet's alleged "concern with sincerity," notably, Shakespeare's splendid efforts "to represent what is in . . . the wounded heart." As Ferry would have it, Shakespeare learned from Philip Sidney that the inward life could not be satisfactorily named because it could not be satisfactorily known. Meanwhile, Calvinists insisted they knew what they were naming with exactitude, although their prodigal selves were only facsimiles in the flesh of the sorrowful—hence saved—sinner, a pietist prototype.[64]

I think Ferry's great divide between the emancipatory skepticism of her sublime poets and the supposed superficiality of cloned or copycat Calvinists is a matter of misperception. Admittedly, advice about doubt, despair, and regeneration was patterned and somewhat predictable. But to see it as trite and nonetheless tyrannical requires a certain contempt for Calvinism and for pietist credulity. Maybe the only ground we have gained is ground cleared of contempt, but the clearing may help us see that Hamlet, left alone with language (as Sidney, Shakespeare, and Donne in their sonnets), faced challenges that each pietist confronted in prayers, meditations, and soliloquies.

Michael Goldman is sure that "at the time *Hamlet* was first performed, no Elizabethan play had ever demanded such intensity of inward concentration." Actors, he says, "must find and project an inner life," and their discovery must "be strong, volatile, and unitary enough to account for . . . the ways that Hamlet's speculation shifts and ranges." I wonder whether the actors' obligations would have been less demanding had scripts been adapted from Greenham's work, Wilcox's consolations, Winthrop's journal, or Perkins's extended inquiry "whether a man be in the estate of damnation or in the estate of grace." After all, the soliloquies reserved for Hamlet and those recommended by Rogers and others required protagonists to "move as [an] extraordinarily burdened mind moves . . . when it is free of urgent stimulation from the outside . . . free, that is, of anything but its history and its power."[65]

When an "extraordinarily burdened mind moves" freely, the burdens sometimes shift, precarious balances are upset, and the mind and its proprietor may get crushed. Pietists acknowledged the possibility. They wrote openly of their fears of utter or final despair. And lately, literary historians favor the idea that Hamlet gets crushed, lost, erased, or canceled. Losing him, however, they think they have found the play or at least have edged closer to its "second esoteric or prophetic meaning that a more subtle deciphering, or perhaps only the erosion of time . . . finally reveal[s]." The words here belong to Michel Foucault, who nevertheless was cautious with invasive procedures undertaken to get from a script's surface to "the secret presence of the unsaid, of hidden meanings, of suppressions." Foucault and his *Archaeology* had other objectives. He wanted to scout out "the modality of existence of the verbal performance as it has taken place," to comprehend "the statement itself," "the already-said at the level of its existence." At that level, relations between statements become particularly important. Describing relations, without imputing influence, one describes—Foucault said "sets free"—a discursive field and a cultural practice. That has been my aim.[66]

Notes

1. James Calderwood, *To Be and Not to Be: Negation and Metadrama in "Hamlet"* (New York: Columbia University Press, 1983), 139, 208. I cannot agree with René Girard that "Claudius resembles Hamlet in his ability to take prompt and healthy revenge on his enemies." Circumstance and others' ineptitude frustrate Claudius's plans, whereas Hamlet brakes himself. The contrast could hardly be more striking, but see Girard's "Hamlet's Dull Revenge," in *Literary Theory/Renaissance Texts*, ed. Patricia Parker and David Quint (Baltimore: Johns Hopkins University Press, 1986), 296. Parenthetical citations in my text refer to act, scene, and lines from the accessible *Complete Pelican Shakespeare*, which follows the so-called good quarto edition of 1604–5 (Q2) but includes important additions from the folio edition (F). For a brief but helpful discussion of textual variations, see R. A. Foakes, *'Hamlet' versus 'Lear': Cultural Politics and Shakespeare's Art* (Cambridge: Cambridge University Press, 1993), 90–97.

2. Calderwood, *To Be*, 146.

3. Cf. Maurice Charney, *Hamlet's Fictions* (New York: Routledge, 1988), 86.

4. John Carey, *John Donne: Life, Mind, and Art*, 2d ed. (London: Faber and Faber, 1990), 43; William Perkins, *Exhortation to Repentance*, in *Works*, vol. 3 (London, 1631), 412–14; Perkins, *A Treatise of Man's Imaginations*, in *Works*, vol. 2 (London, 1617), 477–79; Edward Topsell, *Time's Lamentation* (London, 1599), 264, 305;

Chaderton, *An Excellent and Godly Sermon most needful for the time wherein we live in all Securitie and Sinne* (London, 1610) E6v–E8r; and John Foxe, *Notes Appertaining to the Matter of Election*, in *Treasure of Truth*, ed. John Stockwood (London, 1581) O2r–v.

5. For the "familiar" Hamlet, see A. C. Bradley, *Shakespearean Tragedy* (New York: Macmillan, 1955), 324; but also consult Marvin Rosenberg, *The Masks of Hamlet* (Newark: University of Delaware Press, 1992), 136–41, for Hamlet as "the power intellectual." Calderwood, *To Be*, 78–79, 156–58, shows an excellent ear for "noise" at Elsinore, as does Lee A. Jacobus, *Shakespeare and the Dialectic of Certainty* (New York: St. Martin's Press, 1992), 82–83.

6. Francis Barker, *The Tremulous Private Body: Essays on Subjection* (London: Methuen, 1984), 14–15, 24–25, 40–41.

7. Catherine Belsey, *The Subject of Tragedy: Identity and Difference in Renaissance Drama* (London: Methuen, 1985), 33–36, 40–41, 47–48, 51–52.

8. Jonathan Dollimore, *Radical Tragedy: Religion, Ideology, and Power in the Drama of Shakespeare and His Contemporaries* (Chicago: University of Chicago Press, 1984), 39–40, 159–60, 173–81.

9. *The Complete Works of Montaigne*, trans. Donald M. Frame (Stanford: Stanford University Press, 1967), 239, 244 (*Essay* 2.1) and 849 (*Essay* 3.13).

10. *Works of Montaigne*, 493–94 (*Essay* 2.7), for the lost thread; and Anthony Wilden, *System and Structure: Essays in Communication and Exchange* (London: Tavistock, 1972), 101–2, for Montaigne's fear of "disconfirmation." See Harry Levin, *The Question of Hamlet* (New York: Oxford University Press, 1959), 72, for Montaigne's influence; but also consult Richard Ellrodt, "Self-consciousness in Montaigne and Shakespeare," *Shakespeare Quarterly* 28 (1975): 37–50; and Arthur Kirsch, *The Passions of Shakespeare's Tragic Heroes* (Charlottesville: University of Virginia Press, 1990), 133–37. Howard Felperin watches "conventionalists" closely, looking, he says, "between the lines" for their nostalgia "for universal and absolute authority." See Felperin's *The Uses of the Canon: Elizabethan Literature and Contemporary Theory* (Oxford: Oxford University Press, 1990), 160–67. The yearning for a unified sensibility is difficult, at first, to detect, for conventionalists write rather dispassionately about discursively (hence communally or conventionally) created forces that delimit character. Still, "the undeclared object of desire is identity," Felperin maintains, "defined no longer individualistically, to be sure, but socially." Little wonder, then, that conventionalists indefatigably emphasize the self-erasing elements in Hamlet's antisocial or anarchic gestures and asides.

11. Friedrich Nietzsche, *Die Geburt der Tragödie*, in *Sämtliche Werke*, vol. 1 (Stuttgart: A. Kröner, 1964), 81–82, 131–39. For related reflections, see Ivor Morris, *Shakespeare's God: The Role of Religion in the Tragedies* (New York: St. Martin's, 1972), 204–9. For *Birth* as "practically the hinge," see Henry Staten, *Nietzsche's Voice* (Ithaca: Cornell University Press, 1990), 187, 194–95. Nietzsche, of course, is contested territory, and it is argued that praise or blame for the submergence

of subjectivity has unfairly attached to his reputation. See, for example, Kathleen Higgins, "Nietzsche and Postmodern Subjectivity," in *Nietzsche as Postmodernist*, ed. Clayton Koelb (Albany: State University of New York Press, 1990), 197–98; but also, in this connection, consult Dollimore, *Radical Tragedy*, 250.

12. For telling criticisms of the "ideas-of-the-time approach," see the work of Richard L. Levin, specifically "The Problem of 'Context' in Interpretation," in *Shakespeare and the Dramatic Tradition*, ed. W. R. Elton and William B. Long (Newark: University of Delaware Press, 1989), 90–92, and *New Readings vs. Old Plays* (Chicago: University of Chicago Press, 1979), 147–59. To expand "the horizon of expectations," we persist in asking what Shakespeare's patrons might have remembered when they saw a morality play, contemplated death, pondered pietists' admonitions and exhortations. See, respectively, Alan C. Dessen, *Shakespeare and the Late Morality Plays* (Lincoln: University of Nebraska Press, 1986), 161–64; Roland Mushat Frye, *The Renaissance Hamlet: Issues and Responses in 1600* (Princeton: Princeton University Press, 1984), 219–20; and what follows here. For general but useful remarks on the need for "revisionist" historical scholarship in literary studies (for "effective archival work"), see, *inter alia*, Edward W. Said, *The World, the Text, and the Critic* (Cambridge: Harvard University Press, 1983), 165–68.

13. David Pirie, "Hamlet Without the Prince," in *Shakespeare's Wide and Universal Stage*, ed. C. B. Cox and D. J. Palmer (Manchester: Manchester University Press, 1984), 169–71, 177–78. Also see Sukanta Chaudhuri, *Infirm Glory: Shakespeare and the Renaissance Image of Man* (Oxford: Oxford University Press, 1981), 134–38.

14. Karin S. Coddon, " 'Such Strange Desygns': Madness, Subjectivity, and Treason in *Hamlet* and Elizabethan Culture," *Renaissance Drama* 20 (1989): 51–75.

15. Thomas Wright, *Certaine Articles or Forcible Reasons discovering the palpable absurdities and most notorious and intricate errors of the Protestants' Religion* (Antwerp, 1600) A4r–A5r; John Bossy, *Christianity in the West, 1400–1700* (Oxford: Oxford University Press, 1985), 141, for "asocial mysticism"; and Josias Nichols, *The Plea of the Innocent wherein is averred that the ministers and people falslie termed puritanes are injuriouslie slaundered for enemies or troublers of the state* (London, 1602), 151–52, for "subjects of custom."

16. Richard Bristow, *A Briefe Treatise of divers plaine and sure waies to find out the truth in this doubtfull and dangerous time of heresie* (Antwerp, 1599) 99v–100r, 120v–123r; and Anthony Gilby, *A Pleasant Dialogue conteining a large discourse betweene a souldier of Barwick and an English chaplain* (London, 1566) C3v, "it was never so good world."

17. William Fulke, *The Text of the New Testament* (London, 1589) C6v. For "drowsie" Calvinists, see William Perkins, *Discourse of Conscience*, reprinted in *William Perkins, Pioneer Works on Casuistry*, ed. Thomas Merrill (Nieuwkoop: B. de Graaf, 1966), 11.

18. Nicholas Bownde, *The Unbeleefe of S. Thomas the Apostle laid open for the comfort of all that desire to beleeve* (Cambridge, 1608), 50–51, 60–62.

19. See William Harrison, *The Difference of Hearers or an Exposition of the Parable of the Sower* (London, 1614), 15–16, citing 1 Thessalonians 5:12; and Stephen L. Collins, *From Divine Cosmos to Sovereign State: An Intellectual History of Consciousness and the Idea of Order in Renaissance England* (Oxford: Oxford University Press, 1989), 101–2, specifically describing Richard Hooker.

20. Thomas Spark, *An Answere to Master John De Albines's Notable Discourse against Heresies* (Oxford, 1591), 11–12, 126–27, 271.

21. Frye, *Renaissance Hamlet*, 168.

22. See Kristian Smidt, *Unconformities in Shakespeare's Tragedies* (New York: St. Martin's Press, 1990), 62–63.

23. Rogers, *Seven Treatises*, (London, 1610), 45–47.

24. See Timothy Bright, *A Treatise of Melancholie* (London, 1586), 194. Also compare Bright's diagnoses (notably, 102–8) with those in Stephen Batman, *Batman uppon Bartholome* (London, 1582) 32v–33v, and in John Trevisa's translation of Bartholomaeus Anglicus's *De proprietatibus rerum*, republished more recently as *On the Properties of Things*, vol. 1 (Oxford: Clarendon Press, 1975), 159–62.

25. Bright, *Melancholie*, 184–91, 230–31.

26. Ibid., 216–18, 224–25.

27. Ibid., 236; and, for the differences between the pietists' "complex and conflictual Christian subjectivity" and some previous "conceptualizations of ideal selfhood," see Debora Kuller Shuger, *The Renaissance Bible: Scholarship, Sacrifice, and Subjectivity* (Berkeley: University of California Press, 1994), 112–13.

28. John Downhame, *Guide to Godlynesse* (London, 1629), 357; and *Soren Kierkegaard's Journals and Papers*, vol. 6, ed. Howard V. Hong and Edna Hong (Bloomington: Indiana University Press, 1978), 575.

29. See Richard Greenham, *A Godly Exposition of the XVI. Psalm*, in *The Works of the Reverend and Faithfull Servant of Jesus Christ, M. Richard Greenham*, ed. Henry Holland (London, 1605), 676, for "lumpish spirits"; but also Perkins, *Discourse of Conscience*, 39–40; Perkins, *A Treatise tending unto a Declaration whether a man be in the Estate of Damnation or in the Estate of Grace*, in *Works*, vol. 1 (London, 1616), 365; and John Downhame, *Spiritual Physicke to cure the diseases of the soule arising from the superfluitie of choller* (London, 1600) 4^{iv}, for related remarks on the physiological causes of anger. William Langham's remedies are among the many prescriptions in his *Garden of Health* (London, 1597), 244 (figs), 369 (lemons).

30. The pietists' "comfortable speeches" are quoted in the third volume of Robert Burton's *Anatomy of Melancholy*, ed. A. R. Shilleto (London, 1904), 468–94; for "forgeries" and "fooleries," see 382–83. For Stachniewski's argument, see John Stachniewski, *The Persecutory Imagination: English Puritanism and the Literature of Religious Despair* (Oxford: Clarendon Press, 1991), notably 234, 248–49.

31. Burton, *Anatomy*, 427, 453–57, 478–79.

32. Ibid., 424–26.

33. George Gifford, *A Plaine Declaration that our Brownists be full Donatists* (Lon-

don, 1590), 75. Also see Henry Jacob, *A Treatise of the Sufferings and Victory of Christ in the Work of our Redemption* (London, 1598), 71-72.

34. Thomas Wilcox, *A Discourse touching the Doctrine of Doubting* (London, 1598), 113-15.

35. Ibid., 117.

36. See Bartholomew Chappell, *The Garden of Prudence* (London, 1595) E2r, for the solace in "sorrowes." Without direct citation, Chappell refers to Augustine, whom William Whitaker, on behalf of the pietists, against Catholic apologists, claimed as "wholly and fully ours" on the issue of divine omnicompetence. See Whitaker's *Answere to the Ten Reasons of Edmund Campian, the Jesuit* (London, 1606), 165.

37. Wilcox, *Doubting*, 104-5, 290-91.

38. Ibid., 24-28, 53-56, 273; Thomas Wilcox, *A Right Godly and Learned Exposition upon the whole booke of Psalmes* (London, 1586), 357-58; and Arthur Dent, *The Plaine Man's Path-Way to Heaven* (London, 1601), 268-69. Also see, in this connection, George Gifford, *Foure Sermons upon the Seven Chiefe Vertues or principall effectes of faith and the doctrine of election* (London, 1582) F2ʳ; and Shuger, *Renaissance Bible*, 104-5.

39. Wilcox, *Doubting*, 234-38.

40. L. C. Knights, "Hamlet and the Perplexed Critics," *Sewanee Review* 92 (1984): 230-33; and Ivan Turgenev, *Hamlet and Don Quixote* (London: Hendersons, 1930), 26.

41. Kirsch, *Passions*, 39-41.

42. Calvin, *Institutes* 1.16.2; Jacobus, *Dialectic*, 91.

43. Calvin, *Institutes* 1.17.1; 1.17.11. Also see Roland Mushat Frye, *Shakespeare and Christian Doctrine* (Princeton: Princeton University Press, 1963), 231-33.

44. Laurence Barker, *Christ's Checke to St. Peter for his Curious Question* (London, 1599) H6v-H7r; and Maynard Mack, "The World of Hamlet," *Yale Review* 41 (1952): 504-5.

45. Barker, *Christ's Checke* K5r-K6v; V8r-X4v; and Lancelot Andrewes, *The Wonderfull Combate for God's Glorie and Man's Salvation between Christ and Satan* (London, 1592) 20ᵛ-21ᵛ.

46. For the official position, articulated at Lambeth, see Thomas Fuller, *The Church History of Britain*, vol. 5, ed. J. S. Brewer (Oxford: Oxford University Press, 1845), 220-21.

47. Greenham, *Exposition on the 119. Psalm*, 482-83; Hieronymus Zanchius, *Confession of the Christian Religion* (Cambridge, 1599), 26-31; Calvin *Institutes* 1.16.3.

48. See Nicholas Bownde, *A Sermon containing many Comforts for the Afflicted in their Trouble*, appended to John More, *Three Godly and Fruitfull Sermons* (Cambridge, 1594), 23-25; Niels Hemmingsen, *Commentarius in epistolam Pauli ad Ephesios* (London, 1576), 39-43; but also consult, in this connection, John Pelling, *A Sermon on the Providence of God* (London, 1607), 32.

49. See Fulke, *Text*, 69; and Topsell, *Time's Lamentation*, 227.

50. John Stockwood, *A Sermon Preached at Paules Crosse* (London, 1578), 30–31, 66.

51. John Downhame, *A Treatise of Securitie* (London, 1622), 91–92, citing 2 Peter; Downhame, *Guide to Godlynesse*, 196, 250; and Dudley Fenner, *A Short and Plaine Table orderly disposing the principles of religion*, in *Certaine Godly and Learned Treatises* (Edinburgh, 1592), 92.

52. Keith Thomas, *Religion and the Decline of Magic* (New York: Scribners, 1971), 82–83, 104–5; and Dewey D. Wallace, *Puritans and Predestination: Grace in English Protestant Theology, 1525–1695* (Chapel Hill: University of North Carolina Press, 1982), particularly 191–96.

53. *Sermons of Hugh Latimer*, ed. George Elwes Corrie (Cambridge, 1844), 416–17; and J. A. Sharpe, "Last Dying Speeches: Religion, Ideology, and Public Execution in Seventeenth-Century England," *Past and Present* 107 (1985): 144–67.

54. George Gifford, *A Treatise of True Fortitude* (London, 1594) A6r; and, for Devereux's "fortitude" and influence, see Wallace T. MacCaffrey, *Elizabeth I: War and Politics, 1588–1603* (Princeton: Princeton University Press, 1992), 472–94.

55. Gifford, *True Fortitude* B5r–D4v.

56. Thomas Beard, *The Theater of God's Judgments* (London, 1597), 267–71, 433–34; and Gifford, *True Fortitude* B6v–B7r.

57. See Eleanor Prosser, *Hamlet and Revenge* (Stanford: Stanford University Press, 1971), 33–34, 254–56.

58. See Peter Mercer, *Hamlet and the Acting of Revenge* (London: MacMillan, 1987), 221–22. For Kyd, I have used *The Spanish Tragedy*, ed. Philip Edwards (Manchester: Manchester University Press, 1988).

59. Roger Fenton, *A Perfume against Noysome Pestilence* (London, 1603) B7r–B8r; and Lawrence Tomson, *The New Testament of our Lord Jesus Christ* (London, 1576) 308v, following Theodore Beza, *Jesu Christi Novum Testamentum, Thedora Beza interprete* (London, 1574) 238r.

60. Downhame, *Guide to Godlynesse*, 673. Also see Topsell, *Time's Lamentation*, 264, 311.

61. Rogers, *Seven Treatises*, 407–8.

62. Ibid., 413.

63. For Hamlet's "heroic intellect in its impetus towards renovatio," see Hilary Gatti, *The Renaissance Drama of Knowledge: Giordano Bruno in England* (London: Routledge, 1989), 131–48, 162–63; and Chaudhuri, *Infirm Glory*, 140–44; for "the virus of Hamletism" "infect[ing]" criticism with its obsessions with the prince's failures and tragic flaws, see Foakes, *'Hamlet' versus 'Lear,'* 17–44, 167–69.

64. Anne Ferry, *The "Inward" Language: Sonnets of Wyatt, Sidney, Shakespeare, Donne* (Chicago: University of Chicago Press, 1983), particularly 21–29, 36–41. For telling remarks on Ferry's "romance," see Bridget Gellert Lyons, "*Inward Language:* The Self in Renaissance Poetry," *Raritan* 4 (1984): 115–16; and Stanley Fish,

"Masculine Persuasive Force: Donne and Verbal Power," in Elizabeth A. Harvey and Katherine Eisaman Maus, eds., *Soliciting Interpretation: Literary Theory and Seventeenth-century English Poetry* (Chicago: University of Chicago Press, 1990), 223–52, especially 249–50. For Calvinists' "mature premeditation" and the pietist "apothecary," see Fenton, *Perfume* B6v.

65. Michael Goldman, *Acting and Action in Shakespeare's Tragedy* (Princeton: Princeton University Press, 1985), 34–35, 45.

66. Michel Foucault, *The Archaeology of Knowledge*, trans. A. M. Sheridan Smith (New York: Pantheon, 1972), 28–29, 109–10, 131.

Conclusion

Elizabeth's England was relatively safe in 1599, more than a decade after the Spanish sailed home with that part of the armada left to them by Drake and disastrous weather. So it may have come as something of a surprise when Edward Topsell cited the prophet Elisha to dramatize the timeliness of his own *Time's Lamentation*. Elisha had grieved eloquently for Israel, foreseeing Hazael's rise to power in Damascus, the Syrian decimation of Israelite defenses, and the nearly genocidal consequences of the next invasion (2 Kings 8:12–13). England's defenses, however, had held; God chose not to discipline the realm when he and the Spanish had the chance. Why, then, Elisha? And why a pietist lament?

Topsell perceived that as political and military threats receded spiritual crises were thrown into greater relief. The "drowsie"—Perkins labeled them—saw no reason to fuss. They understood why persons in pain bewailed their fate, yet they could not imagine why pietists "torment[ed] themselves before they feele the miserie." Topsell explained that Elisha, as so many other celebrated seers in the Old Testament, "breake[s] foorth into abundance of lamentation" because "good men do sorrow and mourne for the Lord's judgment before it commeth." Distress was never untimely in the context of Calvinist practical divinity, where proleptic or anticipatory distress was a mark of repentance and regeneration. Paradoxically, the distress afforded assurance of election, security in insecurity, battling against arrogance and complacence. So "good" pietists, "sorrow[ing] and mourn[ing]," were seers as well as self-incriminating confessors, all to ward off the divine judgment that invariably befalls those who never look to, and commune with, themselves.[1]

The roles of seer and confessor were closely related as cause to effect.

Pietists' perceptions of the judgment awaiting both the alert and the "drowsie"—perhaps just ahead—impelled them urgently and "ever" to accuse themselves and "make [their] apprentiship[s] unto sorrows." They

> feele in themselves such terrible horrours, as amaze the strong and confound the weake: From hence it commeth that some in this extremitie think that all that they do is for their condemnation, their meat, drinke, apparrill, health, and libertie are unto many weake minds tokens of the Lord's wrath. Indeed they which are burned with this iron think that every house will over whelme them and everie leafe that falleth on the ground will hurt them, a sharpe word almost killeth them. Terrible is a life led under such conflicts, for every hourre threatneth a thousand deathes, the hart ever accuseth, the memorie witnesseth against it self; his owne reason condemneth him; and his continuall feare is his cruell tormentor. . . . Let us not be discouraged in these woefull torments. . . . A hell thou must have, thou canst not eschue it: therefore chuse it in this world where thou shalt finde mercie with God, comfort in his word, and solace in his church; in the world to come thou shalt have none of these. Make heere thy apprentiship unto sorrows.[2]

It seems, as Topsell remarked, a "terrible" life, made more so by the rule that contrition and consolation necessarily were inconstant. Among pietists there were no exceptions, no saints. Irreverence and irresolution alternated with godly sorrow and a formidable will to repent.

> Oh, to vex me, contraryes meete in one:
> Inconstancy unnaturally hath begott
> A constant habit; that when I would not
> I change in vowes, and in devotione.
> As humorous is my contritione
> As my prophane Love, and as soone forgott:
> As ridlingly distempered, cold and hott,
> As praying, as mute; as infinite, as none.
> I durst not view heaven yesterday; and to day
> In prayers, and flattering speaches I court God:
> To morrow 'I quake with true feare of his rod.
> So my devout fitts come and go away
> Like a fantastique Ague: save that here
> Those are my best dayes, when I shake with feare   (19)[3]

Here and elsewhere in his *Holy Sonnets*, John Donne created illusions of immediacy, much admired and far from irrelevant to our concern with the intensity of pietist self-probing. Donne's sonnets are packed with stunning "idiomatic turns," punctuated with exclamations that cry urgency. "This dramatic language," Helen Gardner nearly gasps, "has a magic that is unanalysable." "Oh, To Vex Me" speaks a different sort of sorcery. It turns inconstancy into a constant and gives dramatic voice to a "kind of fighting" (and terror) to which the Elizabethan pietists had grown accustomed: "terrible is a life lead under such conflicts." And Donne knew or guessed enough about pietism not to expect or script happy endings. His speaker settles for "true feare" and "devout fitts," for fear and fits confirmed that God so loved the sinner as to send doubts and discontent. "Oh Might Those Sighes" begs for distress.

> O might those sighes and teares returne againe
> Into my breast and eyes, which I have spent,
> That I might in this holy discontent
> Mourne with some fruit, as I have mourn'd in vaine.   (3)

"Holy discontent" recalls that "holy desperation" William Perkins attributed to God's "contrary grace." Barbara Lewalski draws together Donne and the sonnet's speaker, and she speculates that fruitless mourning refers to the poet's "love-idolatries," assuming that lovers displaced God and the Catholic church as objects of the poet's affections after his apostasy and before his attachment to reformed religion. We will have more to say—and less to claim—about the relationships between Donne's life and his fictions. For now, though, the speaker's mourning "in vaine" may tentatively be paired with feigned and ineffectual sorrow, for which pietists had no use, as opposed to the godly sorrow they tried desperately to cultivate. The fear, discontent, and wretchedness that the speaker wishes for—and bathes in—as if they were blessings, make the sonnet's sighs seem an echo of the pietists'.[4]

The appeals for sighs, tears, fears, and "holy discontent" amount to a general plea for unfeigned repentance. "Here on this lowly ground / Teach me how to repent," Donne petitioned after having acknowledged that unless one "mourne[s] a space" on earth, sins will "abound" "above" when it is too late "to aske abundance of thy grace." So "Teach mee how to repent; for that's as good / As if thou 'hadst seal'd my pardon, with thy blood" (7).

I cannot agree with Richard Strier that the last line is "counterfactual" and that one's "personal repentance and Christ's atonement are . . . alternatives" here and "not coordinated but equated in value and efficacy." I suspect that "as if" implies that atonement was a source of the "contrary grace" that taught pietists to repent. When the elect learned how to repent, they were thereby confirmed or assured of their election, of the fact that Christ died for them. "My," not "if," should be inflected. When one learns to sorrow and repent, one experiences the pardon purchased by Christ. In "If Poysonous Mineralls," Christ's blood and each Christian's tears "make a heavenly Lethean flood" to "drowne . . . sinnes black memorie" (9). The sonnets exhibit a petitioner's impatience for the results, the grief that only God imparts. "Then turne / O pensive soule, to God, for he knowes best / Thy true griefe, for he put it in my breast" (8).[5]

This "true griefe" looks tame alongside lines from Donne's best known sonnet.

> Batter my heart, three person'd God; for, you
> As yet but knocke, breathe, shine, and seeke to mend;
> That I may rise, and stand, o'erthrow mee, 'and bend
> Your force, to breake, blowe, burn and make me new.
> I, like an usurpt towne, to 'another due,
> Labour to 'admit you, but Oh, to no end,
> Reason your viceroy in mee, mee should defend,
> But is captiv'd, and proves weake or untrue,
> Yet dearely 'I love you, and would be lov'd faine,
> But am betroth'd unto your enemie,
> Divorce mee, 'untie, or breake that knot againe,
> Take mee to you, imprison mee, for I
> Except you 'enthrall mee, never shall be free,
> Nor even chast, except you ravish mee.   (14)

The first quatrain drives the point home so relentlessly that readers may be excused the misimpression that the speaker is a reprobate awaiting—even daring—violent overthrow. But the next lines attest good intent, if poor execution. The sonnet's speaker "labour[s] to admit" God and cannot. The reason of the regenerate Christian recognizes its liege and its duty "but is captiv'd and proves weake or untrue." The remedy is to trade one captivity for another ("imprison me"). "As yet," the speaker has only heard God knock—"Behold, I stand at the door and knock; if any one hears my voice and opens the door, I will come into him" (Revelation 3:20). "As yet," the speaker has only looked for God's radiance and overlooked God's rebuke—"Restore us, O God; let thy face shine, that we may be saved" (Psalms 80:3). But the pietists' appraisals of the sin within and of the magnitude of sinners' offenses dispelled the notion that the faithful can be fit for salvation, as they are, with only a dressmaker's tape. God must batter and burn and "make new" rather than stretch and "mend," if only because the uglier and otherwise unyielding habits of the heart make every reformed Christian one with Christ's crucifiers, no matter how earnestly they wish to be crucified.

> Spit in my face yee Jewes, and pierce my side,
> Buffet, and scoffe, scourge, and crucifie mee,
> For I have sinn'd, and sinn'd, and onely hee,
> Who could do no iniquitie, hath dyed:
> But by my death can not be satisfied
> My sinnes, which passe the Jewes impiety:
> They kill'd once an inglorious man, but I
> Crucifie him daily, being now glorified.   (11)

The "violence of sentiment" strikes Wilbur Sanders as a sign that the sonnets are struggling to "enforce" a meaning that Donne grasps insufficiently to explicate. Sanders laments that rhetoric overwhelms plot, that battering tends to beg rather than answer questions. He suggests, though, that violence appears necessary to prepare or coerce "a stubborn temper" to accept a spiritual good, ill-defined though that good may be. Violence in the poems arrests attention, and Donne's speaker is at no loss for images. The sonnets' virtuosity, in this regard, asserts an "intellectual and literary authority in the very midst of . . . expressions of personal vulnerability and need." The pietists' self-imprecation and prayerful performances show a similar tension between self-display and humility. It is easy to see why they were accused of selling plot for character, self-absorption, and self-promotion, and just as easy to understand why the sonnets are associated with Donne's reputed egocentrism.[6]

Yet the ego in the sonnets is relentlessly and ruthlessly self-incriminating. Petulant and ostensibly arrogant claims are made on God's mercy, but they fall silent as the sestets finish, unlike similarly self-assertive statements that thread through and color all of Donne's earlier love poetry. In "The Sun Rising," for instance, the speaker orders the sun to halt, threatens it with eclipse (in the blink of his eye), and boasts it will find "in [the] one bed" where he and his lover lay all that is worth finding on earth. No eulogy or psalm to the sun's brilliance here; no loving descriptions of a lover's features! One gets, instead, commentaries on how world, lover, and the divine affect John Donne's sovereign speaker. But Donne's poetry, while self-absorbed, is seldom self-admiring. Its self-loathing and "inner coldness," John Carey contends, should be traced to the poet's apostasy from Catholicism: Donne's brother died in the cell where he had been confined for having harbored a priest in 1593; Donne himself defected but was then haunted by thoughts of his missed martyrdom. So, says Carey, he gave his speakers in the sonnets "morbid obsessions" with sin yet kept the cross quite close at hand.[7]

To despise the cross was the grossest of sins, but because the faithful were by nature prone to doubts, a question or worry quite naturally came up: did Christ's cross pardon "the sinne of scorning it?" Donne turned the concern into poetry, arguing the ubiquity and the power of the crucifix. Everywhere one looks, he says, crosses catch the eye; at sea, "the mast and yard" form a cross, as does each bird "rais'd on crossed wings." Crosses are inescapable. Inasmuch as affliction is a sign of God's interest in rehabilitating sinners, "no crosse is so extreme, as to have none." Thus "the losse of [a] crosse were to mee another crosse." Not surprisingly, Christ's cross and atonement most effectively purge, console, and assure when the faithful become their own crosses and confessors, "For when that crosse ungrudg'd unto you stickes, / Then are you to your selfe, a crucifixe."[8]

Pietists presumed the cross "covers" sins; they struggled to confirm that it covers or remits *their* sins. Donne's *Holy Sonnets* are sometimes arranged thematically to chronicle that struggle as a rough trip from corruption through contrition to consolation. But we will never be sure in what order the poems were composed or precisely what Donne intended. It is more prudent, therefore, to set conjectures about sequence aside and to read each sonnet as a discrete meditation on "true griefe" and repentance. Nearly every one of them stages the drama of a therapeutically troubled soul caught between sin and the cross, that is, between knowledge of sin and godly, disorienting sorrow for sin.

Two fine critics and careful readers think they have come upon Donne, trapped in the Protestant paradigm. Richard Strier finds the poet caged in Calvinism, pacing back and forth between petulance and piety, wishing that his sins and predicament could be forgotten because he is unable to sustain the faith that they are forgiven. John Stachniewski discovers the same cage, but his Donne frequently sulks in a corner, more or less resigned to the whims, inconsistencies, and cruelties of his divine keeper.

Strier has an excellent eye for passages that suggest discomfort; the sonnets strain to locate some alternative to the cross, to reassert personal merit or to insist that something sublime swoop down and, in an instant, carry the speaker from sin to salvation: "A Calvinist sense of sin has banished merit as the way to salvation, but nothing—or rather nothingness—has replaced it. Donne finds it difficult to accept being saved as a sinner, and he cannot convincingly imagine being free from sin. In the absence of the capacity to imagine or feel either of these, Donne's deepest prayer must be either to be ravished into chastity or, like Faustus, to escape from God's attention." [9]

That may well be. The pietists certainly paced anxiously, learning grudgingly that discouragement was part of encouragement and consolation. They explained and exonerated themselves, trying to appease an angry keeper and occasionally to threaten him with disaffection. What Strier says about the sonnets—"something goes very wrong with the tone"—could just as easily be said about the pietists' pacing, though in context, "petulant challenges," angry ultimata, "a sense of injured merit," and a wished-for oblivion whip sorrow into godly sorrow and attest an "effectual calling." Strier's telling impressions of the speaker's restlessness tell only against a Protestantism that promises rest and full recovery from sin in this life, a Protestantism infinitely different from the one pietists shaped from the realization that the elect were always sinners as well as saved. The sonnets, then, may reflect their speaker's dis-ease, but Strier is mistaken to think they also exhibit the speaker's or poet's uneasiness with Calvinism.

Nearly the same argument can be made against Stachniewski's reading, although his Donne is less insurrectionary than Strier's and embraced the prevailing orthodoxy because it was "an accurate projection from his own experience of life." Despite his talents and toadying, Donne experienced rejection. Hoping for better, he maintained a humiliating dependence on present and likely patrons. Shifting from life to literature, Stachniewski concludes that the poet's humiliations staked territorial claims on his poetry, that they colonized entire sonnets so that their speaker expressed his maker's irritation and resignation. To illustrate Stachniewski's point, we may cite a sonnet that neatly divides the two, venting irritation in the octave and resignation in the sestet.

> If poysonous mineralls, and if that tree,
> Whose fruit threw death on else immortall us,
> If lecherous goats, if serpents envious
> Cannot be damn'd; Alas; why should I bee?
> Why should intent or reason, borne in mee,
> Make sinnes, else equall, in mee, more heinous?
> And mercie being easie, 'and glorious
> To God, in his sterne wrath, why threatens hee?
> But who am I, that dare dispute with thee?
> O, God, Oh! of thine onely worthy blood,
> And my tears make a heavenly Lethean flood,
> And drowne in it my sinnes black memorie.
> That thou remember them, some claim as debt,
> I thinke it mercy, if thou wilt forget.   (9)

Conveniently, "If Poysonous Mineralls" also illustrates Strier's position: the octave is "petulant," and the sestet seems to echo Faustus's appeal for divine forgetfulness. One could respond to both Strier and Stachniewski with Barbara Lewalski's assertion that the sonnet "enacts the speaker's true repentance and faith." Lewalski emphasizes the importance of Donne's transition from "an almost blasphemous false start" and from the octave's "specious" protests to the sestet's sudden resignation or abandonment of the speaker's initial efforts "to mitigate his guilt or to object to the sentence of damnation he deserves." She is sure the speaker "throw[s] himself without reservation upon Christ's mercy in the earnest hope of justification," but the speaker seems to me less unreserved and enthusiastic than she imagines. Stachniewski, on this matter, is more perceptive; more fear than faith fills the sonnet. But fear has its place, and, as the transition documents, it is not, *pace* Stachniewski, a final resting place. According to pietist protocols, fear drove the faithful forward. So there is no resolution in "If Poysonous Mineralls"—no lasting resolution in pietist practical divinity—but submission ("who am I, that dare dispute with thee") was a decisive step in the right direction.[10]

Perkins, Greenham, Downhame, Dent, Winthrop, and others repeated the right steps in sequence: indignation, sorrow, and submission.

Even if we could stride to Donne's last sonnet, to discover, that is, which one was composed after all the others, we ought not expect of the last anything but another round in that now familiar "kind of fighting," another lap around the "interchangeable course." Frightened and irresolute, speakers exhibit the first symptoms of righteousness; remorseful and submissive, they advance, remaining nonetheless caught between sin and salvation. In other words, signs of struggle punctuate every sonnet; Stachniewski splendidly describes them as "the wriggling movements of a mind pinned by the contemporary phrases with which it is compelled to understand itself." "Thou Hast Made Me" "wriggles" to stave off utter or final despair:

> Thou hast made me, And shall thy worke decay?
> Repaire me now, for now mine end doth haste,
> I runne to death, and death meets me as fast,
> And all my pleasures are like yesterday,
> I dare not move my dimme eyes any way,
> Despair behind, and death before me cast
> Such terrour, and my feebled flesh doth waste
> By sinne in it, which it t'wards hell doth weigh;
> Onely thou art above, and when towards thee
> By thy leave I can looke, I rise againe;
> But our old subtle foe so tempteth me,
> That not one houre I can my selfe sustaine;
> Thy Grace may wing me to prevent his art
> And thou like Adamant draw mine iron heart.   (1)

But Stachniewski points out, as if he were raising an objection, that the speaker "can muster no confident anticipation" of God's forgiveness and settles for a "sense of being at God's whimsical mercy." If, as he argues, John Donne's problems with patrons and preferment were projected on the poem's soterial predicament, this, "no-confidence" reading is plausible. But if one features a different context, the late Tudor religious cultures of doubt and despair, it seems less so. Can we say whether the text leans one way or the other? [11]

Stachniewski's case for divine whim and for the speaker's failure to "muster . . . confident anticipation" builds on one word, on "may" in the sonnet's penultimate line. Grace, it says, "may" save the speaker from his "subtle foe," from the diabolical intruder who was believed to dis-

suade pietists from godly sorrow during their soliloquies and to confis-
cate dissuaded and damned souls. "May" suggests that God may not save
Donne's prayerfully delinquent speaker. Fair enough, but Stachniewski
overlooks the choice four lines above, "when towards thee / By thy leave
I can looke." Had the poet supplied "if" for "when," the delinquent's gestures would be hypothetical as well as conditional, and the case against
the speaker's confidence would be closer to closing. But "when" suggests
that a favorable reply to the prayer, "repair me now," is certain, albeit
deferred. Donne dramatized anguished experiences of uncertainty—no
argument here. But he staged his drama in light of the doctrine of divine
election and not in the shadow of an angry God. When God finally
"draws" the faithful, then grace "may" keep them from the devil's devices, may momentarily let them lapse, but will ultimately and irresistibly
retrieve them from sin.

The text "leans" both ways. The colleagues who stress John Donne's
apostasy, guilt, insecurity, and narcissism pull in one direction; I tug
in the other, all the more insistently because Calvinism is as popular in
the study of early modern temperament as public spending in an age of
mounting deficits—one must do it, bring Calvinism to bear, yet one is
obliged to deplore it. Arguably, the influence of Calvinism on character
was deplorable because those peddling it hawked the horrors of human
existence and harped on "a guilt in creatureliness itself." Calvin, after
all, held that human will never yields to God unless powerfully compelled. He sanctioned, some scowl, coercion and intimidation. Much of
the force, of course, came directly, internally, gently from God, through
grace, but powerful and "painful" preaching, along with the warnings,
strictures, and censures in devotional literature, inclined the faithful
advantageously. So, against the grain of each ordinary, unsensationally
edifying life, Calvinists set what Jean Delumeau, referring to Donne,
Perkins, Greenham, and other pietists, called "an evangelism of fear."
Thus runs the indictment.[12]

By attending to the Elizabethan pietists' dialectics between fear and
hope, following their "changeable course[s]," and, to an extent, referee-
ing their "kind of fighting," *Prayer, Despair, and Drama* has tried to "plea
down" its clients to a lesser charge, to identify extenuating circumstances
that explain why pietists had to lose themselves in despair to rehabilitate
and find fresh and prodigal identities. What happened when the familiar
consolations of the Catholic culture of penance vanished was analogous

to what happened when Machiavelli demystified the state and, according to Jonathan Dewald, when "the individual seem[ed] more real than the community." Dewald goes on to show how the aristocrats in France composed memoirs "to display the continuity of the self within an often irrational, fluctuating, political environment." Pietists also courted continuity, though more in terms of repetition.[13]

By now, though, repetition has ceased to be a virtue, and I owe the last word to the poet whose *Holy Sonnets* fashion the prodigal self as dramatically as did the pietists' prayers, with which we started. Perhaps, then, patient readers will not be disappointed and think themselves ill served if I conclude by simply saying "Donne."

Notes

1. Edward Topsell, *Time's Lamentation* (London, 1599), 179.

2. Ibid., 264–65.

3. Numbers in parentheses refer to those assigned in H. J. C. Grierson, *The Poems of John Donne*, 2 vols. (Oxford: Clarendon, 1912). I have consulted notes and commentary furnished elsewhere, particularly in *John Donne, The Divine Poems*, 2d ed., ed. Helen Gardner (Oxford: Clarendon, 1978) and *The Complete Poetry of John Donne*, ed. John T. Shawcross (Garden City, N.Y.: Doubleday, 1967). I am persuaded by Gardner's dating of the composition to the first decade of the seventeenth century (xlix–l).

4. Cf. Barbara Kiefer Lewalski, *Protestant Poetics and the Seventeenth-Century Lyric* (Princeton: Princeton University Press, 1979), 267. Also see Roger B. Rollin, "Fantastique Ague: The Holy Sonnets and Religious Melancholy," in Claude J. Summers and Ted-Larry Pebworth, eds., *The Eagle and the Dove: Reassessing John Donne* (Columbia: University of Missouri Press, 1986), 145; and Gardner, *Donne*, xxxii.

5. Cf. Richard Strier, "John Donne Awry and Squint: The Holy Sonnets," *Modern Philology* 86 (1989): 357–84; quote from 372.

6. Wilbur Sanders, *John Donne's Poetry* (Cambridge: Cambridge University Press, 1971), 120–38. For "expressions of personal vulnerability," see Arthur Marotti, *John Donne: Coterie Poet* (Madison: University of Wisconsin Press, 1986), 253–60.

7. John Carey, *John Donne: Life, Mind, and Art*, 2d ed. (London: Faber and Faber, 1990), 9–10, 32–35, 43, 85. Also see Marotti, *Donne*, 156–57; and Thomas Docherty, *John Donne, Undone* (London: Methuen, 1986), 92–93.

8. Donne, "The Cross."

9. Strier, "Donne," 384.

10. See Strier, "Donne," 382–83, where he distinguishes his position from Stach-

niewski's, which first appeared in "John Donne: The Despair of the Holy Sonnets," *ELH* 48 (1981): 677–705. For Lewalski's interpretation of "If Poysonous Mineralls," see her *Protestant Poetics*, 269–70; but also note John Stachniewski, *The Persecutory Imagination: English Puritanism and the Literature of Religious Despair* (Oxford: Clarendon Press, 1991), 278, for an alternative reading of the transition, "But who am I that dare dispute."

11. Stachniewski, *Persecutory Imagination*, 262, 282–83.

12. Jean Delumeau, *Le Péché et la peur: La culpabilisation en Occident XIIIᵉ–XVIIIᵉ siècles* (Paris: Fayard, 1983), 613–16; Calvin, *Institutes of the Christian Religion*, trans. Ford Lewis Battle, ed., John T. McNeill, 2 vols. (London: SCM Press, 1960) 3.14.6; and William Bouwsma, *John Calvin: A Sixteenth-Century Portrait* (Oxford: Oxford University Press, 1988), 42, for the "guilt in creatureliness."

13. Jonathan Dewald, *Aristocratic Experience and the Origins of Modern Culture: France, 1570–1715* (Berkeley: University of California Press, 1993), 44.

Index

PETER IVER KAUFMAN is a professor of religious studies at the University of North Carolina, Chapel Hill. His books include *Redeeming Politics* (1990) and *Church, Book, and Bishop* (1996).